Letters in a Helmet:

A Story of Fraternity and Brotherhood

Ron Sorter
Bob Tierno

2019

To my beautiful partner in life Karen
- Bob

To my lovely wife Michelle
- Ron

You Might Also Enjoy Reading

"The Prostate Chronicles: A Medical Memoir. Detours and Decisions Following My Prostate Cancer Diagnosis." by Bob Tierno, Mind Over Bladder Publishing (2019)

Table of Contents

III. Bob: Karen and Brother X (1969-1970)

V. Bob: The Corrections

VI. Ron: Captain Ahab and the VA

Kērothen Philoi Aei;
Friends From The Heart, Forever
— Delta Kappa Epsilon motto

Foreword

As Executive Director at Delta Kappa Epsilon, I'm always looking for stories that illustrate the unique advantage of our fraternity. Stories that not only inspire, but speak to the benefits of fulfilling one's education with a lifelong commitment to brotherhood.

"Letters in a Helmet" is such a story. It speaks to the "raw material" of two pledges at our chapter at the University of Oklahoma in the late 1960's, spanning fifty years of fully-actualized lives.

Ron Sorter graduates and receives a commission as a second lieutenant in the Army. He is severely wounded, while serving as an infranty company commander in Vietnam. We follow Ron on his journey from a MASH Unit in Chu Lai to his Rehabilitation Hospital in Denver, where we intersect with Brother Bob Tierno, whose unique military family connections have been a comfort to Ron's family.

While Tierno serves stateside in the Army Reserve, Sorter recovers and becomes a prosthetics specialist with the VA, helping to heal hundreds of other wounded veterans over the years. Not to be outdone, Tierno joins the Federal Prison System, earns an MBA from Pepperdine, makes the jump to Intel Corporation, and runs a bed & breakfast in the California gold country with his wife for a dozen years.

You can't make this kind of stuff up, and luckily I don't have to. Sorter and Tierno display sophisticated narrative skills.

At times I thought I might have been reading Ernest Hemingway or Stephen Crane. This book is a real page turner.

What really speaks to me here is the longevity of bonds formed in youth. Recently, Tierno was diagnosed with prostate cancer and Sorter lost his wife of twenty-five years to a degenerative cerebral disease. Brother Tierno is now cancer free, and Sorter is able to confront his profound grief, knowing his DKE circle is there for him.

This is just the story of two Dekes. I am sure there are other stories out there, as yet untold and equally profound.

Doug Lanpher

Introduction

Don't walk in front of me, I may not follow.
Don't walk behind me, I may not lead.
Walk beside me and be my friend
— Albert Camus

I would rather walk with a friend in the dark, than alone in the light.
— Helen Keller

Turning 70 means you reach a summit, an elevated place where you can turn and see your life with an unusual clarity. And it's not just the age, it's the circumstances as you embark on your eighth decade on the planet.

Facing a fatal illness like prostate cancer or losing a cherished spouse will also give you tremendous insight, but don't go looking for it.

One thing you learn is that your friendships endure, especially the ones that are built on bedrock. What's surprising is how friendships formed inadvertently when you were a college freshman, ones that you almost stumbled over, can last over fifty years and be a constant source of support.

There's something profound about someone knowing you at the start of the journey, who was there for you along the way. Even if you haven't seen them for several years, it only takes five minutes to get back in the groove.

A Focus on Fraternity

Upon reflection, some of the most influential associations we've made are with our fraternity brothers. It took us over 40 years to reconnect with some of them, but every day we get a text, email, or Facebook comment from one of our brothers. We crossed paths with several brothers (Fred Streb, Bill Nation, and others) at various points in our lives.

Delta Kappa Epsilon was founded 175 years ago in 1844 at Yale. There have been many famous "Dekes" over the years, notably: Presidents Teddy Roosevelt, Rutherford B. Hayes, the late George H.W. Bush, George W. Bush, and Gerald Ford, as well as J.P. Morgan, Robert Todd Lincoln, William Randolph Hearts, Dean Acheson, Henry Cabot Lodge and Astronaut Alan Bean (4th man on the moon).

In the spring of 1968, Bob pledged at the Rho Lambda Chapter of Delta Kappa Epsilon at Oklahoma University and moved into the fraternity house the fall semester. Admittedly a bold move for a guy who barely got accepted to college following a less than an illustrious run in high school graduating with a 2.2 GPA. Ron pledged in 1966 and moved into the house for fall semester. He admits he might have raised his hand too often when volunteers for office were requested.

As Bob recalls, "Ron and I met at the University of Oklahoma in the fall of 1968. Ron was a junior. I was a sophomore; two different worlds. Ron was high up the brotherhood as Brother X and I was a pledge, a lowly neophyte during 'Hell Week,' ultimately earning my DKE pin as a newly minted brother."

Bob studied hard his freshman year forgoing beer, women, and song, and the result was a 2.5 GPA . Fraternity life was like the movie Animal House, but the friendships and the bonds will last a lifetime.

Ron's struggles to balance OU's social and scholastic worlds were not uncommon. There was that one standout semester in senior year, when he made the Dean's list but the rest was just a straightforward push.

The house mothers Mom Harris and, upon her retirement, Mom Moran, trained us in all things genteel. Mrs. (Momma) Southard, our cook, did wonders with frozen fish, breaded shrimp , and french fries.

We were fortunate to have an alum who operated a food distribution company and gave us the broken boxes of perfect food that could not be returned or sold. Momma Southard made the best Danish and cinnamon rolls on the planet.

We were a creative group of brothers. We acquired an old Coca Cola machine and discovered that it could dispense 11 0z Coors Beer bottles. We had the machine converted to accept quarters and one row was reserved for Fresca so that we would be "legal". We never could keep that beer machine full.

Bob's roommate Bill Nation met his late wife Karleen through our Deke sweetheart group. Bob married his Deke sweetheart Karen. It took Ron longer to find the love of his life but Michelle finally, thankfully, arrived.

This yarn about Bob's and Ron's lives and brotherhood includes their connections with extraordinary women. They've both found and love wives who've become a part of them until the end. This may be a tale of fraternity, but the women in their lives are a vital part of that story.

Reunions and Revelations

We didn't always keep in touch with our brothers over the years. In 2014, a core group of Oklahoma University Rho Lambda chapter Deke alumni brothers started hosting a reunion during the University of Oklahoma homecoming weekend.

It has been over 40 years since we tipped a beer together. Some things never change. The tales of years past get larger in scope, funnier by the word and, yes, we've all put on some poundage. Dang!

When you meet a fraternity brother again it almost feels like yesterday. George Otey, an attorney from Tulsa (who would have thought it?) drove the creation of a new chapter at Oklahoma State.

Our house folded in 1972-3. Our sense is that most of us were from out of state and there were not enough in-state members to keep the house alive. It was also a time when fraternities were losing popularity. Larger houses were likely to survive with strong local alumni support legacy and pledge classes. Small houses were doomed.

Over the years our house was sold and a small fraternity gave it a go, then the University bought the property at 700 Elm St. and a shiny new building was erected dedicated to a deep-pocketed alumnus with no evidence of our existence. Not even a plaque.

Our current annual homecoming reunion is held on the grounds of 700 Elm, the site of the DKE House, which is appropriate because that address has seen some parties. On the plus side, at our '60s and'70s parties, there was no social media or smartphones, just Party Pix or Kodak cameras with film that had to be developed.

Maybe even a Polaroid camera taking instant pictures. Good thing, because in today's environment we would all be tarred and feathered for getting shit faced (versus black face which never happened in our house). We have our yearbooks, pictures, and memories of our time at OU. Nobody can take that away. Thanks to Brothers George Otey, R.J. (Bob) Pickup, Fred Streb, Dennis Clowers and Richard (Burnsie) Burns for spearheading the DKE Roundups!

A man's life connections and influences start with parents, teachers, and in college, our fraternity experience.

When Bob was diagnosed with prostate cancer, he reached out to all of them for support. He got needled (versus a rectal), but everyone rallied to his "cause." Several of the guys shared their brother's experience with prostate cancer and everybody shared their age driven maladies.

We were still jolly good fellows but technology-assisted with hip and knee replacements, shoulder surgeries and heart monitors.

Reenergizing these relationships has been awesome. Friends from the heart, forever.

Intersections

We embarked on the effort of writing this book to tell you the story of two fraternity brothers, separated by two years in age, with a deep friendship that has spanned fifty years, prostate cancer and the loss of the love of a lifetime.

The important part of brotherhood is that the bond remains intact forever, despite the lapses in communication or the frequency of visits. When you go back to the well, even after decades, the fresh water flows.

There will be two junctures of extreme importance in this story, the first, following Ron's wounding in Vietnam, and the second, this past year, when Bob was diagnosed with prostate cancer, and Ron's wife Michelle passed away following a lengthy illness. These are the major intersections.

The rest of this book is about some very interesting periods in our lives and careers, where the normal cadences and events shaped us, with brotherhood beneath us a foundation.

If you know us, we'd like you to come away from this book saying, "I had no idea!"

And if you don't know us, we'd like you to say, "I wish I had a brother like that in my life."

Enjoy the movie. Please silence your cell phone and pass the popcorn.

Bob   Ron
Denton, TX   Sequim, WA

Editor Note

In a world full of interesting stories, it's a surprise when something magical comes along that is remarkable in its poignancy and raw power.

I first met Bob Tierno in 2018, when we began work on his first book, *The Prostate Chronicles*. Ron Sorter was an integral supporting cast member in that book. Soon after the publication of *Chronicles*, Bob and Ron approached me to discuss the "Brotherhood" project.

Over three months, Ron "opened a vein" and gave me 80 cinematic chapters of material. I then circled back to Bob to get his side of the story. When all the chapters are captured, it is known as the "giant hairball" phase. It's my job to sort it out.

I'd like you to think of Ron and Bob's combined story like the double-helix of a strand of DNA, looping and intersecting in an elegant manner, with the final result a resounding "yes!" to our humanity, and our ability to form friendships in youth that can last a lifetime.

With two male contributors, there's a lot of testosterone coursing through these pages. Ron's chapters remind me of the measured approach you find in Hemingway's *A Fairwell to Arms*, blending battlefield bravery and tenderness on the home front. Bob is more of the comedian and improviser, possessing the savvy, entrepreneurial, anti-establishment skills you find in Kesey's *One Flew over the Cuckoo's Nest* or the war memoir of Tobias Wolff, *In Pharoah's Army*.

I wanted Ron and Bob to tell their stories separately, to create a sense of authenticity (same root word as "author"), rather than attempting a blended narrative, where both voices are subsumed into a single narrative voice.

This book captures the two voices, alternating back and forth, first Bob and then Ron. There are section headings to guide you as to who is telling the story, or you can consult the Table of Contents.

Additionally, you will enjoy the "Greek Chorus" of added voices of OU Deke brothers, who provide their stories in interview format and as submitted chapters. It helps round out what you will learn from Ron and Bob.

It is my delight to share with you the *Sorter-Tierno Chronicles*, inseparable by design, drawing on a power greater than all of us.

Jon Obermeyer
Durham, NC

I. Bob
An Entrepreneur in the Making
(1949 - 1971)

Rocky and Carmela

Rocky Tierno, Pearl Harbor, January, 1941

1
I'm From Everywhere

"So, Bob, where are you from?"

"I'm from everywhere."

I'm an Army Brat, a "Post Toastie," whose parents chose the life of gypsy travelers, forgoing planting roots until late in life when Pop retired after 32 years of distinguished military service.

Pop passed away July 12, 2012. I have only begun to appreciate his influence on me as a man. You only need to read Rocky's distinguished military career record, and it's not difficult to see how he shaped me as an adult.

2

Ralph Thomas "Rocky" Tierno, Jr.

Ralph Thomas Tierno, Jr., aka "Rocky," my Pop, was born in 1923. A second-generation Italian immigrant, he graduated from Pleasantville, NJ High School.

He applied for an appointment to West Point. He once told me that the Irish congressman wouldn't grant him an appointment because he was Italian.

He chose another path to his goal. He enlisted in the U.S. Army in January, 1941 and was assigned to Schofield Barracks at Pearl Harbor, HI. He was a member of B Company, 3rd Engineer, C Battalion, 24th Infantry Division from the West Point Preparatory School.

On December 7, 1941, the Japanese attacked Pearl Harbor. That morning, he and fellow soldiers were heading to the USS Arizona for breakfast after attending Mass.

They didn't make it to breakfast. For the next three days, his unit spent day and night building beach defenses that still exist today. He was given the choice of going either to West Point or The Naval Academy or accepting a promotion to Sergeant and ship off to Guadalcanal.

He chose West Point and entered the Academy in July of 1942 (nearly all of the personnel who chose the promotion were killed in action).

He graduated in 1945 and was commissioned a Second Lieutenant in the Infantry. He had a brief tour as part of the Combat Invasion Unit in the Philippines then spent thirty-eight months assigned to MacArthur's staff in the 441st CIC Detachment HQ, rebuilding Japan.

He returned home to marry Carmela Pasquino, the girl next door, on May 31st 1947. Mom recounted her journey by ship to Japan and it was quite a journey leaving Paulsboro, NJ. More on Mom later.

Rocky was a "ring knocker," the term used to describe an officer produced by West Point. He was a "lifer" through and through, committed to the Army life and his family.

He was deployed in the Korean Conflict and was wounded in action in December of 1950. He was awarded the Purple Heart, his Combat Infantryman's Badge (CIB), and a Bronze Star with Valor (three medals that he shares in common with my co-author). His memories of Korea was that it had to be the coldest place on earth. He and his men were never warm. His visit to the Korean War Memorial in Washington D.C. brought back those memories. Fifty years after the ceasefire, South Korea recognized our military for their sacrifices by giving them a medal of thanks.

Following rehabilitation at Valley Forge Military Hospital, he was assigned to the Infantry School at Fort Benning, GA. He was an instructor until deployed to the 5th Infantry Division in Augsburg, Germany followed by a transfer to the 7th Infantry Division, Fort Ord, CA.

From 1957-59 he earned a Masters Degree in Electrical Engineering at the University of Oklahoma. He then transferred to the Command and General Staff College at Fort Leavenworth, KS, graduating in 1960.

He was named a White House Fellow and assigned as a Defense Systems Safety Officer for the Atomic Energy Commission (AEC) and moved our family to Sandia Base, NM (near Albuquerque) from 1961 - 63. He was then assigned to the 7th Infantry Division, Eighth U.S. Army, Korea commanding a Mechanized Infantry (Buffalo) Battalion defending the Demilitarized Zone from 1963-64.

Upon his return to the U.S. he was assigned as an advisor to the Research Analysis Corporation, McLean, VA from 1964-1967. As I graduated from high school and shipped off to Oklahoma University in the fall of 1967, Rocky was assigned to the U.S. Army War College. He graduated from the War College in 1968. From 1968-71 he was assigned to the Institute of Advanced Studies at the War College.

He aspired to become a Brigadier General. It was pretty clear that he'd have to go to Vietnam to get that promotion. He'd had enough of combat. Through his connections in the Pentagon, and some luck, he was assigned to command the U.S. Military Group in La Paz, Bolivia from 1971-74.

He packed up Mom, my sister and brother and headed to South America. Rocky returned to the War College as an instructor and retired in 1975.

5

Rocky's military career elevates him to "hero" in my mind. A young Italian kid from South Jersey rising to the rank of Full Colonel. I've been asked how he shaped me as his first born son.

As one of the Greatest Generation, he never talked about Pearl Harbor until late into his 70s and 80s when the press would interview him and the Pennsylvania State Legislature would honor Pearl Harbor Survivors. He walked in parades until his knees would not permit it.

When pressed for an opinion after South Korea awarded Korean War Veterans a medal and the Korean War Memorial was established in Washington, DC, he just said, "the Red Chinese attacked, I got shot in the hand. We beat them back that night."

When watching the movie *The Code Talkers*, which was about American Indian Code Talkers, he broke into tears remembering losing one of his Indian Code Talkers in a firefight.

3
Learning Math with Match Sticks

I was not the brightest bulb in the box, but Rocky was there
every step of the way to help, cajole, or even discipline me. He
knew how to use a slide rule before calculators. The nuns at
school claimed I could not add or subtract. I was either
dyslexic or perhaps just plain stupid! He asked my mother
to buy a box of match sticks and we spent hours until I could
visualize 2+2 = 4.

There were certainly frustrating moments but his persistence
paid off. I was not going to fail 3rd or 4th grade. What I
observed as a child was a father committed to my success in
whatever endeavor I chose. I learned to adapt to my role(s)
and to not be afraid to try anything that might interest me.

He didn't push the idea that I should attend West Point. I had
that notion. Frankly, it would have relieved a big financial
burden but going to college was the goal since he was the first
in his family to graduate from not one but multiple colleges.

Rocky also understood the role my mother would play in
managing the family through all of our moves. He was the
breadwinner and earned every promotion and raise. Another
lesson for me. You must earn it. Don't count on your employer
to hand you the keys to the office.

My Pop influenced my Roman Catholic faith: confession every
Saturday; Mass every Sunday and Holy Day; meatless Fridays.

Rocky was a strict disciplinarian. Corporal punishment was the norm. We were to be seen and not heard around other adults. He influenced my love of sports: Dizzy Dean and the Game of the Week on Saturdays; NFL on the black and white television. Pop loved his Falstaff Beer and a cigar.

He was my Little League coach at Fort Leavenworth and showed no favoritism towards me.

One time my mother grounded me on the day of a big game. I was suited up and ready to head to the game. He came home to change clothes, applied a generous amount of corporal punishment with his swagger stick and benched me, leaving me home.

About 30 minutes before the first pitch, he called my mother and told her that he didn't have a second baseman. My neighbor was heading to the ballpark and I hitched a ride with them. I had three hits, 2 RBIs, no errors and threw a runner out at the plate. Pop said absolutely nothing. We won the game. I was put back in my cell, my bedroom without dinner. I can assure you that I didn't screw up again for a long time.

He encouraged me to work at a young age to make my own money. He put up with my anti-Vietnam War attitude, later agreeing with me. He knew that leaving the protected "Post Toastie" life and heading into a pluralistic world I would have many choices good, and bad.

4
High School Waterloo (Not!)

The inflection point in my education was near-failure in high school during my junior year at my third high school in as many years. Pop had meetings with all of my teachers trying to break the code on what interested me.

The breakthrough came when he met with Mrs. Flores, my world history teacher. Mrs. Flores noted that I showed an interest in historical events.

She proposed testing that interest by assigning a research project, so, since we were studying French history, she gave me some choices. I talked it over with Pop and chose the battle of Waterloo.

Pop had some very good history books, so I was able to understand how the battle started and was fought by Napoleon Bonaparte's army and Wellington's British. Napoleon lost this battle because he chose to mount a charge on a rain-soaked, muddy hillside. I received an "A" for my work, complete with hand drawings of the battlefield action, and the rest is history!

Pop did not demand that I become a career Army officer but demonstrated that it was a good living. Frankly, if there had not been a war it would have been encouraged. When I did complete a two-year Army ROTC program he was very proud to commission me as a Second Lieutenant in December of 1971.

9

He later ran into one of my ROTC instructors in Panama. The instructor told Pop that I should never have been commissioned in the Army. I was not "suited" for military service. Pop told me he just laughed and said "That's my boy! He'll prove you wrong." And I did! He taught me to accept the challenge before me and make every effort to overcome it.

5
Carmela "Mom T" Pasquino Tierno

Carmela Pasquino Tierno was an Army officer's wife and
a "Force of Nature." In the 40's, before Social Security was
established, she changed her name to Bond because she was
of Italian origin (sound familiar?). The dentist she worked
for commented when she had to register for Social Security
deductions from her paycheck that he knew all along that she
was Italian because of the olive color of her skin as well as her
big nose.

More important was how her father Luigi Pasquino abused
her mother and while she would not disclose the abuse
(verbal and physical) she endured, my grandfather had a
violent streak and a short fuse. Italians by nature are screamers
and Mom followed suit.

In the '40s Carmela and Rocky left South Jersey and vowed
never to return except for visits. She married Rocky in 1947
and took a train from Philadelphia to Seattle through Chicago.
She boarded the General Langfitt on October 29, 1947, sharing
a cabin with three other women. It was a rough, stormy ride,
arriving in Yokohama, Japan on November 16, 1947.

Mom was a risk taker, leaving home to a war-ravaged Japan.
Mom and Pop captured every moment in Japan with visits
to Nagasaki and Hiroshima where the U.S. had dropped the
Atomic Bomb. Their albums are full of pictures from their
adventures and their walls are covered in art.

11

My mother martialled us through every move, taking care of everything once Pop received his orders. Judging by the scrapbooks of pictures over the early years they were very busy starting a family and had it not been for several miscarriages there would have been seven or more children in the family.

It wasn't unusual to see large families on posts. I remember our friends the Truscott's who had ten children. They were given an entire duplex on posts.

It was the role of Army Wife to hold the family together. There was also a guide book, *The Army Wives Handbook: A Complete Social Guide*, which was mandatory reading. It covered all facets of a wife's responsibilities. I'm not sure but that may the source of "children should be seen and not heard."

They were our parents; superiors, but not friends. We were Major Tierno's children. Our behavior reflected on my parents which could impact Pop's career. You didn't dare receive an incident report from the post military police (MP).

When we went to Mass on Sunday we dressed like it was Easter or Christmas. We sat in the first two rows near the post commander.

One time I stood upon the pew and declared that I couldn't see the movie. We used to go to see movies at a local drive in. Very embarrassing but comical. If we misbehaved at Mass, our breakfast was at risk.

Mom T was a gourmet chef. She sous cheffed for Julia Child, Martin Yu, Joanne Weir and other distinguished chefs of her day. She also taught classes at the Cooking Shoppe in Carlisle, PA. As an Italian she loved to make homemade spaghetti, gnocchi, meatballs, stuffed squid (Christmas Eve), all things Italian.

This talent was passed down to the kids. We were given a large rolling board and a hand-cranked pasta machine. She taught us how to make tomato sauce from scratch. Karen and I had vegetable gardens in the early years of our marriage and canned our own tomatoes and sauce. Mom T shared her talents with Karen who learned how to make Italian cookies, her famous Italian cream cake and other recipes.

Mom T, like most housewives of the '50s, was a student of Julia Child cookbooks which simplified the art of cooking, introducing the wives of America to different meals from around the world. She shared every cookbook with Karen and her recipes were meticulously typed and filed by type.

More important was teaching us how to set the table for dinner and for formal dinners, and which of the silver utensils were to be used for the salad, soup, main course, dessert, etc. She shared her love of crystal by buying us a starter set of our own and formal table cloths as well as linens. She taught me how to wash and iron my clothes. When I wanted starched oxford cloth shirts she bought the spray starch and showed me how to do it myself rather than send the shirts out to the cleaners.

Mom was a child of the Depression.

The experience of scarcity as a child resulting in her buying two, even three of the same item. Two sets of china, silverware, even clothes. We did not appreciate it until she passed and we had to sort all of those items for disposition.

A large number of linens, cooking items, china, and clothing were donated to the local battered women's center in Carlisle, PA. She volunteered there and was recognized by the organization for her contribution.

I think later in their marriage things became strained because of the pressure for promotions my father endured and, frankly, menopause for Mom. Despite her tantrums Pop wouldn't think of divorce but kept her happy with fine jewelry, remodeling her kitchen, trips etc.

They were married for 65 years but the last 15-20 were not very pleasant. She wouldn't let me shave until I was fifteen, thinking that her "boy" should remain with a peach-fuzz face. Pop finally took me into the bathroom and taught me to shave. He was my hero. Mom lost it when she saw my new "mug."

Menopause began as my teen years hit full stride. She was a screamer and I was a teenager in search of myself. It was an oil and water relationship. Pop tried to intervene without being over-protective, coaching me on what not to do or say. There were many "I told you so" moments from Pop.

By the time I made it to my senior year in high school, Pop had made the decision to send me to college as far away as possible from Mom. Looking back it was a great decision but I really didn't appreciate my mother's love for me until she passed on. The last ten years of life she was plunged into the darkness of Alzheimers.

Mom, like her father, lost her hearing and needed hearing aids. She was very vain about this and wouldn't wear the expensive aids my father bought her. This may be the source of her screaming. Who knows?

Mom T was all about appearances at times. When I went to work in a Federal Prison as a correctional officer (guard, hack, bull, etc) she told every friend in Christmas letters that I had a career in the "correctional educational system."

They collected Japanese ceramics, artwork and an appreciation for the cuisine. At Pop's 70th birthday was a Japanese gentleman who was an officer in the Japanese Army and had worked with Pop. He shared that Pop would collect C rations and canned goods and give them to his hungry Japanese family and neighbors.

Mom sailed home on the USAT David Shanks on October 28, 1948 from Yokohama arriving in Seattle, WA on November 8th, 1948. While waiting for Pop to arrive she spent six weeks with her parents in Paulsboro, NJ then moved on to Fort Devans, MA from January 1949 to August 1951.

Mom T was a "fashionista", always dressed "to the nines." In her working years, her typing and shorthand made her a top-notch secretary. I will be forever in her debt for making me take typing and shorthand in high school. Typing was a lifesaver in college and my professional life. I only wish that I had paid attention in the shorthand class.

Mom's relationship with Karen got off to a rocky (no pun intended) start because Karen ate like a bird and, oh, had a "big nose" too. Once the rough years passed and they discovered their mutual love of cooking, they truly developed a wonderful relationship which lasted 40 years, until Mom's passing.

Post Toastie

6

The Winner Arrives

I was born June 15, 1949 in Waltham, MA. I was the first-born child. Robert means "The Winner."

From August 1950 to April 1951, Mom and I stayed stateside while Pop was deployed to Korea where he was wounded.

We moved on to Fort Benning, GA where Pop was assigned to the Intelligence Unit at the Infantry School. We lived in two houses on post. Battle Park Homes and Custard Terrace. I visited Custard Terrace when I was in basic training in the summer of 1969. Very small three-bedroom, single bath homes. For three of us, very comfortable I'm sure.

My sister Susan was born June 30, 1950 while stationed at Fort Benning. We transferred to Augsburg, Germany, leaving on Seaboard and Western Airlines enroute to Frankfurt, Germany. Mom's notes recounted that all of the children on board got sick except my sister and I (until we got to our apartment). My brother Skip was born October 3, 1955.

We left Germany March 23, 1956, transferring to Fort Ord, CA via a short stay at Mom's parents where I got to meet Pop's parents and brothers. He had four brothers, John and Joe (twins), Andy and Carmen. All fought in WWII except Joe who was a Merchant Seaman, chief engineer. Their stories weren't told to me until my thirties. They all returned to post-war school and jobs.

Uncle Joe was a career Merchant seaman, shipping items of interest from foreign lands to my folks. Andy and Carmen were pipefitters for Socony Oil Company and settled in Woodbury, NJ. John worked for a manufacturing plant in Lycoming, PA. All have since passed on.

It took eight days to drive to Fort Ord, CA in our '53 Chrysler.

No air conditioning and a water bag hanging off the hood in case the engine overheated. Imagine three children in the backseat including baby Skip. "Are we there yet?" "You kids better behave or I'll pull over and spank you," were common themes.

We lived in two houses at Fort Ord from April 1956 to May 1957. I attended Kindergarten, first and second grade on Post. My First Holy Communion was in the Fort Ord Chapel which is still standing even though the post is now University of California, Monterrey. I had chicken pox in 1957.

We headed to Norman, OK May 17, 1957 via Disneyland, Knott's Berry Farm, Petrified Forest, and the Painted Desert. We arrived in Norman on May 23, 1957. We stayed in the Norman Courts Motel until June 16, 1957. We were introduced to tornados and spent several evenings in the motel's storm shelter.

One evening we went to a professor's home for dinner. A storm rolled in and I saw my first funnel cloud. We drove back to the motel in a rain storm flooding the campus streets.

Water came up through the floorboards and I thought we were going to float away. Several students pushed our car through the water to higher ground and we made it back to the motel.

I went to St. Joseph Catholic School in Norman for third grade. It was an old wooden building with 2nd and 3rd graders in one classroom. This is the school where the "matchbook math lesson" occurred.

There was no physical education. The school was similar to one that had burned down in Chicago that year. Frightening thought.

James Garner, the actor who played Maverick on TV, visited us on the playground on his horse. I played little league baseball but we practiced on sand lots. I played second base. Bobby Richardson from the Yankees was my role model. Kids football was in its infancy.

I received a helmet and pads from my folks for Christmas. I played on a Pop Warner team that wasn't very good. Pop made me wear ankle-high cleats to protect my ankles. The helmet didn't have a face guard on it like most helmets. One fellow player got a bloody nose and never returned to practice. I never got hurt but we lost most of our games.

We rode our bikes behind the DDT sprayer in the summer and other fun adventures. When dark came we were in the house. If I got in trouble at school or in the neighborhood I suffered corporal punishment as well as the ultimate embarassment: loss of my bike for a week or two. Ouch!

Rocky completed his Masters in Electrical Engineering, and we were off to the Command and General Staff College at Fort Leavenworth, KS on June 23, 1959. We moved into one house from June to September. Then we moved to newer quarters until June 22, 1960.

I played Little League baseball, was in the Cub Scouts and swimming league. I took boxing lessons (won my first fight in the ring but lost my first street fight), and served as an altar boy, learning the Latin Mass and all of its ceremonial trappings.

7

Extended Family

My grandparents on Pop's side weren't very influential. His father died when we were at Sandia Base in New Mexico, and his stepmother was out of the picture. She was very strict with the boys and Pop wanted nothing to do with her.

On Mom's side my grandparents were very influential, both good and bad. Good for their cooking, and small farm with chickens , fruit and vegetables etc. Bad because Luigi was very gruff and often yelled at grandmom. Mom would try to intervene and she'd get her share of the screaming. It was very confusing because it was mostly in Italian.

Uncle Lou lived next door with Aunt Kay. She died of cancer when I was in high school. There were fun memories like going to Ocean City, NJ and enjoying the boardwalk as well as the beach. A great-uncle owned a small grocery store there, too. The folks bought live crabs and hauled them back to Paulsboro. Watching grandmom chase one around the kitchen was hilarious. I can hear her now after asking her a question. She'd respond, "I dunno?" with her hands in the air. Italians talk with their hands.

I'll always remember Uncle Lou telling me after the funeral to go to college and not become a pipefitter like him. I did go to college but he got the last laugh because in 1972 he and my father's brothers were all let go when the EPA regulations went into effect. They all received a huge sum of money. I was struggling to get a job.

Uncle Carmen and Uncle Andy used to take me fishing for flounder off the coast of New Jersey. I really looked forward to those trips except when it rained. One time, a U.S. Navy blimp flew very low over us and disappeared into a cloud bank. We later learned it went down into the ocean and all on board were killed.

Uncle Carmen and Aunt Marion were the youngest and I really liked them. When I was growing up they shared a story about getting married and wanted to buy a house near the local Catholic Church. The pastor refused to allow it. He and the neighbors were Irish. Eventually they were able to locate property nearby. The Irish weren't too kind to Italian immigrants back then.

As an Army brat I was never exposed to that sort of discrimination. Rank talks and the military is based on respect for the rank a person holds.

8
"Post Toastie"

Another road trip. We headed to New Mexico on June 22, 1960, arriving at the Sandia Base on July 15, 1960. As a common theme we would be moved into temporary quarters until the officer's quarters were vacated by the previous resident. So, after a stay in the Visitors Officers Quarters (VOQ) for a week then to temporary housing, and finally on November 18, 1961 we moved to 1822 18th Loop .

I remember the inside doors of the storage closets in the carport. Previous officers' families had left messages and where they were headed following this assignment. I went to Holy Ghost School in town for 6th and 7th grades. Starched grey uniforms with a red tie. These were sent to the post laundry and came back starched and stiff as a board. Very uncomfortable.

I played little league baseball and was a Boy Scout. Since we lived close to the Post Chapel I served Mass as an altar boy plus weddings. The dinero was muy bueno for a kid. I was selected for an all-star baseball team but the game was the same week as Boy Scout summer camp at Bluewater Lake. I chose camp and nearly drowned in the lake. My mother wanted me to play in the all star game. My dad let me make the decision. It led to my becoming a swimming instructor lifeguard, and Water Safety Instructor a few years down the road. Of course had I chosen the all star route I could have signed a major league contract with the Yankees. Not!

I delivered the post daily bulletin every Friday on a route earning twenty cents a household, August until December 1962, until I moved up to a Sunday Denver Post delivery route until April 1963.

Catholic school was not a good experience. No sports, no physical education and nuns who were more worried about discipline than education. I think this is when my rebellious period started. No one was happier than I when we moved off post to town when Pop went to Korea. I got my first experience as a "townie" attending 8th grade at Sandia High School. Physical education, soccer and no uniform.

This was probably the most challenging time for Mom while Pop was assigned to South Korea. They bought their first home in town. (I became a townie) and I was plunged into the morass called 8th grade. I made friends fairly easily but most shied away from our house because Mom would scream at the drop of a hat then the capper was to ring a bell to signal us to get home for dinner.

One night Skip, Susan, and I decided to not come home at the tinkling of the bell by Mom. It was after dark when we stumbled in and we were sent to our rooms without dinner. Skippy was pretty agile so we had him low crawl to the kitchen and get crackers from the pantry while Mom watched television.

The next morning we had dinner for breakfast. Pork Chops over rice and smothered in canned tomatoes. We were never late again. When the bell was rung, we ran to the house.

I had a terrible time in school "earning' my first "F." You can only imagine Mom's response with my father in Korea. I survived that year, though.

On November 22, 1963, JFK was shot in Dallas. Like most eighth graders I was at a loss as to the magnitude of this tragic event. At home we sat glued to our black and white television set and watched every moment, including JFK's funeral. Everybody of my generation remembers where they were on November 22, 1963.

That year, I learned how to make smoke bombs. One night, I got a box of matches and a test tube from a chemistry set. I shut the door to my bedroom. With my brother Skip observing, I inserted match heads into the test tube.

Once it was full I thought I had enough room to insert a cork and put it away for later use. As I inserted the cork there was a spark and the bedroom filled with smoke. Skip put clothes under the door and I opened both windows hoping the smoke would exit quickly.

Enter Mom, thinking the house was on fire. All I remember is her screaming at me, striking matches in my face scaring the crap out of me. My brother and sister looked on in horror. I was reduced to a bucket of clabbered puke.

Mom sold the house in May and we moved into the VOQ on post which was next to the officers club and pool. Pop returned home in June, 1964.

Upon Pop's return we headed to Vienna, VA for his new assignment at the Research Analysis Corporation (RAC) in McClean in civilian clothes. We moved into 1537 Bowling Green Drive in Vienna. In April, 1965, the address was changed to 2636 Bowling Green Drive and the school boundaries shifted by a couple of blocks.

I had been attending ninth grade at James Madison High School in Virginia. With the boundary shift I was required to go to G.C. Marshall High School in Falls Church. Pop fought this but lost and I'm off to my third school in as many years for 10th, 11th and 12th grade. I struggled with most classes, did well in drama, becoming a thespian, but low grades kept me out of varsity sports.

My social life was limited until I finally got a driver's license at age 17. I was promised this when I turned 16 by my father, including a Red Ford Mustang for Christmas. The driver's license didn't happen, of course, and the red mustang was a model car under the Christmas tree.

He ultimately bought a 62 Blue Comet for my use. He traded it for a '66 VW Bug which became my college ride. Dating wasn't as problematic for a post toastie in 9th and 10th grades. I was banned from dating due to my grades.

In 11th and 12th grades, dating life picked up but I soon learned that heading to Oklahoma after graduation shortened the life cycle of my dating relationships.

Pounding beers made up the other half of my teen life. Pop monitored this closely and enforced an early curfew on weekends. The prom was a big deal but the after-party was even better. My senior year, I had hit it off with a girl "Jane." She was an Army brat, too, so we had something in common. Our parents liked the relationship. When I asked her to the prom another guy was asking, too, "Ben," a good old boy from Texas whose father was in D.C. on an assignment. Ben was heading to the University of Texas upon graduation. I hadn't learned to hate the Longhorns yet but you can see where this is going.

Jane asked me to consider Ben's request as he was heading back to Texas. I relented figuring that would build capital for me following the prom with Jane. Well, it did not. We'll leave it at that. I did take Sandy to the prom and also extolled the, "this is the last time we'll see each other." message. She married a Marine. I certainly will have better luck in college.

After graduation night, I was heading to the celebration parties. Pop gave me a watch and asked that I consider not drinking that night. I didn't drink and had a reasonable time and got home early. Time to prepare for college.

My job for the summer was being a lifeguard at Dunn Loring Swim Club a couple of blocks from home. The manager of the company that manages pools decided that after two years of employment he wanted to promote me to manage a pool in a largely white-trash apartment complex. It was more responsibility, slightly more pay.

One day I opened the pool, swept the pool floor, changed filters and set up to open for the day. I had a few minutes before opening the pool to the residents when Joe Pizzuto entered the office while I was on the phone. He was a 19-year-old dishonorably-discharged Army guy who was dating a twelve-year-old who hung out at the pool. Admittedly, she was an attractive girl but she was a 12-year old child.

Apparently she told Joey that I was hitting on her. Joey had paid a visit to defend her honor and I beat the hell out of his fist with my face! I had him arrested for simple assault. The trial was short and sweet and he got 30 days in the local jail.

I moved back to my home pool but not before a group of fellow lifeguards who were also football players settled the score with Joey's crew, surprising them my last day at the pool when the crew showed up to beat me up. My fellow lifeguards made short order of the crew.

I moved on very quickly.

OU was in my sights!

9
Boomer Sooner

Oklahoma University was a good fit for two reasons. Pop had connections on the faculty who could help me when I needed academic support.

The second, and most important reason, was that I was accepted to OU and no other university! OU was growing by importing out-of-state students with GPAs as low as mine (2.2), who were willing to pay out-of-state tuition.

In August of 1967, I flew out to Oklahoma City from Washington D.C. and took a shuttle to Norman. I moved into Baker House, an independent dorm. I arrived a week early to get the lay of the land, so I didn't have a roommate for two weeks.

The new class of freshmen were assembled together in Owen Field, the football stadium. Dr. Cross, President of the university welcomed all of us. He asked us to look at the person to the left and the person to the right. He predicted that two out of three of us will not graduate from the university.

Well, that was a sobering prediction.

10
The Nose Guard

The dorm counselor assigned roommates by alphabetical order, and I drew Richard Tolbert a 5' 10" nose guard from Texarkana, TX. His goal was to walk on and start for the freshmen team, eventually working his way to the varsity.

If you had a hunch about Richard, you are right. Richard was the only black student in the dorm. It made absolutely no difference to me and we got along well. He would bring over to the dorm varsity football players like Granville Liggins (All American Nose Guard) and others, which made us very popular. He also snored like a freight train which took some getting used to but we made it work.

On Sundays, Richard would call my mother and say "Good morning, Mom!"

When I took the phone back the first time she asked me, "Is your roommate a Negro?".

We both damn near peed our pants! I don't recall any racist comments by residents of Baker House. I did get into a fight with another dorm resident where I beat the hell out of his fist with my face, breaking my nose in the process. Little did I realize how that broken nose would affect my plans in the future.

11
Avoiding the Math

I enrolled in Army ROTC. Keep in mind this was 1967 as the Vietnam War escalated. I am not sure if it was mandatory but the Colonel (my dad) said give it a try as another way of earning a commission into the Army.

Knowing my dislike of math and love of history I enrolled in Chemistry VI, a general class that if I passed I would get a pass on math requirements for the duration of college. History, English, Psychology with a Water Safety Instructor class elective rounded out my freshman year. No drinking, no partying, no dates the first year, as failing was not an option for me.

It was a curious time. I observed a student jump to his death from the 12th floor of his dorm. I decided to walk the oval and find out who exactly the Students for a Democratic Society (SDS) represented. Oklahomans thought they were all long-hair commie hippies. Their agenda was clearly against the draft and the Vietnam War.

I had just received my draft card and I definitely didn't want to go to Vietnam so it was difficult to disagree with their position. My roots as an Army Brat, though, had me committed to a military career but I decided to compete for West Point after my freshman year once my grades improved and I could achieve an acceptable SAT score.

The Chem VI class nearly ran me out of school, as each test throughout the semester was worth a higher percentage grade and I was towing a D or C- as I recall. I remembered that a friend of my parents was an OU Chemistry professor, so I sought his counsel.

He informed me that in the Chemistry Department library there was a file cabinet which contained all of the professor's exams for the past decade. They were color coded so he would choose one or the other and add a new question every semester. I obtained the last two test papers (four in all) and four of my dorm mates studied those questions night and day until the day of the exam. Several others scoffed at us saying that it was impossible to be that easy.

The day of the exam arrived and it was supposed to take three hours. The professor handed out the exam. In the back of the class the dorm mates who scoffed at my strategy were heard saying a muffled, "Oh, shit, Tierno was right!" It took me 20 minutes to take the test. I spent two hours resisting the temptation to look at my answers. I had memorized every question and answer except, of course, the new one which I missed. I scored a 98 and my adjusted grade was a B for the course. No math for me!

12
DKE

The second semester was equally hard with no social life.
When the wind blows across the plains in the winter, it gets
awfully cold.

Spring arrived and I decided to participate in fraternity rush,
ultimately pledging Delta Kappa Epsilon ("Deke"), Rho
Lambda Chapter.

Upon my return to school following summer break I moved
into the Deke house with initiation prior to classes, which
started the first couple weeks of September.

Growing up a gypsy traveler I drove a stake in the ground
for establishing long-term friendships through my fraternity membership. I'm positive that had I not pledged Deke, I
wouldn't have graduated from O.U

Neither parent had much to say about my choice of pledging
Deke. They paid my tuition and room costs for the first two
years and I worked to pay the remaining two years. I think
overall they were pleased with my choice "brothers" and felt
more secure about my chances to graduate.

I think I was comfortable with the Dekes because there were
brothers from New York, Chicago and out of state. I was
offered to pledge houses that were mostly Oklahomans or
Texans.

I was my own "man" and my brother was six years younger than me. No impact but as the oldest son, in the late '60s, I naturally entered the "black hole" of being a teenager, rebelling against everything. My brother and sister went to Bolivia to finish high school. Both left for college, Skip to West Point and Susan to Marymount College.

I was on my own while the family was in Bolivia. I have no connections to my highschool classmates, most of whom attended Virginia universities while I took off for Oklahoma. I attended the 20th reunion of the G.C. Marshall Class of 1967 and no friendships were rekindled.

Joining DKE meant terra firma for the rest of my college life with a sense of brotherhood, academic discipline, and social life. I would not have survived as an independent when two out of three freshman would not make it to graduation.

The parties were as advertised, such as the Graveyard Party every Halloween. "Hanging" Hank Helton over the lunch hour on the big tree in front of the house was good for a scream or two along with the gravestones of the most unpopular school administrators and deans. Our annual formal party was an opportunity for the brothers to don a tuxedo and dance the night away with their dates.

1968 was a chaotic year for the country. I retook the SATs and qualified for an appointment to West Point. I headed to Fort Sill in late October or November to compete with a group of high school kids. I passed every one of the physical tests.

The physical was another matter. Remember the fight my freshman year in the dorm? When the eye, nose, and throat doctor examined my broken nose, he declared me 4F, which disqualified me from West Point.

I called Rocky and gave him the news. Policy dictated that I was not to have been told until after all of the tests were done. Rock was livid and called the superintendent at West Point. That led to a call from the "supe" to me at school.

He told me that I should get my broken nose fixed at Valley Forge Military Hospital in the spring. Then, wait for it, enlist, go to basic training and enter the academy's prep school. I did the math. Had I taken that route, I would be a 28-year-old second lieutenant. I decided to get my nose fixed over spring break and pass on West Point.

The saga continued when I dropped a class (Italian). That dropped my hours from 14 to 11 and triggered a notification to my draft board in Falls Church, VA. This was within days of dropping the class. I looked at my draft card and noticed that Joyce G.'s signature was on it. We graduated from high school together. The call didn't go well and I'm bracing for my draft notice, "Greetings from the President of the United States, your presence is requested to serve as a conscripted soldier." (that is how I remember it).

Do I evade the draft by heading to Canada? I didn't want to threaten Rocky's chance to be promoted to General. I didn't want to become fodder for a war that made no sense at all.

36

Brother Wayne Hughes was in the same predicament.

We evaluated our options and checked into the two-year Army ROTC program. We headed to the Armory, signed some papers, and were sworn in. The next step would be heading to Fort Benning , GA for six weeks over the summer break.

Summer at Fort Benning was hot, muggy and a miserable experience. I developed a respiratory infection two weeks before graduation and wound up in the hospital. Two well-starched Lt. Colonels with their swagger sticks visited me. They recognized my last name and asked if I was Rocky Tierno's son. Then they asked what I had learned over the training period. To their dismay, I responded,"Don't be first, don't be last, and never volunteer!"

I returned to my unit and prepared to graduate and head back to OU. Wayne and I drove straight through to Oklahoma. I dropped Wayne off in Yukon, then headed to the Howard Johnson Motel in Norman where the manager, DKE alum, Rex Beckenhauer let me bunk until the house reopened in late August.

The following year I headed to Fort Sill, OK for six weeks of advanced training. I spent my 21st birthday drinking 3.2 beer and watching tarantulas cross a road.

I did, however, catch a break when the ROTC department recruited cadets for flight training. I had 20/20 vision and passed the rest of the physical.

We flew Cessna 150 aircraft out of the old naval base near campus. I wasn't required to attend drills, I got to wear a flight jacket, and I let my hair grow longer.

Ten hours of solo time and a near collision with an idiot who cut me off on final approach made me think better of flying. With too many classes and the student store pressure.

I voluntarily quit the program.

The Student Services Store

Student store to open soon

Deke Brother Fred Streb (left) and Bob Tierno (right) prep for the store opening

13
Shelf Life

You say you want a revolution
Well, you know
We all want to change the world...
— "Revolution," The Beatles (1968)

I was looking at my transcript from OU recently. Other than Military Science (oxymoron) and Water Safety Instructor (an elective), there was nothing of any career-advancing redeeming value. I went to college to graduate, a feat only accomplished to date by my father Rocky (West Point '45).

The true benefit of the college experience was establishing relationships with a broad spectrum of people. The Deke experience established a "home" at college with a group of brothers that were indeed Gentlemen (most of the time), Scholars, and Jolly Good Fellows, the Deke motto. The Student Services Store was an experience like no other for me as a student and while I had many experiences at OU, this one stands out.

Ripped Off Among Radicals

You never have enough money in college. Everybody around me at OU was complaining about getting ripped off by these off-campus 7-Eleven and Lil' Red convenience stores, and their high prices. The times were ripe for change. The one-year tenure of OU's president came to an abrupt end and a temporary president was appointed.

The OU Student Association (OUSA) was led by an upstart Afro-American, Bill Moffitt (a huge afro), hailing from Bedford Stuyvesant, NY, plus a small cabinet of politically-astute students.

I joined as a cabinet member, I'm guessing, because I was white, a fraternity member (perceived conservative) and in Army ROTC. The ROTC professors were not very happy with me, of course.

During the post-Kent State anti war protests, I was the go-between with the campus police, the protestors and anti-protesters, especially when the protest was moved to Owen Field, the Sooners' football stadium.

Rumors ran rampant concerning guns being found around campus and farmers with pitchforks coming to quell the rebellion.

The administration threatened to cancel the Jimi Hendrix concert in the Field House. We had to insure that all went well. Oklahoma State Troopers were stationed outside while everybody got high enjoying Purple Haze, and Hendrix's rendition of the National Anthem. This was to be one of his last concerts before dying of an overdose. We did well. No one died.

Back to the Student Store. The OU Student Association Senate heard their constituents and demanded that Moffitt's crew address the issue most affecting students' pocketbooks.

41

Learning Retail on the Run

I did some research about student-run stores and cooperatives. I contacted the University of Texas and even UC Berkeley to understand the challenges of setting up a student store. My inner entrepreneur kicked in and said, "I'll lead the effort to start a student store." My Deke fraternity brother Bill Nation and I figured out how to get the money to fund it while learning how to open a store on campus.

We talked to a member of another fraternity whose dad owned a chain of grocery stores. He gave us a quick primer on how to open a store. His dad was very helpful but, frankly, thought we were nuts. We had to navigate some really tricky waters.

We borrowed $10,000 of student government money, then signed the lease to rent space on the first floor lobby of a 12-story dormitory tower for pennies per square foot. Imagine twelve stories of hungry students above the store, a 1500-square-foot pop up on the first floor operating 24 hours a day, seven days a week. There were three towers on that block. One was a U.S. Postal Service training dorm. Two were for students.

We had a captive market of students. From the first day we opened, the receipts were incredible. At the time, we didn't want to disclose how much money we were taking in, or the lease would have been up for renegotiation. For safety reasons, I split the day's deposits between our accountant and our security cop.

More Reefers (the other kind)

Our Deke brother Fred Streb built the walls, installed the doors and finished out the store space of 1,500-square feet. Some aspects were simple. We quickly learned we could negotiate with different vendors, and the vendors would come in and install the shelves and the gondolas and reefers, the refrigeration units.

They would even stock the shelves. Our soda can sales were incredible. Coca-Cola would park their truck at the dorm on the weekends so we never ran out of soda! We also had a storeroom in the basement for canned goods and nonperishable items. Cigarette sales were supported by a tobacco rep.

As founder and manager, I turned over all responsibilities for paying the bills and revenue accountability to Bill Nation. Many a night were spent counting cash and preparing deposits while sitting on the floor of our fraternity room.

14
The Safeway Book

The hardest thing about starting the OU store was getting a
food distributor to sell to us. I was in a flight program. My hair
was a lot longer and I had on these really bright, striped bell
bottom pants. I wore my flight jacket to the meeting, but that
didn't really matter. He was giving me a lot of lip service.

He said, "Here's the 7-Eleven book."

I asked, "Why would I want a 7-Eleven book?"

He replied, "Well, that's everything you need." He meant all
the inventory lists and the pricing that 7-Eleven relied on, a
grocery insider's dream.

"I want the Safeway book," I said, because that's what I
learned from the fraternity guy's dad. Items would cost less
allowing us to lower prices.

This distributor was getting a little upset with me and said,
"We don't even think you're going to make it. Why should I
do this?"

I took out the $10,000 check and put it on the counter.

He stared at the check and said, "Here's your Safeway book."

And that was that. He set up an account for us right then and
there.

We learned the grocery business by doing. Several of the guys in the Deke house were business school students, so I went over to the business school at OU to talk to the business professors about what we were doing, and they threw me out on my ear. Their job was to produce corporate, IBM-ready graduates, not entrepreneurs. I find it interesting that 50 years later, they have a school for entrepreneurial studies, of course.

And we did it in real time. We opened the store, managed it, we stocked it, ordered and restocked all while we were full-time students.

We priced soda at a quarter per can and the business was strong, especially on weekends. The Coca Cola Guy and the Pepsi Guy would bring a truck and leave it parked right outside the tower and just swing by on their own to restock. It was amazing what was flying out the door. We grossed about a hundred grand that first year.

15
Afro Picks

Who is the man that would risk his neck for his brother man?
(Shaft) Can ya dig it?
— Isaac Hayes, "Theme from Shaft"

A dose of reality. We had an Afro-American student working for us. He told me, "The black student association is really upset that you don't have any black products in the store."

"What do we need to stock to make them happy?" I asked.

"Afro picks and stuff like that."

I got out the Oklahoma City phone book and found the distributor. The rep. They sent out a guy who reminded me of Shaft from the movie *Shaft*.

He told me, "You're going to make a killing."

He laid out all this stuff and told me he would put a rack in.

"How much is this pick?" I asked.

"It's going to cost you 50 cents, but you can sell it for $10.00."

This was outrageous to me. I looked at his price list and quickly made a decision. We brought everything down, with no respect to profit margins.

We brought everything down to below market, but we were still making money.

Then someone in the black students association decided to write an editorial about how our store's racist policies were ripping them off with high-priced Afro products.

I had to go testify at an OU student association meeting.

I walked in with the price list and said, "I'll answer all your questions, but first you have to consider this. I am charged 50 cents for this hair pick and *your* sales guy, who represents your race, says I should charge you $10.00. So, if you want me to get in line with the market, what everybody else in the world outside of OU pays, I should just knock it up to ten bucks."

We were selling the Afro pick for $5. Basically, half what we could charge, and they were flying off the shelves.

"So what's the problem here?" I asked them. "Unless you want me to do it for free. In that case, I'm just going to take the whole thing out."

The student body president was black. He understood my explanation.

And we cleared another hurdle.

16
Fridges, Bicycles and Egg McMuffins

We ran a retail store. We had issues with shoplifting. We were open 24 hours a day and everything was strictly cash.

Bill and I decided to add to the store's complexity. We expanded to rentals of bicycles and refrigerators.

When the university-run grills got shut down, I negotiated with the university and said we wanted to lease the grills and reopen them because of where they were located.

We started tweaking the menus at the grills.

I remembered how my dad used to make us egg sandwiches and I never thought anything of it, but it was really the first Egg McMuffin. We introduced those at school and they just flew out the door.

That's my story and I am sticking to it.

17
To Beer, or Not to Beer

The *pièce de résistance* for our store was the liquor license. If the Student Union can sell beer, why couldn't we sell beer as well? I didn't realize how easy it was to apply for an ABC license. I completed an ABC license application and the next thing I know, I get the license in the mail.

Bill Moffit, the OU student body president, and the staff all wanted to know, "When are you going to start selling beer?"

It wasn't if, but when. I replied, "I'm really not sure whether we're going to sell beer or not. I'm still thinking about it. The beer companies are already calling me."

The next thing I know there is a story about it in the Norman *Transcript*. We don't know who told them. I certainly didn't. Next, I get a call from the OU interim president's secretary, summoning me to breakfast the next morning. That is never a good thing.

I get up early and put on a typical fraternity/collegiate look and went over there for breakfast. The OU president starts reading me the riot act and then he pulls out the Norman *Transcript*, and wants to know what I had to say about the liquor license article.

"It's our policy in student government to not comment on newspaper articles." I told him.

He went red in the face. I could see the veins were popping out as he exclaimed, "If you think you're going to sell one can of beer in there, your ass is mine!"

"We're still thinking about it," I said, cooly.

It didn't bother me that much because I was so close to graduating.

18
Coda: Payback

Fast forward on your cassette players to 1973. My new wife Karen and I went back to visit her parents and go to an OU football game.

The university had made a decided shift to the right since I graduated, moving away from a more left-leaning, moderate position. They came down really hard on drug use after a decade of tolerance.

You had to be a student to run the store. When I got commissioned and was heading to the Army, my roommate Bill and then Fred Hager ran it. The store had moved to a new location, one that I organized, taking over space in one of the other towers formerly operated by the OU Bookstore.

I walked in looking for the manager. He was wearing an army fatigue jacket. I didn't say who I was. The manager was a "B" student as in business school. Wow, have times changed.

"When did you guys move in here? This was really a great space compared to the one in the other tower that opened several years prior."

The new manager said, "I don't know who the idiot was that set this up. They didn't have a clue what they were doing."

"Meet the idiot," Karen said, as I walked out the door.

We helped thousands of students save thousands of dollars. With our tower lobby locations, we also saved them time running off campus for high-priced items. We understood the demand, and came up with an ingenious method to meet it. Some individuals did not appreciate our inspired entrepreneurship. We provided employment and paid a good wage, plus discounts for store purchases.

In 1985, I was living in Dallas and went down to an OU alumni association meeting before the OU-Texas Red River Rivalry football game. Dr. David Burr, who was VP of student affairs when I was a student, made a beeline for me at the reception. He walked right up to me and said, "If you were in college today, I would have your ass in jail." It was comical. With a drink in one hand and a cigarette in the other, I responded, "Great to see that you are still alive." Unfortunately he died several years later. RIP Dr. Burr.

I understood why he said that. We had gotten one over on him, and he never forgot it. By the way, we paid back the $10,000 loan to student government, in the first year. We broke no laws, and were transparent with our business practices and were full-time students. Brother Bill Nation rented the rental refrigerators and bicycles.

Brother Richard Hager supported Bill, who ultimately joined Kroger Stores and retired several years ago as a vice president. I turned down offers from the Coca-Cola distributor, Budweiser, and others because I had other plans and I wasn't coming back to Oklahoma for a long while.

II. Ron
An Officer in the Making
(1946 - 1970)

Upperclass Cadet Captain Ron Sorter (far left, in glasses) marching the freshmen in formation (Norman, OK, 1968)

Colorado
(1946-1964)

19
The West

My story is a story of the West. It takes place in Colorado, Oklahoma, California and Washington. Even the events that take place in Panama and Southeast Asia have Western style.

There are Wild West aspects to my personality that I chalk up to my kin who helped settle the West. There was a toughness from my parents who survived the Dust Bowl, and a respect for straight-talk. We're polite in the West, but only until we circle the wagons. If we say nothing to you, we're good. If we don't care for you, we'll find a way to tell you in person.

My dear wife Michelle, like a lot of us, traveled the country before settling out here. We met in San Diego and for 25 years we made our home in the high country of Redstone, CO (pop. 92), a place where you can be exactly who you are while keeping arm's length from Aspen and all its billions.

My wanderlust and love of the road were influenced by that modern western, *Route 66*. There's nothing like getting behind the wheel of a classic big-block Corvette and heading for the open spaces and mountain ranges that make men look miniscule. Those places must be in my blood.

20
Viola

Viola Breitling was born in 1920 in Wishek, ND. Her parents were of German descent by way of Russia. Catherine the Great had encouraged Germans to settle in the Volga River basin in the 1700's, to introduce their industry and ability to her people. She assured them they could keep their language and customs, but by the 1800's the Cossacks had different ideas. Thus, their exodus past the grand Copper Lady in New York Harbor and eventually to North Dakota.

In the 1920's Gottleib Breitling bought a piece of dry Oklahoma prairie and my mother, then a toddler, and her brothers and sisters became children of the red dirt country. They would later regal their own children with tales of their life on a shrieking prairie during the Dust Bowl.

She remembered the dust as a swirling red powder. And every bit of white clothing turning pink in the wash. The flour-like dirt made its way into the house despite closed windows and doors. They dared each other to find the barn in a windstorm. They tied ropes between the house and the barn so they wouldn't get lost on the way.

My mother had chicken pox, resulting in a profound loss of hearing. She was sent home by her teachers and labeled "too retarded to attend." Fortunately, it was just her hearing. She spent time at home helping on the farm, while the other kids went to school. She finished second grade, and that was it.

The harvesting combines came in waves through Texas and Oklahoma to harvest the wheat crop. Local families were, by custom, to feed the combine drivers. Viola was such a good cook she hired herself out to neighboring farms as a teenager to cook for the combine crews. She took great pride in her young reputation.

In 1940, she became a hairdresser and lived outside of Custer, OK. Bill Sorter lived in town and he had a car, which the hairdressers noticed. "The front end is leaving town before the rear end gets to town," they said. It was a small town.

Viola and Bill dated. They won a local jitterbug contest. In 1944, they got married and honeymooned in Glenwood Springs, CO, near Ft. Carson where he was stationed.

My uncle Skip lived nearby in Palisade, CO. After Bill returned from Europe, my parents moved to Palisade, too. And thus the family's diaspora continued westward.

21
Grand Junction

Grand Junction, CO (elevation 4,483), is a dot on the map where the Rocky Mountain Uplift relaxes and the Colorado River, augmented by the Gunnison River, turns its precious waters west. Rails and roads followed the river into the Great American Desert, hauling freight and people to San Francisco, Los Angeles and everywhere in between.

Grand Junction is just west of the little town of Palisade, which nestles in vast fruit orchards. The trees are irrigated by a big canal of river water and the fruit grown there is wonderful. Palisade peaches? Man, they're the best. As an extra treat, the entire area is a sportsman's paradise. Take that, Louisiana.

South and west of town is the Uncompahgre Uplift and the Colorado Monument, which hold some of the finest deer, bear and elk hunting in Colorado.

East of town, topping out at over 11,000, feet is Grand Mesa, the largest flat-topped mountain in the world. It's capped with a flat volcanic flow holding countless lakes filled with rainbow, brown, and cutthroat trout.

It instantly became a winter playground with the invention of snowmobiles. If you have the nerve, you can shut your eyes and fly flatout on top of ten feet of snow. Of course, one can catch the tip of a ski on a hidden fence line and bury oneself in deep powder but I'd rather not talk about that.

22
Autumn Leaves

On October 4, 1946, I was born to Viola and Bill Sorter on a
sunny October day. As my mother held me in her arms in St.
Mary's Hospital, the yellows, oranges of russets of autumn
would be painting the cottonwoods and elms outside her
window, opened to the warm breezes of late summer.

She would have seen similar hues on the flanks of Grand
Mesa. The fiery aspen forests up there were even visible down
here in town, a mile below. My mother always reminded me
that all of the beautiful autumn leaves were a birthday present
made just for me.

There was no more important connection and rite of passage
than when my own mother passed me into this world. What a
saint she was. She now had a family of two boys and I've had
autumn leaves as a birthday present every year since. It's true.
Mom said.

Mom was rarely vulnerable and tough as nails. As my older
brother and I grew up, we never forgot that there was a belt
hanging on the wall of the back hallway, a brown belt, heavy,
with a brass buckle that matched the hook from which it hung.
I always gave it a wide berth. Lesson one, don't push Mom. In
our house there was no room for pushing back on the
critical lessons of life.

23
Dad

Bill Sorter was a fly fisherman and hunter of local renown.

When I was six, I begged to be allowed to cast his fly rod rigged with "double dries" and after a few ridiculous attempts to throw the heavy fly line he was helping me reel it in when all hell broke loose. We pulled in two nice rainbows, one on each fly. I was beside myself with joy and asserted, "This is so easy!" Of course, it's not, which I've learned over a lifetime.

My dad was a contractor so I swept a lot of floors as a kid to earn an allowance and eventually was allowed to pound nails, shingle roofs and finally use the table saw, a monster with giant wheels and sliding hand bars.

By fourteen, in t-shirt and gloves, I could run wheelbarrows full of concrete across planks and pour them into the forms. I slipped off the plank once and mixed the wheelbarrow, the concrete and me into a gummy pile in the bottom of the trench. The laughter from everybody was a great lesson, though, red-faced, I didn't notice at the time.

In 1962 I insulated a garage of what Dad said was the very first house ever built in Vail. Like most places in the West's high country it was being created by a mad flurry of men and machines in a place where a few months prior there had been nothing but grazing sheep. It was a hot summer, yet I wore a hat, my long sleeves buttoned, hands in thick leather gloves.

Sure, it was a dry heat, but I was still sweating like mad, stuffing fiberglass insulation into the ceiling rafters overhead. The fibers would get in my eyes, down my shirt collar, and I was sure I'd breathed in enough to insulate me from teenage heartbreak but, as anyone will tell you, that didn't work. It was good money, though.

Evenings were spent in our construction trailer playing poker, my dad ridiculing guys buying the surrounding land for $600 an acre when it was worth, maybe, $100. We reminded him of that, later.

Interstate 70 made Vail, and eventually that monster would consume the entire valley. See what we started?

I packed away lessons I learned swinging a hammer. And the beginnings of a work ethic, the discipline to do good work even when no one is watching. And one never knows when one might need to build a house for a fabulous woman. More on that later.

24
Tribe

1946 marked the birth of the Baby Boom, so I had tons of pals. We all took it for granted that there'd always be crowds of kids ready to play baseball, play snowball wars and Kick the Can every day until dark.

The sound of a tin can bouncing across the pavement still awakens those memories of a carefree youth and my initial brotherhood of constant pals on Linda Lane.

At the time, I assumed that bands of friends like this were just a part of me, my rightful tribe.

Everything was so innocent for us in the fifties. Can I just make that blank statement? America's kids played with their friends, relatively unscathed by the recently-ended world war. One trusted that everything would always be just like this.

One summer day when I was 11 or 12, things took a decided turn. Marshall and I were playing Army in the backyard when my pal Owen strolls over to the house, hair all combed and says, "Hey, let's go down and watch the girls at the pool."

We looked at him like he was crazy.

I said something like "Girls? Girls are stupid, man! Me and Marshall are playin' Army!"

I'd once heard Dad say he'd played real army with Patton at the Battle of the Bulge.

One day, surreptitiously looking through my parent's forbidden chest of drawers, I saw a weird box filled with little balloons and, at the very bottom of the drawer, a badge. A light blue rectangle with an antique musket, and a silver wreath surrounding it.

In the living room we had a picture of him wearing his uniform with only that badge. I nonchalantly asked him what it was one day and he told me it was a Combat Infantryman's Badge, awarded to soldiers who've been in close combat. Then he changed the subject.

The connection from the moment I saw it to this moment right now exists in this room where I'm writing these words. Over there on the wall I have my own CIB, plus a Purple Heart, a Bronze Star, captain's bars and all the rest. But in 1958, that was a dozen years in the future.

By the end of that summer my days of playing play army were over and Owen and I were leaning into teenagerhood, eyeing those beautifully transformed creatures down at the swimming pool.

25
Puberty

Puberty is fun, isn't it? First it twists your head around a couple of times then grabs you by the scruff of your neck and pulls you right through the eye of a needle.

On the other side is the same world but you know you've been changed, big time. One grows hair. And then unexpected things start happening...down there.

Shirley was shy and I thought she was pretty. I was still getting my bearings about all that. She sat behind me in ninth grade English class and one day when the teacher wasn't looking she tapped me lightly on the back and when I turned around she hissed, "Turn back around!"

Then she tapped me on the elbow away from the teacher. I sneaked a look and saw a folded note, so on the QT I slowly moved my hand down and took it. The teacher pounced and, strutting back to the front of the class, he adjusted his glasses as he read the note to himself.

Assured there wasn't anything completely obscene in her note, he dramatically read it to the entire class. I was surprised and embarrassed, too, to first discover from the teacher how Shirley felt about me. It wasn't exactly Shakespearean but still... She said I had nice eyes.

Shirley was red faced and didn't speak to me for a week.

66

But finally she did. Apparently, she was a member of Rainbow Girls and needed a date for a special dance. I agreed and my dad taught me how to tie a tie, my mom taught me how to slow dance and Shirley's parents taught me how to nervously pin a corsage on Shirley's nascent bosom without ever touching it. At all.

We went steady for about three years, even dancing the Spotlight Dance when she finally became President. After she was crowned on a glittery round dais, I held her hand as we stepped down onto the floor of the gym, the single spotlight lighting us in the dark as the other couples and parents stood in a wide circle.

By then we were pros. We danced around the circle as others joined us and she was on cloud nine. Later that evening, our double date with Kathy and Stan continued on Lookout Point, where she and I had such a wonderful time in the back seat.

We ended up being the couple in high school who'd gone steady the longest. But finally we bought matching sweaters and I think that was the death knell. Apparently it was time to see other people and so we did. I saw her and her husband at our twentieth reunion and she had a wonderful family, living in Los Angeles. I remember her mostly for those lovely first acquaintances with young love and the unbuttoning of a person of the opposite sex.

26
The Jeep

Dad bought a used '46 Jeep. We painted it with scrub brushes, inside and out, added a folding top and a trailer hitch and then drove it to the end of every backcountry road we could find.

We'd tow it up to Grand Mesa and follow faint dirt tracks to hidden lakes all over its volcanic table top. We'd "turn the hubs" to get it into four wheel drive, shift it into the under range and crawl through every muddy hole on the road. He once stopped where the road crossed a rocky creek and, after wrapping some waxed paper around the distributor and, while we stood up holding onto the windshield, he drove through that creek while water ran up over the seats.

He'd love to bury us in some hole then shout instructions to my brother and I on how to get us out of the jam. My take? Don't get in a jam in the first place but if you do, know how to use a chain and come along because you can go anywhere and bring back fish that will astound the neighbors.

Once, when it was parked at home, I broke a major rule. I was speed shifting it while it sat there and the stick suddenly went all sloppy in my hand. Good God, I broke the tranny. I found some tools and taking a deep breath, removed four bolts holding the stick mechanism to the floor. I slowly lifted the stick mechanism up and peeked underneath it. Two half round things stuck out and they looked exactly like two matching channels down in the gear sets.

68

I carefully slid the half rounds back into the channels, rebolted the shifter plate in place and the rest is history. Which I've shared with no one until now. Dad is comfortably in his grave so I'm safe there. I recite my lesson often to my grandsons: "Rule one, don't get in a jam. Rule two, if you're threatened with death, just dive in and fix things."

27
Fast Cars

The biggest thing that happened in high school was JFK's assassination. They gave us the afternoon off at school and I sat on a park bench confused. It was as if the America we baby boomers had enjoyed as fixed and wonderful forever had fallen on its face. Uncertainty had leapt into our world in a single day. And life sped on.

You've seen *American Graffiti*, right? Grand Junction was precisely like that. Owen and I had a friend, Sam, who talked his uncle at the Studebaker dealership into letting us take a shiny new black Avanti for a test drive.

Something happens when you actually get to physically experience a dream like that. You get closer to convincing yourself that you can live that dream. Drifting a corner around curves in Debeque Canyon in a brand new Avanti definitely qualified as living the dream.

A few months later, I saw Sam and Owen standing outside the window to my math class smiling and waving a set of keys so I grabbed my books, told the teacher I was feeling sick and had to go home.

In the parking lot sat Sam's brand new 1962 Impala Super Sport #409, four speed, light metallic blue. We respectfully got into that cathedral of coolness. And split.

We can debate whether the Muscle Car Era started with the '49 Olds Rocket 88 or the '55 Chrysler Hemi but I'm voting for that day in '62. It seems like only days later, cars just like Sam's were everywhere.

Me? I was saving money for college. I drove a '53 Chevy beater.

28
Tina

Why I did work at the A&W root beer joint? It was one of the two main hangouts/cruising stops on North Avenue, the main drag in Grand Junction. Wait, that's not the real reason. It was Tina. She was the head cheerleader at Central High, our arch nemesis. Of course, we all hated Central. We were the Tigers, Orange and Black to the core. They were the Warriors. Their colors were Red and...I forget, but I know one color was red. Let me tell you why I remember that.

Free at last with driver's licenses, my tribe attended a basket-ball game at Central and their bleachers were crammed with people screaming for their team. We were doing the same on our side with our cheerleaders who were, between cheers, kneeling courtside facing Central.

Tina and her band of cheerleaders were kneeling down, facing us. A few of us began to notice that when Tina got particularly excited she'd grab her little dress and quickly flap it up and down, showing her distinctly red...you know. I'm sure she had no idea. Did I say we noticed? There were guys elbowing other guys, "Jeez, look at Tina."

She made Marilyn Monroe look average. It was a sin, I know, but that instant we all became Central fans despite questioning looks from our other bleacher mates. We cheered for more Central baskets! Lots of boys my age were pigs; sorry.

Immaturity is often transformed into maturity by undergoing certain rituals of initiation like that. Guys have undiscussed rituals, women do, too. It's the method whereby we change how we think. One can begin by hooting together at an attractive female and learn later how immature it was when one learns that all along that female was and is actually a very nice, humble person. Having a daughter drove that home to me with chrome-like clarity.

As a young male, I needed a job and there weren't many gorgeous cheerleaders working on Dad's job sites. Tina was a carhop at the local A&W so I immediately started as a menial rootbeer gofer. I had a crush on her the size of Texas and in my teenage mind I saw a wonderful future for us. Late one night at closing time, her boyfriend showed up and parked his customized '57 Chevy Bel Air next to where I, in a dirty apron, was hosing off sticky rubber floor mats in the parking lot.

They, and I, were covered with root beer stains as boyfriend leaned against his car waiting for Tina and asked me nicely to keep the water off his car. Jeffrey Conger was his name and he was the former state heavyweight wrestling champion.

You were totally expecting that, weren't you? It's the way romantic movies work. Sometimes we don't get to star in them, but are forced to watch the happy lovebirds drive away as we hose off a floor mat that reeks of broken dreams and root beer. Yeah, it was heartbreaking as she said, "'Night." as she passed me. I was sixteen. But I still had fantasies. Someday, on the road, in a Vette...

73

29
Skiing with Stein Eriksen

I learned to ski when I was ten. As soon as our drivers licenses put Aspen within reach, we'd tell our parents we'd be on sleepovers and drive up to Aspen Highlands on Friday night. We'd sleep in the parking lot so we could be skiing when the lifts opened.

Before Aspen became so moneyed, skill on skis was the only currency. And when one talks about skill on skis, Stein Eriksen's name always comes up. He was the legendary Director of the Highlands Ski Patrol, and winner of the Giant Slalom gold medal in the 1952 Winter Olympics. He gave lessons, too. Let me tell you about the one he gave me.

One sunny day I was coming fast off the mountain, not skiing breakneck, but for me pretty fast. Someone flashed past me on the right and I recognized him. The King, wearing a robin's-egg-blue one piece, tanned, blond. He barely moved, making graceful small motions but, man, he just flew by me.

I usually went to the lodge by hanging a right off this slope onto a narrow catwalk through the forest then down to a little bunny slope and over to the lodge. It looked like Stein was going that way, too, so I leaned into it a little and brought my skis closer together to maybe keep up. I shot into the shadows of the catwalk, the mountain on my right, an abyss of trees on my left and suddenly I saw him abruptly slow, do a thing with his poles and catapult over the left edge into the trees.

I was actually falling down the mountain while still on my skis. I madly shifted weight, put my edges crossways and shaved speed while asking myself what the *hell* I was doing. I couldn't believe I'd decided to follow him. Before I could stop I shot over the edge behind him into deep, steep snow, right through the trees, one branch almost taking my head off. I pulled my weight back to lift my ski tips above the snow, falling fast but still somehow skiing.

Then I was out, going hell bent for the lodge and all its windows. I glimpsed a man in blue taking off his skis as I turned a little then whipped hard over to spray snow, finally slowing, slowing, slowing until I barely, finally came to a breathless stop right next to the ski racks. I was alive. I was still upright. I was amazed.

No one noticed me but I saw several beautiful women by the doorway of the lodge, and I could see Stein through the windows. I'll never forget one of the women by the door. She was smiling at her friends and fanning her face like she was going to faint.

Here's what Stein Eriksen taught me: ski with the very best and do whatever it takes to keep up. I think it's one of my life's greatest lessons, regardless of the activity.

I also got to see how certain men can leave molten women in their wake. Stein Eriksen doesn't know me from Adam but to this day I love to tell anyone who can grasp it, "Sure, I skied with Stein Eriksen."

30
Route 66

As I got closer to graduating, my connections focused on my pals and my sainted mother, that's it. My dad? By that time he was out of the picture. I knew my mom was devastated but I wasn't. His fathering skills had evaporated entirely after my brother and I reached puberty. His enduring lesson was to try to convince me I was "too stupid to do a goddamned thing."

My brother joined the Air Force after he graduated the year before me. I took him to the train station and waited as it began to roll. The train horns blasted and I saw him arrive at the curved rear window at the end of the last car as the wheels started rolling. We didn't wave, we just stood there looking at each other until he finally disappeared.

My last memory of Grand Junction? If you're of a certain age, you'll remember the TV show, *Route 66*. It was about two guys roaming America in a new Corvette, looking for fun and adventure with fascinating women. The Corvette used in the show was once trailered through Grand Junction to a shoot somewhere in Utah. A crowd of us saw it and drooled on it as it camped overnight at a local motel.

Seeing that car in the flesh helped me form a fantasy that night, that somehow, someday, I'd be taking road trips in Corvettes with the most fabulous woman in the world riding in the passenger seat. It took me decades, but my dream eventually unfolded and her story begins in section VIII.

31
Summer of '64: It All Turns to Dust

On Graduation Day, we moved our tassels from one side to the other of our odd square hats, and went outside for pictures. Mom went to get the car. Excitement of a new life filled the air with shouts of, "See you at the party tonight!"

Guys ran by, yelling at Owen and I, "Don't forget the kegger at Dean's house!" These were the people who would stay in Grand Junction. Maybe forever, who knows?

I was leaving, confused but hoping there was a transformation waiting for me in Oklahoma.

Mom had the Buick idling at the curb. Owen and I finally shook hands in a confused way, "See ya."

I walked into the gym and tossed my hat and gown into a big box that should have been labeled Finality.

I went outside and got in the car. We stopped at the A&W, got one last burger and left that town behind.

Oklahoma
(1964-1969)

32
CO to OK

Road trips are cathartic for me. I sort things out while looking down a highway. In the long silences, I can see a car coming at me, pass me, then disappear behind. I understand the flow. I can sort things and figure out what I need to do. But on that long ride to Oklahoma I was only seventeen and I was definitely not yet up to roadtrip speed.

Mom and I alternated driving straight through stopping only for gas and to call her brother long distance to let him know when we'd arrive. We didn't speak much. Mountains turned into flat land and two lanes ran straight to the horizon. Each oncoming semi took its turn pushing us around.

When Oklahoma City finally appeared at the horizon, the hot wind through open windows had become ceaseless. The car was an oven and for me the exciting road trip had become a blur of nothing but endless wheat fields.

We were the Joads returning to the Dust Bowl.

33
Uncle Matt

We finally arrived at Uncle Matt's driveway in Oklahoma City. I turned off the engine. We just sat there. The lack of road noise was peculiar, and I think we were both unsure of what to do next. We didn't even want to get out and knock on the door.

Then the garage door creaked open, and there stood my favorite Uncle Matt, his wife Sally and the kids, all smiling and Matt motioning to me, "Hey, park the car in the shade."

I carefully eased the car inside. We were helped out with this greeting: "Great to see you, how was your trip, come in the house, we have some cold lemonade, we'll bring your luggage later!"

Mom and I had floated to the surface. I was old enough that day to finally appreciate the true value of family and to appreciate the damage Dad had done to Mom. Or, so I thought.

My appreciation didn't extend to Mom's younger sister, Ella. The next day an offhand, cruel comment from her drove Mom from the house in anger. I'd never seen her do anything like that. Matt and I looked for her, rolling slowly through intersections, searching down each sidewalk.

He glanced over at me with a foul look on his face, "Bill left her in a rough way. Did she tell you?"

He pulled over, engine idling.

"Tell me what?"

He looked through the windshield and his words came out fast: "A couple weeks before Bill left he convinced Vi that a second mortgage on their house was the only way to buy a bunch of road equipment to rebuild your family's construction business. When it came time for her to sell your house to move here, she had to clear that mortgage. Bill told her if he sold the equipment to pay off the mortgage he wouldn't be able to come through with any of the money he promised for you to go to college."

He looked at me: "If that's your plan."

He eased the car back onto the street. "After paying off both mortgages herself, she ended up with a couple thousand dollars. That's it. After twenty years of marriage to that sonofabitch. Two thousand dollars."

He wasn't finished. "And all that food she packed for you guys to come down here? She could only eat the soft stuff because like some last goodbye from that crappy town a charred kernel of meat in a hamburger broke one of her teeth."

I couldn't believe it. She'd told me what I thought was everything, but not any of this.

"What are you going to do?" he asked me.

"When are you going to get a job? You need to be the other adult now."

I didn't know. I was seventeen and had dropped into a strange land with no map or compass. I was too embarrassed to tell him I didn't know where to begin.

We soon found Mom sitting on a park bench looking out at a small pond.

When we pulled up she looked over at us and said, "Hey, guys, give a girl a ride?"

She was smiling when she got up. The woman was made of steel.

We found an apartment that weekend. On Monday morning, thanks to Matt, I was a warehouse assistant in a Uniroyal tire distribution facility.

34
Stacks of Rubber

Do you remember the final scene in *Raiders of The Last Ark*? That gigantic warehouse?

At 8:00 a.m. sharp, I walked into a similar giant warehouse filled to the ceiling with tires. There were huge excavator and tractor tires leaning in ranks against every empty wall. Passenger and truck tires of every size were crammed into pallets stacked to the ceiling in long aisles of black rubber. The place smelled of fresh hot rubber. It was so hot I was already sweating.

A guy came out of a little office, huge belt buckle, torn cowboy boots, mouth full of chewing tobacco, carrying a paper cup. He leaned against a big forklift that had a gigantic empty pallet on its front forks, looked at me and asked, "You Ron?"

I said I was, so he put out his hand out. After we shook, he spit in his cup. He made it quick: "We ship tars to six states, ya see these orders?" Did he say "tars?"

He showed me a clipboard packed with papers. "We gotta fill these b'noon. Y'ready?"

I tried to be as business-like as possible, asking, "Yes. Where do I put my lunch?" I showed him my brown bag.

He looked at me, spit again and jerked his thumb towards the office, "In there. Take a piss if ya gotta 'cause you're gonna be ridin' this pallet all mornin'. Hurry up."

I did, then stepped onto the pallet, as he scanned the first order. He put the clipboard down, looked at me and said, "You afraid of heights?" I didn't know what he meant. "Hold on!" he yelled as he started the forklift and accelerated around a corner.

As it gained speed, I instinctively grabbed onto the lift's risers. We sped down a corridor and the pallet began lifting me towards the ceiling. He rolled a halt, yelling up at me, "Gimme sixteen of them 230s."

"What?"

"On your left. Look at the label on the bin. The tires have the same label. Make sixteen stacks, one high. Keeps the load balanced. Keeps the order on one level. Hurry up!"

I was holding on for dear life. I looked down. It was ten feet down to the concrete floor. It must have been 100 degrees.

I started loading hot tires onto the pallet, each one covered with little flexible black hairs. Then I would hold on as we sped over to other stacks, sometimes on the floor, sometimes up high. It was like being on an elevator with wheels and a crazy man at the controls. But he knew where every tire he wanted was located, and we worked methodically across the warehouse, filling the pallet as we went.

85

It wasn't long before there was no place left to stand. I found myself laying on top of the pallet's tires holding onto the risers, hoping I could keep them from falling off with me.

When a pallet was full, we'd race for the shipping dock, offload the pallet, pull the pink copy of the order, tape it to a top tire and get another empty pallet. He'd throw his full spit cup away, get another one and yell, "Drink more water, take a piss, hurry up!" I would then run to get on the pallet before he disappeared into the stacks.

All morning, diving into piles of sticky new tires, pulling out a few, stacking them as we raced to a new pile, sweating, sweating, making sure the count was right, dreading the top stacks where the metal roof radiated like a furnace, never stopping.

Merle Haggard songs floated through the stacks with us. Sometimes the cheaper tires would collapse in on each other like pancakes, throwing off my count. The bigger tractor tires could be rolled along the floor later, wheelbarrow tires went inside the truck tires.

I thought I'd worked fast packing peaches in Colorado but it was nothing like this.

There was an antique Coke machine where we'd have a free cold Coke for ten minutes at ten o'clock then begin again. By lunch I was more tired than I'd ever been in my life. I inhaled my lunch listening to Buck Owens and we began again.

In the afternoon, the semis began arriving. Orders were located, brought to the dock and loaded. Between loads, we'd pull more orders. I swore my watch was broken because time had stopped.

Somehow I made it until quitting time. Sitting in the office with Bill waiting for my ride, he surprised me by saying in a kindly way, "I been doin this alone for four years, with no vacation. Two guys can do the work of three so I'm gonna teach you how to run this place for a week while I go down to Houston and screw my honey."

As we were walking out I heard him tell the facility manager, "He'll do. First day jitters but he'll do fine." I didn't tell them I was going to hop a freight and be long gone by tomorrow.

But I didn't. Mom told me she'd gotten a job at a fabric store. We decided to work, put money away and decide our futures in time. I collapsed on the bed, went to work the next day and the day after that.

After a month I pretty much knew the ropes. Bill would even load tires and let me drive sometimes, spitting into the cup in his shirt pocket.

One day he said, "I think you're ready. I'm gonna take a vacation in two weeks." And he did. The manager had asked me if I knew anybody who'd work cheap for a week, so he hired my cousin Freddie. Freddie was my age so with his help I successfully ran the place that week Bill was gone.

I drove the forklift and Freddie got to load the pallet. He hated it, he told me so constantly. I laughed.

In July, I made a weekend trip to Oklahoma University with another uncle who'd gone to school there. Stately old brick buildings, 22,500 students, in-state tuition. It'd be barely do-able if I could get a part time job somewhere. I told Freddie I was going to go for it.

By the end of the summer I'd proved that I could run a shipping warehouse at age17. It made me more confident, more certain that I could make it in college.

I applied and was accepted. I had the feeling that once I knew where the road was going I could put the pedal down. Since I'd only then be limited by the speed of the vehicle, I could fix that by buying a faster car. I'd heard Corvettes were nice. I'll get a degree in business, make some money and buy one.

By the end of that summer, I had found my compass.

35

Threshold I: What the Hell is ROTC?

1964 was full of threshold moments. Early one September morning, I drove Mom to work at the fabric store and before she got out, she made a point of saying, "Good luck, you'll be fine."

I turned on the AM radio. As I drove to Norman, an hour south of Oklahoma City, I reviewed all of the things I'd packed in the car: clothes, local checks, drivers license and most importantly, the list of classes I would be registering for as soon as I got there. I'd checked everything twice the night before. I had no idea how little that I knew.

There was no place to park on campus. I found a parking place off campus and joined other students streaming to the massive basketball arena up ahead. Inside the door someone asked for my last name, directed me to a long line and I slowly inched up to a long table. I gave the lady my name, she pulled a big card, handed it to me with a pencil and said, "Next!"

I looked at her and said, "Wait. What do I do?"

She handed me a paper. "Read the instructions, here, next!"

Apparently, one went line to line registering for the classes indicated on the card. I located the first class I needed and got in line. I registered in that class, then on to another line. This shouldn't be too hard, I thought. And the first few weren't.

–English 101, Required, MWF, 9AM
–Math 206, Elective, TTh, 2PM
–ROTC 101, Required, TTH 10AM

Wait, what the hell's ROTC?

I noticed the ROTC table had a stack of brochures, so I went back and got one. It said that since OU was a "land grant" college, two years of ROTC was required for every male student. OK. I liked to play army as a kid, I'm sure this would be easy.

The building was getting hotter, crammed as it was with so many people. I remembered that there were 22,500 students and apparently they all knew each other. It was a cacophony,

"Hey, Betty, nice to see you. We're gonna be in English together!"

"How was your summer?"

I didn't know a soul and was confused. I discovered that day that I had no idea at all about how to strike up conversations with people.

As I filled my registration card with classes, I'd get in lines for the remaining classes I needed, only to find none of the available times fit my schedule. I overheard someone say to register anyway, then go back and reschedule another time for the first class.

So I did that as more time passed, more time, more classes. By then it was afternoon, I was hungry and the building was hot and humid. The sea of people was starting to ebb. I kept telling myself at least I wasn't having to load tires.

I'd noticed many people talking together, doing all this with such ease, obviously veterans of this crazy free-for-all. I noticed some girls who wore clothing with matching Greek letters on them.

By the time I was finally finished, I walked back to the car, opened the doors to let it cool off and just sat there. I'd registered but I'd also discovered that I was adrift, alone in a sea of people.

I was afraid to even strike up a conversation with someone. How could that be? Hell, I still had to find my dorm.

36
College Man

It took me another hour to locate the building, inching slowly along with other cars apparently doing the same. I parked in a temporary unloading space and went into the building. I was given a key and a reminder I had to move my car.

There was a guy playing the bagpipes outside the open window. I admired this guy.

You can do whatever you want at OU as long as you don't mind someone tossing a shoe at you. I'll remember that.

I found my room, the door was open and my two new roommates were sitting on the two bottom bunks. We introduced ourselves. They pointed at an empty closet and I went out to get my stuff. They were gone by the time I returned.

I put everything I had in the closet, locked it and pocketed the key. Dead tired, I went to the car and drove slowly through campus again, and then I headed for the highway and home.

37
The Barbecue Ritual

That night the entire family was at Matt's for a barbeque. I walked through the house and noticed the glass patio doors now had OU Sooners decals pasted all over them. Nice.

I just wanted to sit down.

As I walked into the crowded backyard, my Uncle Matt asked, "So, are you an official student at OU?"

I nodded. He gave me a cold beer and everyone lifted their drinks and sang "Boomer Sooner," the official OU song.

I looked over at Mom, who seemed pleased. We had escaped Grand Junction, my dad, her past and my childhood. Family looked after family. I had the instinct then that this barbecue was an important rite of passage.

Apparently, I'd managed to join a very popular tribe hereabouts. Somebody told me that Fred was going to go to Oklahoma State, our arch-rival second only to the University of Texas. I'd have to give him some hell at Christmas.

In the crowd of cousins and relations in the back yard was Uncle Marvin, Matt's older brother. He was wearing his OU '52 jersey. As I made my way over to see Matt, everyone started talking at once, "How did it go? What's your major? Can you get us discounted football tickets?"

I laughed. I just said I was happy it was over.

Marvin had been a Big Man On Campus at OU, which held some rank. He'd graduated with a 3.96 average on a 4.0 scale, so I seriously respected the man's brain.

He drew me aside, leaned in and quietly asked, "Did you see some gorgeous women?"

I nodded, "Yep."

"You're a college man now, Ron," he said. "Don't study every night, OK?"

He elbowed me in the ribs, grinned and walked away. Marvin was a hound. Who knew?

I waved at his wife.

The sweet smell of barbeque filled the air. Matt was by the grill wearing his OU apron and Sooners hat. He packed the last few corn cobs onto the grill's top shelf and wiped his hands.

Then he gave me a grownup handshake, dug into a cooler and handed me another beer.

He turned to the crowd and bellowed, "To the newest Sooner in the family!"

Everyone lifted their drinks and started singing "Boomer Sooner" again.

I looked over at my mom, surrounded by her family. I could tell she was proud of me.

Hours later I lay in bed, thinking about all that Matt had done for me. I hadn't attended a single class yet but I couldn't deny that I'd registered at a storied university after a summer of learning the ropes at a real job.

At 17, I may not have officially been an adult but the more I thought about it, the more I convinced myself that Matt's ceremonial barbeque was his way of arranging for the family to celebrate this transition of mine. It had meant something to everyone.

High school graduation had been a transition, but a transition into an unknown future. This transition had a future. I'd mapped it out, class by class, that morning in the field house and I didn't intend to let my family down.

38
Threshold II: First Day of Class

That first Monday morning I was up early. I went to the
cafeteria, opened the door and it was bedlam. Food trays clat-
tered onto rails, clean plates and silverware were thrown on,
then an empty glass, everybody in line was hurriedly shuffling
towards steaming bins filled with food of some kind. I quickly
got in line, too.

"What's that?" someone would ask. "That" is the dorm word
for food. One ordered by simply pointing, saying, "Gimme
some of that." It was still a few minutes before sunup and
it was already hot. Steaming food added clouds of smells. I
could see the bacon. I wanted some of that.

A few food tray veterans in line had first stopped by the
coffee urns for a cup of coffee. Damn, great idea. The clamor of
loud conversation reverberated around me as I silently inhaled
my food, watching many of my fellow foodmates
nervously eyeing the action. Me, too, I guess, inhaling a
serving of first-day jitters. If one had an early class to make,
there was no reason to be here so I and others were leaving as
quickly as other new students arrived.

Back in my room, I grabbed the books I would need for the
day. My new books were used, cheap, and underlined. I'd
scanned them the night before. One thing was apparent: college wasn't going to be about hanging out with my pals taking
easy classes and cruising town afterwards.

I had to admit, I was wearing some pretty cool clothes for the first day. I wondered about the vast majority of the other guys I'd seen in the cafeteria. Some of them had been wearing *penny loafers*. For God's sake, one had even been wearing palomino-colored penny loafers with yellow socks. And a button down shirt! Man, how could a guy wear such sissy clothes in public? I had on some cool Beatlemania threads from high school, black boots, black pants, white tab collared shirt, open.

I found the room where my English class would meet and grabbed a seat close to the wall. The first few older students found seats by the open windows where it was cooler, and everybody else seemed to think that was a good idea, too. I vowed to do the same tomorrow. The teacher, a drop-dead gorgeous woman, walked in, introduced herself and sat on her desk, crossed her legs in my direction and began to say a bunch of stuff I barely remember. She was stunning.

"For how many of you is this your first class at this marvelous institution?" The majority raised their hands. I wasn't alone.

"We'll start with introductions and you can go first," she said, looking directly at me.

She waited as I tried to speak. I knew my name, I was sure. After a few seconds I said, "Ron."

She looked at me.

"Uh, Sorter," I said.

She said, "And you are from…?"

"I'm…from Colorado," I croaked. I heard snickers.

She covered some other topics and at the end of class explained that our homework would be the preparation of a two minute speech we'd each give the day after tomorrow regarding the importance of the proper use of English. Then something else, something else as I tried to focus on her face and then class was over. Everybody scrambled for the door.

Jeez, a speech, I hated the idea completely. Loved the professor, though.

In the hallway, I began to walk faster, trying to get out of this building, fighting masses of students going down stairwells. I was taking the shortest distance between two points, to a math class hidden in one of the older university buildings up on the North Oval.

I barely made it, taking one of the few empty seats in the back. One wall had windows but the other three had wall-to-wall blackboards. The blackboard in front had another one hanging above it, so the professor could pull it down and cover it with equations, too.

I liked math so I knew this would be a fun class. Plus, no speeches. His first sentence is seared in my mind: "This first day I'll only be summarizing what you already know."

He began speaking in a language I'd never heard before. I recognized a few words but I didn't recognize any subject I knew. I did notice that most of the other students looked older than me, and only a few were taking notes. I left class dazed.

Chemistry class was no different. More sanskrit. More older students.

After class, I found a private carrel desk hidden away in the stacks of Bizzell Library where I unloaded an armful of basic math and chemistry books.

That desk became my second home. The next two weeks would be daunting, playing catch up with the classes I was taking.

39
Dropping Out

After several weeks of studying night and day, I wasn't catching up. If anything, I was falling further behind. I couldn't share that realization with anyone but I did get up the nerve to go by the Admissions office. I asked one nice lady, "If I have to drop out would I get any of my tuition money back?"

Apparently that wasn't an unusual question.

She didn't bat an eye and handed me another brochure: "It's all in there. You can get most of it back but only if your advisor signs the withdrawal document."

She looked at me. "You don't know who your advisor is, do you?"

What a pathetic weenie I was. "No."

She sighed, went to the rear wall, thumbed through some records and finally stabbed her fingernail at something. "Found you. Professor Abernathy, Abbott Hall, room seven." With that she was done with me and walked to the other end of the counter. I went back to the library to think.

The next Monday I sat sweating on a hard hallway chair, trying to imagine how I was going to tell my family, especially after that wonderful barbecue, that I'd only made it for two weeks before having to leave OU.

A man with a briefcase walked towards me, his heels reverberating in the empty hallway. As he unlocked the door he looked at me and asked, "You waiting for me?" I said I was. He opened the door and said, "C'mon in."

He lifted a stack of papers from the only chair and dropped it onto an equally overflowing desk. "Sit down. What can I do for you?" I told him my story, saying I had to admit defeat and I imagined that, like my brother when he left college, I would join the military or something.

"Do you have your class schedule with you?" he asked. I pulled it out of my pocket and laid it on his desk. As he pondered it, he asked, "Why are you taking all these advanced classes?"

"They're the classes the university said I have to take," I said.

"These classes are usually for sophomores and juniors, not freshmen. How about I just change your schedule?"

As he filled out a class change approval, he explained how it probably happened, high SAT scores and my place in my high school graduating class.

He signed it with a flourish and handed it to me with a smile. "Take this to Admissions. I don't think you'll have any more problems." I couldn't believe it. Damn, I get to stay?

I found the same lady at Admissions. She said, "You again."

She could tell by the smile I was back on track and I never looked back. I got an A on my English speech about Bill's fractured but effective use of English in the tire warehouse and that made me a proper freshman. With a future.

40
Dorm Rats and Frats

Eighteen American presidents have been fraternity men. According to the Center for the Study of College Fraternity, fraternity men make up 85 percent of U.S. Supreme Court justices since 1910, 63 percent of all U.S. presidential cabinet members since 1900, and, historically, 76 percent of U.S. Senators, and 85 percent of Fortune 500 executives.

In the Sixties, it seemed that the privilege and rank associated with fraternities would always be a permanent part of college life.

In the abstract I admired the brotherhood of it but not the attitude. I knew nothing about them, really. My family had been wheat farmers. It seemed to me that rank had to be earned, not bestowed. And yet....

I began to notice more dorm guys wearing jackets bearing greek letters. They'd pledged a fraternity and were wearing the proof. And don't forget the cadres of beautiful girls on the sidewalks wearing matching sorority jackets.

OU had more fraternities and sororities than any other large university in the country. A dozen stately houses sat just off campus and as many more houses clustered down on Fraternity Row. A kid from Grand Junction who didn't know what or who he was in social terms knew he wouldn't fit into that tribe, no way. I was just a dorm rat.

Most of the guys in my dorm lived close to home, so on weekends it was almost empty. I envied their ability to return to friends and family each weekend for a re-up (real meals and clean laundry).

I had no car at that point and no friends, so I wandered around campus or studied in my dorm room. The library had Byzantine, hidden areas that offered privacy. Hiding, that's what I was doing. I was hiding.

To me it seemed the only people left on campus on weekends were us fools who still thought our high school clothes were cool and had nowhere to go but the library. I was an unproud member of the lonely fraternity of people who have zero skills at meeting people. God, even Buck Owens wouldn't sing a song like that.

I knew the professors had no concern whether students attended their classes or not. First semester, freshman year was designed to cull the herd.

I just said screw it. I went to the library, put my head down and did what I had done last summer. I loaded tires onto pallets.

41

Threshold III: Dinner at the Deke House

One night in November, 1964, I was propped in my upper
bunk studying Roman generalship for the next day's ROTC
class when Jim and Alex walked in and Alex asked, "Notice
anything unusual?" Who could miss the fraternity pledge pins
on their shirts. He walked over so I could see it close up.

"Delta Kappa Epsilon," he said. "Dekes, we're called."

We, Kimosabe?

"Our pledge class will be initiated in spring, and then we'll
be getting more sex than Frank Sinatra." They both broke up
hysterically. Frank Sinatra? I returned to Rome. I was getting a
serious rash about the high society associated with the Greek
system.

A week later, Alex returned from his weekend at home dressed
in new clothes. You guessed it, penny loafers, hopsack jacket,
tie with the Deke emblem on it, chinos with a cute buckle in
the back and, I'm not kidding, an ascot. He spent some time
with the mirror that night.

Jim began sporting a sartorial look, too. I chalked it up to
hanging out with Sinatra. The next Wednesday, I was shocked
when they asked me if I wanted to have dinner at the Deke
house. What would you say? I knew I wasn't fraternity
material. Curious about having dinner with aliens, I agreed.

The night arrived and Alex and Jim deposited me in a line of potential new pledges being introduced to the house mother. She was not alone; she had an escort. Culture and code.

When it was my turn, I heard her escort say, "Mother Harris, may I present Ron Sorter? Ron is a roommate of Alex and Jim, whom we pledged last week."

Wow. Formality for me?

She extended her hand, I took it and as she looked at me she smiled and said, "It's a pleasure to meet you. I hope you'll enjoy your evening with us."

Mother Harris was easily 85 years old, formerly married to a Phillips 66 oil executive. She would wear a 1920's flapper dress to every dance, like a character in an F. Scott Fitzgerald novel.

Her escort was already turning to the next guy as another member took my elbow and introduced himself as my guide for the rest of the night. Which was cool, as I was totally lost.

I was used to living in a WWII barracks with a cafeteria serving God only knew what. Here we were in a beautiful three-story mansion with a dining room glittering with matching china and polished silverware. I smelled real food. I was starving, but my guide gave me the full tour of the hotel-like accommodations upstairs. It was built in the twenties but it seemed to be nice enough. I'd learn later who actually kept it that way.

Finally, a gong sounded, we went back downstairs and, after the housemother was seated at the dining room's head table, everybody else sat down. The opulence was glaring. A spotless white napkin rested next to several silver forks.

I noticed every knife, like mine, had its edge aimed at the gold rim of the plate, I guess to guard it from all the spoons next to the knife.

The DKE fraternity crest was fired into the center of every piece of china in the room. On display was a service for fifty including every kind of salt and pepper shaker, soup tureen or accessory imaginable, in either polished silver or Deke china. Of course I was impressed, wouldn't you be? That was the plan.

Everyone put their napkin on their lap. So, I did too. Apparently we were all waiting for the housemother to begin eating and when she did, we began. Very Emily Post.

All I remember of that dinner was everyone laughing, myself included.

42
I Join a New Tribe

I must not have embarrassed myself too much, because I was asked to pledge the next week. It took a few days for me to work out the entire financial obligation in my mind. I'd have to go from working part-time to full-time, but I could do it, just barely.

It turned out to be one of the most fortuitous decisions of my life. Since I'd changed to freshman classes my grades were doing well but I hated the isolation. I was even considering other paths, not college life. I had no friends, no life and I knew that had to change. I couldn't survive, I didn't want to live in a perpetual shell.

I admitted that even without a closet full of ascots, the Dekes had treated me kindly.

How did Groucho Marx put it? "I don't care to belong to any club that will have me as a member." In this case I would and, overnight, it changed my life.

I had scorned it, I knew, but deep down I also realized I needed to be a part of something like this. I had learned how to work in the adult world with Bill that summer at the tire warehouse. Now it appeared I might be able to join a tribe of like-minded brothers who knew how to socialize and live in this world. I chose to join that world. To put it more fundamentally for me, they chose me.

I joined other pledges polishing the oak dining room floors, the silverware and windows on Saturdays. That was standard drill for pledges at every fraternity, along with the housemother teaching one how and when to use what utensils when dining, how to make introductions at parties and the requirement to graduate with a good game of bridge and a great game of golf.

I was initiated the next year, and to this day I still value those particular rites of passage. One crosses paths with certain brothers whose paths begin to cross with repeated meaning as the years go by.

A brotherhood can last a lifetime.

Bob Tierno and I can both say that. I was the Initiation Master the week he got his pin. His and my families would intersect repeatedly in the ensuing years. But that's all to come.

In 1965, there were legendary parties, a few pranks and serious study, too. Sooners football was always a full time obsession.

43
Football, Parties and Sorority Girls, Oh Man!

By the time I was a junior at OU, I'd dated a lot and finally bumped into Kathleen Eileen O'Connor. My, my. She was an Alpha Phi, with red hair and green eyes. And, yes, she was Irish and gorgeous. Her father had been the captain of an aircraft carrier in WWII, and he was now working on his Education doctorate.

She and I met at a mixer and ended up laughing all night. It was love or what passed for it in 1967. A few months later we were pinmates, then bedmates and more. I didn't want to get married yet. She did but we never really discussed it. I saw nothing but Vietnam in my future. My brother, in Vietnam at the time, wrote me a letter calling me an idiot.

Apparently, his wife, Sharon, whom he'd had to marry, was living with Mom while he was in 'Nam and she'd become friends with Kathleen when we visited. Kathleen had told Sharon that we didn't use contraception and she didn't mind since, if she got pregnant, I'd marry her and she could escape her dad who was a dick.

This letter was like a bolt of lightning from the other side of the planet. I asked her about it, she said something like "So, what, I thought you loved me." I soon bid her adieu and vowed to be more responsible. She threw my pin in a sewer and that was that. I started dating other girls as the Republic of Vietnam began to elbow everything else out of the way.

44
Mother Harris

It was lunchtime at the Deke house, and Mother Harris was casually rocking in her rocking chair next to her escort, elbow on the armrest, chin in her hand. They were discussing the matters of the day. I was sitting across from her in the living room, and next to me sat Taylor, the psych major.

After a few moments, he couldn't resist saying, "You know, Mother Harris, rocking is a form of masturbation." All the guys in the living room looked at Taylor then looked at Mother Harris. This was going to be good.

Her rocking stopped as she turned her gaze upon Taylor. We waited, looking first at her, then Taylor. She cooly considered him as she began rocking again, then looked back towards her escort and continued their conversation. She was imperturbable. Droll. An accomplished house mother, the only true adult in the house. The bell clanged. The round was over. Unanimous decision: Mom Harris, TKO.

She ruled her dining room. She would summon the house boys by ringing a small brass bell. During my time as the kitchen manager, I heard that bell. A lot.

At our weekend house parties, tradition required that she dance the first dance with one lucky soul. Never a waltz. No, she'd always wear the very same red fringed flapper dress she'd worn in the 1920's. Man, she could cut a rug.

Everyone would cheer when she cut loose because she was totally fearless. Then she'd return to her suite, probably to insert her earplugs and have a double martini so she wouldn't have to hear the soon-to-be drunken brotherhood screaming "Louie, Louie" into the band's microphone.

Her husband had passed away some years before. He'd been an executive with Phillips Petroleum. She liked to tell the story that, before a formal party somewhere in South America she, in her formal dress, had sewn up a tear in fellow Deke Henry Cabot Lodge's tuxedo pants, while he was still in them.

Her contribution to the brotherhood's poise and polish cannot be overstated. In many ways the thought of college men in their late teens and early 20s needing a house mother may seem ridiculous now.

But in the 60s, it was the final years of ceremonial, procedure-driven cultural life and Mother Harris was an invaluable avatar, teaching a bunch of Dekes, most of us admittedly uncouth, how to enter the world of grown-ups and thrive there by using the social mores of the day to advance ourselves. I found it invaluable in the military.

When she retired, I pocketed her bell. I still have it.

45
ROTC For Real

"What size are ya!?"

Teams of ROTC staff were throwing uniforms onto the tables as we newbies stuffed them into duffle bags.

"Move it, move it!"

Back in my dorm room I and my roommates began what would become a perpetual ritual, Brasso our insignia, polish our shoes, be "parade ready."

Freshman and sophomore years of ROTC, Reserve Officer Training Corp, were comprised of military studies and, every Tuesday evening, being marched to a nearby parade ground.

Upper-class student officers would try to keep us in formation but we were all new to this, looking ridiculous in our new, ill fitting uniforms.

" Ten-HUT! Dress right, DRESS! Ready, FRONT! Left FACE! Forward MARCH! "

That's what we heard while we looked to find anyone who knew what that meant. I knew how to stand at attention but what's this stuff about dresses? The upperclassmen tried their best. A bunch of college freshmen in uniform appear cartoon-ish at first.

As the years passed, that view was transformed to become something deadly serious.

It focused everyone's attention. Let me describe ROTC math.

If you flunked out, you were immediately drafted and sent to Vietnam. If you graduated you were immediately drafted and sent there. If you completed ROTC you went to Vietnam as an officer. If you didn't return from Vietnam, the value of that college degree reduced to zero. If you're in uniform and refuse to serve, then treason requires you to be shot. Clear enough?

Enlisting in the Air Force or Navy offered very low odds of combat, but with a four-year term of service. The Army's was a two-year term.

I made my choice of Army in 1964. Vietnam was an unknown backwater. I graduated in December 1968 when there were 500,000 troops in Vietnam. Most of the draftees wanted no part of it, nor did the soon-to-be draftees rioting in the streets. Returning soldiers were being spit on in public.

Each of us dealt with our choices in our own way. Some of them paid off. Some of them didn't. This may be an alien treatise to young males of today who have no such math to consider. But if the draft were to return, so would the riots. One's draft status focuses one's mind considerably.

It was like Bingo where the winners go to Heaven, and the losers go to Hell.

114

My railroad tracks led out of town to some sort of dark adventure, and I was locked on the rails. I would only learn much later how much I loved being an infantry officer.

The upperclassmen bought their own "Class A" dress uniforms, complete with ROTC rank and insignias. The optional third and fourth years included a stipend which I also needed.

These classes for juniors and seniors were taught by officers who, by that time, added depth to the discussion of combat with their actual experience in Vietnam.

By 1967, we'd all been steeped in the progression of the war. And war it was. There were disagreements about whether it should be called a "conflict" or a "war," since our national survival didn't depend on its outcome. Yet to the young infantryman bleeding out his last blood for his country, whether in Pleiku or Normandy, it was war.

"Every week we lose a hundred fine young men," as Johnny Cash put it. Anti-war riots were beginning everywhere and the draft waited like the grim reaper for anyone who left school.

46
Pick a Branch

Each ROTC class now revolved around nothing but how to be an effective combat officer, and more precisely, how to be in command. It was the only class I had in college that actually taught one how to direct others to accomplish anything. My management classes taught that concept only in the abstract.

And then it became time to be even more real. "What branch are you choosing?" That was the question posed constantly amongst the juniors in the Deke house, where I now lived.

The day was arriving when we would have to list the top three branches of the Army we wanted. The guys on the Dean's list got their choice of any of the fifteen branches but the rest of us had to choose the three combat branches: Armor, Artillery, Infantry. But which one to put first?

The Artillery shoots shells. So does Armor but with more speed and shock action. The Infantry is the point of the spear. And I do mean point. They don't call them combat branches for nothing. I distinctly remember looking at the card, fiddling with my pencil, considering the finality of the choice I was about to make.

Of course, I remembered that deep dive into my parent's chest of drawers and finding my dad's CIB. I wanted to choose anything but the infantry just because my dad had been a grunt. But I'd decided to walk my own path. I wanted the Infantry. I slowly wrote, in capital letters, I, N, F. It was done.

116

Since I'd always had to work and attend class I hadn't been able to attend enough of the classes I needed to graduate in four years. After summer school and another semester, I officially graduated from OU and was ready to be sworn in as an officer in the U.S. Army. I couldn't believe it. Finally.

47
Shavetail

Before Christmas, the graduating class of officers gathered in the ROTC Armory, in uniform, standing and swearing our oath to the Constitution. We officially became "shavetails," a term referring to second lieutenants in the U.S. Army. It dates back to when the Army used pack animals, and handlers shaved the tail of newly-broken animals to distinguish them from those more seasoned. That was us. Rank, no seasoning.

We were each given our own pair of gold bars to take to the pinning ceremony. At the exit door, we received our very first salute from the Armory's First Sergeant. We each gave him a dollar, proud to pay for the ritual. He made a quick hundred bucks for his Christmas party fund.

We carefully put our hats on and, shoulders back, head high, walked to a different building packed with proud parents, family and friends. My mother was happy, she patted me on my cheek and said, "I'm proud of you."

The ceremony was quick. When the commander of the regiment asked a loved one to pin on each new officer's bars, I gave mine to Mom and she took her time to do it right, putting one on each shoulder, just so. Dad was standing nearby but he had no part in this. After all his promises in Grand Junction, he'd never given me a dime to help with school. I looked forward to another legendary barbecue at Uncle Matt's house. When the ceremony was over, Mom and I drove straight to his house.

118

48
1969 Chevelle

When we got to Matt's, I told Mom I'd be right in so she went
inside while I wiped the dust off my new car. I'd bought it the
day before, a brand new 1969 Chevelle, 396 Super Sport, cobalt
blue, white interior, four speed. It was faster than stink.

In my pocket were a few new credit cards that had just shown
up in the mail. Three weeks ago I couldn't afford a pack of
cigarettes but now that I was a college graduate and military
officer, the banks surmised I could do no financial wrong. I
wiped the dust off the toe of each shoe with my finger, stood
up and walked to Matt's front door. You should have heard
the welcome I got from everybody. I yelled at Matt, "Hey,
Mathew, want to see my new car?"

The next year, President Nixon decided he wanted to create
a volunteer, not-drafted force, to hopefully escape the effects
of draftee riots. On December 1, 1969, a lottery was held on
national TV and the numbers were pulled at random, each one
associated with a different birthday, which allowed everyone
to see exactly the chances of them being drafted.

001 meant you were going. The odds decreased to zero as the
numbers called approached 365. Overnight, our fraternity and
the entire male population of America was split in two: those-
going to Vietnam, and those who would not. I can't remember
my number. I didn't care. I was an infantry platoon leader at
Ft. Carson. I'd be in Vietnam soon enough.

III. Bob
Brother X and Karen

Mom Moran (front row, center) and the Little Sisters of the Rampant Lion. Karen Jones (back row, center beneath the DKE crest. (YEAR)

49
Two Paths

Ron signed up for the Army in order to go to Vietnam. I signed up in order not to go.

Ron ended up in the jungle as a platoon leader, avoiding anything that looked like a jungle path, because even the faintest trail could lead to an ambush. In less than a second, you could lose one of your men: here one moment and gone the next.

I was a 2nd Lieutenant in the Army Reserve, drilling a squad in the safety of a blacktop surface, with no one shooting at us. I served as a range officer too. My only fear was being shouted at for having my hair too long, or having a lightbulb go out in the classroom projector.

I also held on tight to my "wheels of shame" Transportation Corps branch insignia. Over the next fourteen years several generals tried to hand me infantry crossed rifle insignias.

I was last in my class and the cadet in front of me shocked the group by proudly selecting Infantry. I had won the branch lottery selecting the Transportation Corps. I left the reserves after fourteen years holding the rank of Captain.

From our days at OU in the Deke house, our paths diverged. There was no "high road" or "low road" in the late 1960's. You did what you had to do. We each served in our own way.

What matters in Brotherhood is that we were there for each other when it counted. My military upbringing not only prepared me for how I approached military service, but it allowed me the connections and knowledge to help Ron's family navigate a very difficult time.

We see military veterans wearing their uniforms or fatigues in the airport all the time now. In the early 1970's, you dressed in your civvies when you flew or took R&R, even though your crew cut identified you straight away as being in the service.

At a time when many Americans were abandoning their soldiers, I was going to stand by my brother.

50
Brother X

I first met Ron Sorter during rush week and my subsequent pledging Deke at OU in the spring of 1968. Ron was "Brother X" during my initiation. Ron was very articulate and got the attention of my neophyte class that week. He was a senior and an ROTC cadet.

Ron always had something funny to say as well as always tinkering. For example, he made a bar out of a bookcase, painted black, with an electric motor spinning a styrofoam cup with sparkles that, lit up under a blacklight, professed something obscene; very disco era. I inherited it upon his graduation.

As I recall, he graduated in December 1968 and was commissioned as an infantry officer in the U.S. Army. I didn't give much thought to the possibility of Ron going to Vietnam.

For Thanksgiving, 1969, I drove to Fort Carson, Colorado to meet up with Ron and go skiing. I really liked Colorado and thought perhaps one day I'd live there.

On Thanksgiving Day, we stopped at the top of the Rockies near a bubbling stream of water (think Coors Beer). We cracked open a case of C Rations (C Rats) and had a canned turkey loaf dinner. I figured that at this altitude the water must be pure (think Coors Beer) and made a cup of cocoa (cold).

After a twelve-hour drive back to Norman, I checked into the campus hospital with a case of dysentery syndrome. I don't remember the next five days but it was a miserable experience where I nearly died according to the doctor. It was also very lonely being the only person on a ward during the holiday break.

51

The Great Date Substitution

Karen Jones was introduced to me by one of my Deke
brother's girlfriend. It was a blind date.

But if you want the real story, let's have Karen tell it:

"I met Bob my freshman year in 1968 while I was 'pinned'
(pre-fiance) to a wonderful young man from another fraternity
named Bill.

"Bill was home for the weekend visiting his parents. His dad
was the owner of the bank in his hometown, and Bill was
studying accounting plus economics so that he one day would
take over the bank from his dad. My Mom and Dad had met
Bill, loved him and his history/prospects.

"Since Bill was away for the weekend, one of my dorm mates,
a spirited redhead named Samatha (Sam for short) came into
my room . She told me that there was a great guy who had just
broken up with his girlfriend. He was date-less for a big Deke
fraternity party that weekend. Sam asked, 'Would I go this just
once?' I said yes, as Bill was with his parents.

"Bob called to introduce himself, tell me a little bit about his
background, and arranged to pick me up at my dorm that
evening. I had him spell his last name for me, as he is
Italian and I'm not. Cutting to the chase, Bob called me from
the lobby of my dorm when he arrived to pick me up.

"I walked downstairs to greet him, and within thirty seconds I knew that this was the man I was supposed to marry. It took Bob three and a half years to come to the same conclusion.

"In the meantime, I broke up with Bill, seriously breaking his heart. I didn't realize how much until the next semester's Spanish class started and tap,tap,tap on my shoulder from a beautiful redhead sitting behind me. She asked me if my name was Karen, and I replied in the affirmative. She looked at me for about thirty seconds then said 'My boyfriend has your pictures on his bulletin board.' I asked who her boyfriend was, and of course it was Bill, whom I dated before I met Bob.

"As fate would have it they went on to be married following graduation. Bob and I were married within a year of graduation and have been married forty-seven years."

52
My Townie

Karen was a "townie" in Army Brat terms. She grew up in a small home with her two brothers and sister. Her father Dale was a veteran of World War II, a SeaBee who came home to become a pastry chef at the Oklahoma City Golf and Country Club. Karen's mom Floretta was of German stock who had immigrated from Germany to Kansas and ultimately to Oklahoma.

All of the Jones children went to the same schools. Karen played violin earning a music scholarship to OU. Her older brother Jim played golf on scholarship at the University of Missouri.

When I was introduced to Karen's family they were not very welcoming and weren't sure of my intentions. Of course wearing a tie-dyed tee shirt and brightly colored bell bottom pants raised an eyebrow or two.

Over the years, we'd visit Dale at the country club. He made the most beautiful wedding cakes, pastries, breads, and donuts. His ice carvings were also a wonder. Unfortunately, in his later years, the hands-on carving ice took a toll on his health with arthritis.

What was it that attracted me to Karen? First of all her beautiful eyes, and she was an attractive young woman. As you may recall, I left home to flee a screaming Italian mother.

The second reason I was attracted to Karen was that she was not Italian nor was she a screamer when upset. She was committed to her education, quietly reserved but fun to be with in public. She did not blink an eye about taking a road trip and travelling with me.

Did I know I was going to marry her at the outset? Of course not! Or at least would not admit it even though we spent night and day together the final two-three years in college.

With the exception of Army ROTC boot camp and Advanced Camp, we were inseparable throughout our college experience. I pinned Karen, and she became a Deke Sweetheart of the Little Sisters of the Rampant Lion.

We drove to Padre Island over spring break, camping on the island near a place called Oyster Island. You could walk into the water and harvest oysters for dinner!

Of course, the weather turned bad near the end of our week and when we heard a tropical storm was approaching we packed up my Volkswagon Bug and raced north towards Oklahoma. It was dark when we hit the road and Karen had her hair in large rollers. Think orange juice cans.

We drove all night. At dawn we pulled into a rest stop and Karen removed them from her hair so she was presentable when we arrived at her home. I remember her mom met us as we arrived, relieved that I hadn't run off with her daughter. I sheepishly left for Norman.

Karen and I went to football games, OU-Texas and concerts. The Deke parties were always a hit.

While we didn't talk about marriage, my father, the Colonel, flew in from Bolivia to pin my U.S. Army Lieutenant bars on. Karen assisted. Next thing I get is a picture from Armed Forces Newspaper in Panama, showing my commissioning and identifying Karen as my fiance. There had to be a plot.

Bill and his pinmate Karleen joined us in selecting the first stocking order for the Student Services Grocery Store. They added a "woman's touch" to our choices, so we stocked accordingly. I didn't go to visit my family in Bolivia my last two years in school. I basically commuted between Oklahoma City and Norman visiting Karen.

53
What's Happened to Ron?

Ron was deployed to Vietnam as a platoon leader. What is burned into my mind is a photograph he sent me of a helmet full of letters being mailed home by his troops, and in particular, one letter addressed to me at the Deke house.

I don't remember much about our correspondence but I do remember that Ron had experienced the loss of a few of his troops and having firefights in the jungles. I was against the war but I was committed to support my brother in arms.

On a rainy night in October, 1970, I was pumping gas at Lil' Reds store on campus corner in Norman. I got a call from Joel Ketonen from the house and was told that Ron had been wounded in Vietnam but no details. Ron's mother had called the house with the news.

We all were concerned so I called my father, Colonel Tierno, who was at U.S. Army War College in Carlisle, PA. I asked if he could look into Ron's situation. It turned out that Pop had a good friend "Red," who was in charge of personnel records for the Army in the Pentagon. Red knew the status of everybody in the Army.

Every morning, I would get a call with an update. Rocky would first preface the call with, "You can tell Ron's mom this but not that, as that's the Army's responsibility." I would agree. "Yes, he was injured in the field."

131

A couple of days later: "Ron's in Chu Lai, and it does not look good for saving his leg."

The next call was that Ron was enroute to Tokyo.

Finally, several weeks later: "Ron's headed to Fitzsimmons Army Hospital in Denver, Colorado."

Ron was alive and that's all that mattered.

Several years earlier, Brother Randy Morrison had died saving wounded soldiers as a combat medic. We were not going to lose another brother in Vietnam.

IV. Ron
The Eye of the Needle (1969-1970)

1LT SORTER - Plt. Ldr.

Vicksburg to Vietnam

54
Vicksburg (March, 1969)

Mississippi River	8 miles
Vicksburg, Mississippi	8 miles

I sped by that highway sign in my Chevelle, windows down, southern rock blasting from the radio tuned to some local AM station. A beautiful spring day in March, barreling down I-20 in Louisiana. I loved driving this car. It had velocity, but the acceleration, wow.

Out of state cars were treated warily by the state patrol down here, so I was just cruising. Plus, second lieutenants got black marks for speeding tickets; "conduct unbecoming" it was called. I kept my eyes open, approaching Vicksburg.

The day before, I'd bid Mom and my family farewell for a while, dropped down from OKC to Dallas to miss some late spring snow in Kansas, and turned east on I-20 heading to Ft. Benning, Georgia, The Home Of The Infantry.

I had plenty of time so as I crossed onto the bridge over the Mississippi and marveled at the size of Old Man River. It was gigantic. I'd never been east of this river so I stopped in Vicksburg for lunch. A little cafe had a nice view. I stopped and went inside to watch the river barges.

I had an OU T-shirt on and when I sat down near an older gent at the empty counter he looked over at me.

A waitress gave me some water and a menu and stood there as I read it.

The man asked, "So, y'all from Oklahoma?"

I could just barely understand his accent. I said I was. I studied all the fried foods on the menu, told the waitress what I wanted and she yelled it at an old black man in the tiny kitchen.

Then she turned back to me, and asked, "So, Oklahoma. Was y'all Yankees or Rebs?"

I couldn't believe I knew the answer. At dinner, one of my frat brothers had once described how Oklahoma wasn't a state at the time, but that thousands of the Five Civilized Tribes had sided with and fought with the Confederacy.

I regaled the waitress and Old Gent with that trivia and we became instant pals, being Official Rebs and all. My food arrived and while I ate they described The Siege of Vicksburg by that vile General Grant and his army of blue bellies and the huge cemetery just up the road.

I told them I was on my way to Ft. Benning for Infantry Officer Training and the effect was strange.

The old gent said, "Well, son, I wish you all the best. Take the time to visit the army memorial just north of town before ya go." Then he left. The waitress wandered away.

I wandered the trenches and bunkers, all well mown, with small signs showing who did what to who and when. I'd studied all this, with maps, as different battles were instructive in different ways. Vicksburg was a classic example of starving the occupants inside a perimeter before breaching it.

It was sobering to see how closely the thousands of soldiers from both sides had lived to each other and what it must have been like to shoot down hills with muskets during the day or sneak up hills with bayonets at night, slowly butchering thousands of each other. I walked the vast cemetery holding most of the thousands who'd died during the siege.

Forty seven days. By winning the The Siege of Vicksburg, Grant succeeded in splitting the Confederacy in half. The beginning of the end for the Rebs.

I left with a new appreciation of those massive fields, overflowing with marble gravestones. Each stone marking where an infantryman fell, an infantryman who believed in his cause, fighting for himself and his buddies. At the tactical level, in the trenches, the glory of whatever side one fights for fades and it becomes only about whose blood soaks the grass.

55
Ft. Benning

I hear, I forget. I see, I remember. I do, I understand.
—Confucius

The next day was muggy, overcast, and in the afternoon I approached the main Benning gate, slowed to a stop and showed my new military ID to the military policeman manning the gate. He looked at it, told me to go to the ID office soon to get a car sticker, then handed my ID back, took a pace back and saluted me. I didn't know what to do. I saluted him back. He dropped his hand and motioned me forward.

I found my barracks and nirvana in the parking lot. It was filled with dozens of the coolest muscle cars I'd seen in one place with license plates from everywhere. Obviously most of the other lieutenants had bought new cars as well. Nice ones.

That night I met my new roommate. He'd just graduated from Ranger school and we talked over what we knew about the officer training course and what we could expect. He laughed at me for saluting the MP and said he'd done the same thing his first day. One doesn't do that, apparently, for safety reasons. We went to the officers club with some other guys for some booze.

As the next two months passed, everybody became seriously better equipped to assume leadership positions in an infantry company.

All of the instructors had CIBs, many were Airborne, Rangers, or both. All veterans of combat in Vietnam. We ran fast map exercises, called in mortar fire missions at night, we even learned the rudiments of constitutional law.

We experienced the amount the iris opens in complete and utter blackness. After half an hour in a huge, dark theater, someone said, "I can see it. There, on the left wall." I couldn't see anything but in a few minutes I could make out the outline of a tank with its gun elevated. After ten more minutes we could see we were surrounded. I was amazed at the depth of my night vision.

The instructor then showed us what flares do to night vision. "Everyone look up. Do you see anything?" We all looked up.

He triggered a strobe light. Damn, the pain! Everybody cursed the asshole. But the lesson was this: if a parachute flare ever pops and you don't keep one eye closed to preserve that hard-won night vision, you are screwed.

We reviewed how to situate interlocking fields of fire using machine guns. One evening we were trucked to a firing range and climbed into bleachers. When it was dark we witnessed the effectiveness of overlapping fields of fire demonstrated by perhaps 30 different machine guns firing tracers at the same time. Impressive isn't the word. The sound was incredible, as were the ricochets tearing up into the darkness.

Back to Confucius. I saw. I knew I would later do.

Approaching the end of our training we'd learned how to fire every weapon and earned whatever marksman badges we were entitled to. Most importantly, we were now ready to assume command for the first time of a line infantry platoon. In another few weeks, we'd be sent to various Army bases all over the US to do just that.

56

The Million Dollar Display

The final week of training included Santa's Christmas present, in April. It's impossible to describe but let me try.

It was called The Million Dollar Display.

We assembled in a huge set of bleachers. Arrayed in front of us was a vast firing range, replete with rusted out tanks, demolished jeeps and cars and rusting military equipment of every kind. A Sergeant Major walked to the microphone, replete with stripes and chevrons around a star. His starch alone was holding him at attention.

He welcomed the assembled lieutenants, other officers, their families and friends. He bellowed, "The assembled lieutenants will soon deploy to Vietnam to lead men in combat. Sirs, here is a display of, and the sounds of, and the impact of the firepower which we will make available to you. First Sergeant Adams, please proceed."

About 100 meters in front of us was a white sheet tied around a human-sized target. First Sergeant Adams, his chevrons and rockers surrounding a diamond, marched out to the target, pulled an automatic out of his holster and shot the target once in the stomach.

The white sheet, filled with a red bag, bled its contents all over the ground. We looked at each other. This was a million dollars?

He stuffed his pistol back in his holster and marched back to the microphone and stood at parade rest, his hands locked behind him. He bellowed into the microphone, "Sirs, you have just witnessed me issuing a *coup de gras* using my sidearm, the 1909 Colt .45 caliber automatic."

A squad of infantrymen with M-16s and an M-60 machine gun had replaced him on the range and proceeded to disintegrate the target, sending a thousand bloody pieces flying up into the sky. The first sergeant described each of their weapons as they appeared, their calibre, effective range and kill zone.

After that a dozen men with LAWs, light anti tank weapons, came out, kneeled down, extended their fiberglass tubes, fixed their sights and disintegrated a few car bodies, after which they cracked their empty tubes over their legs. By then, we were all cheering the blasts, the smell of gunpowder, all of it.

It accelerated. Teams of troops ran out, assembled mortars and sent them arcing out to rusty truck targets, the First Sergeant explaining the art of 60 and 81mm mortars. A Jeep-mounted 106mm, M-40 Recoilless Rifle, an antitank weapon, blew some rusty treads off of an ancient Sherman tank.

There was more. The synchronicity of it all was mesmerizing. Armored personnel carriers crisscrossed with .50 calibers blazing, then artillery marking rounds appeared in the sky followed by a ground-pounding fusillade of noise. The shrapnel raised spouts of dust in every direction. The cheering was deafening.

Another rank of sheet-covered targets tilted up down range as a self-propelled 8-inch howitzer sped out, sliding to a stop 50 meters in front of them. As its rocking stopped, its spade on the back dropped, digging into the ground and the SP quickly reversed onto it, locking itself into the earth. The First Sergeant intoned, "Flechette round, range: Deadly Close." The gun fired, and thousands of holes spurted red, the targets torn to shreds by the winged nails in the round.

Cobra helicopters criss-crossed 100 feet above the ground ripping the area with cannon. Machine gunners hung out both sides of little egg-shaped, four-bladed Loach helicopters and worked their weapons over the ground, dropping red smoke grenades to mark enemy locations.

Just like that, the range cleared. The canisters continued to slowly discharge their sanguine billows into the motionless air. For the first time in half an hour it was deathly still.

What a crescendo. This display of firepower, soon to be available to young Lieutenant Sorter, was mind blowing.

We heard or, I guess, felt is the right word, an atmospheric tremble, an approaching turbulence coming from somewhere behind us...then suddenly two Phantom jets blasted over the bleachers at treetop level, heading away, pulling up, disappearing, one to the left, one to the right. And we saw, tumbling lazily down towards the earth but moving so fast, twin polished aluminum canisters. The Phantoms had released them right over our heads. Napalm.

They impacted the range and detonated, smearing giant gouts of flame, consuming the entire range.

Ink-black smoke filled the sky.

The sound had a shuddering echo as it took its time to burn. We were stunned, stoned, agape. The pornography of weaponry is intoxicating.

All of it was mine. To use as I saw fit.

Welcome to the infantry.

The impact of this kind of firepower became clear in combat. It is both obscene and necessary.

If you're in a killing zone, you understand.

57

Leadership versus Command

One leads from the front.
One commands from the rear.
— Ft. Benning truth

This truth would inform every order I would ever give and every action I would always take. It's a fancy way to say, "Here is the point, up front, and behind it is the spear. You need both."

The infantry badge is a silver shield, with a field of blue displaying a single silver bayonet.

On its top are the words FOLLOW ME.

The badge is relevant when it appears on an officer at the point of the spear. The platoon leader.

It doesn't say: "You guys go over there."

It says, "Follow Me."

I and a couple of fellow infantry lieutenants loaded our gear in my Chevelle the day we were released from Benning. I drove for awhile and later crashed in the rear seat. I awoke to Dave doing a hundred through the swamps of Louisiana. We made Houston the next morning.

58
Ft. Carson

The sound of typewriters filled the orderly room of Bravo Company, my new home at Ft. Carson, Colorado. I'd been assigned to a mechanised infantry outfit, part of the storied Red Diamond, 5th Mechanized Division.

First Sergeant Elfego Gomez, the lifeblood of Bravo company, welcomed me to the company and pointed out a chair where I could wait to meet the company commander, so I had a seat.

An enlisted man marched in, snap turned in front of Elfego's* desk and, locked at rigid attention, shouted, "First Sergeant, Private First Class Bennett reporting as ordered!"

Elfego didn't look up. A slow minute passed. He signed a paper, then cooly considered the soldier. As he readied himself to chew Bennett's head off, his intercom buzzed.

He picked up the phone, "Yes, Sir."

I got ready. "Yes, Sir."

He replaced the phone and pointed at a door. I strode over, knocked twice, when I heard, "Enter", I did.

I marched to his desk, locked myself to rigid attention and saluted, saying, "Lieutenant Ron Sorter, reporting for duty, Sir."

Captain Jim Gardner returned my salute and said, "At ease." He was maybe thirty. He leaned back in his chair, all 5'8" of himself, replete with glittering captain's bars, jump wings and Ranger tab. He was wearing a West Point ring.

"Tell me a little about yourself, Lieutenant Sorter", he said.

I gave him a quick summary of my life.

He smiled, "So, I take it you're not married?"

"No, sir, I'm single," I replied.

"Well," he said with a smile, "let me be the first to congratulate you on your marriage to Bravo Company. The other platoon leaders are married so you'll have time to do great things for Bravo Company. I'm giving you Third Platoon. They really need help, if I can be blunt. Let's see. Do you like weapons?"

I didn't know where this was going, but I jumped in. "Yes, sir, every kind."

"Fine, you'll also be my Armory Officer. As soon as we're finished here I'll introduce you to the Armory Sergeant. Wait, are you hungry?"

I was. I'd skipped lunch to make sure I arrived here on time.

"Just a little," I said. Are we going to the Mess Hall? Cool.

148

Captain Gardner's smile got wider. "Fine, after we're done at the Armory, I'll introduce you to the Mess Sergeant. He can give you a snack while he gets you up to speed on your duties as Officer of the Mess. Any questions?"

"No, sir."

That was my introduction to the stateside army.

59
My First Platoon Sergeant

I met with the Armory and Mess Sergeants. Elfego introduced me to my new platoon sergeant, Staff Sergeant Walls. This introduction was the most important of my military life so far. He was maybe 35 years old, from Arkansas, a Combat Infantryman badge (CIB) over his left pocket, with Expert Marksmanship badges for rifle, and pistol hanging just beneath.

Platoon sergeants decide whether platoon leaders will succeed or fail. An officer gives orders but the Army's sergeants, its "non coms," actually make things happen. Listening to them is essential because they know. Everything.

A new platoon leader's first order of business is to convince the platoon sergeant that his opinion is valuable, needed and welcome. To earn that conviction, words from me would count little. Only actions count. It starts with listening.

I asked Sgt. Wall's opinion about the platoon and listened. He was not happy with the platoon's performance, either. Just back from Vietnam, he adroitly convinced me the platoon wasn't happy with the "Mickey Mouse rules" that the last platoon leader had imposed.

He thought the platoon was embarrassed, too, for being considered a troop of losers. We agreed that we wanted the same thing: to make Third Platoon the best in the company. When we decided that, it was a done deal.

No bond is more vital than the one between an officer and his men. The trust either exists or it doesn't. It affects everything and the lack of it can be deadly in combat. The officer must remember that he leads only because they agree he does.

The platoon leader eats only after his men have eaten. He sleeps only after he's assured himself that his men are cared for. When C-rations are delivered in the field, his men choose first; the platoon leader takes whatever's left. An officer is superior in rank only. If he lords it over his troops, he's done.

Over the next ten months Sgt. Blaine, the armorer, taught me how to use, clean and control the flow of every weapon, bullet, flare, grenade and mortar shell in a company's armory and ammo bunkers. Mess Sergeant Mink taught me the intricacies of serving three hot meals a day to a hundred soldiers in any location, while maintaining a level of perfect cleanliness.

Sgt. Wall and I worked every day, demanding the best, and telling the platoon they were the best and helping them prove it. That summer, Bravo company was chosen for a chemical warfare test. Ever live for a hot summer week in a full hazmat suit?

Waking up from a deep sleep while wearing a gas mask is like discovering you're being smothered with a rubber pillow. CS gas and tear gas was everywhere, churned up by our tracks as we ran chemical war games with armored personnel carriers at night. Growing stubble in a sweaty, rubber gas mask was a riot.

At week's end, the company was celebrated for doing better than the Camp Pendleton Marines had done a month earlier. The CO told me Third Platoon had been exemplary.

Captain Gardiner was the finest officer I met in the Army. When he rotated to Vietnam he was replaced by a Special Forces captain who immediately made me his Executive Officer. I was honored when he later gave me a 100% Officer Efficiency Report. It was endorsed by my battalion and brigade commanders. I can't tell you the effect it had on me.

Bob came up during Thanksgiving. We loaded our gear into the Chevelle and drove up to ski at Breckenridge. We spent some time drinking, running scenarios of our futures.

We'd just landed somebody on the moon so anything was possible, right?

60
Elfego*

I call him Elfego here, because I came to admire the man. I only ever addressed him as "First Sergeant."

As I left for Panama, he said: "You're the only real lieutenant in this whole goddamn company."

Hearing that from him was like getting a medal.

61
A Python (Panama)

"Anybody afraid of snakes?" The question hung in the fetid, humid air. "Nobody?" he said, scanning our faces. It was just like old times, my Ft. Benning pals and I sitting in a bleacher, a Ranger instructor down in front. Our fatigues were soaked with sweat, and the Panama heat sweltered out of the surrounding jungle

The Ft. Sherman Jungle School was built in 1912 on the Atlantic side of the isthmus to protect the Canal. We were the latest rotation of soldiers to train in Vietnam conditions. Venomous spiders as big as salad plates. Venomous snakes, as many as you like. Iguanas, pretty green ones with weak venom and fierce bites. Heat, jungle, swamp… Panamanian paradise.

No one was dumb enough to raise their hand to the snake question. We were seasoned platoon leaders since Benning, some were now Rangers, Airborne and Green Berets. We knew the drill. Somebody was going to end up with a snake so we all pointed at Darryl. "Darryl! He hates snakes!"

It was a harmless prank. We were all going to Vietnam to die. Snakes were nothing in that equation.

Darryl was a terrific officer from the South who told everybody how cottonmouths, water moccasins and snakes in general we're not his cup of tea. "OK, Lieutenant, front and center."

Darryl shook his head then, smiling, gave us all the finger and clambered down from the bleachers to a chorus of cheers. He stood next to the instructor and behind him a Ranger captain silently slipped out of the jungle wearing a huge brown python on his shoulders.

He floated up behind Darryl as the instructor looked at Darryl and said, "OK, Lieutenant. Do. Not. Move."

Darryl closed his eyes for a few seconds and opened them as he felt the captain gently balance the weight of the python around his shoulders. The bleachers went silent.

Darryl froze. The snake slowly writhed around his neck, making itself comfortable. Great bravery is only present with great fear and it is awesome to witness.

Darryl pasted a smile on his face. After a minute or so , the Ranger retrieved his snake.

Darryl climbed back up into the bleachers, grinning. He gave all of us the finger again, and we gave him a standing ovation. This was our going away party, so we were going to have fun every available second we had.

After a smoke break we climbed back into the wet wooden bleachers as it started to rain again. I carefully stowed my smokes and lighter in a plastic bag inside my shirt and poncho. The jungle shed its water onto the ground and collected in greasy puddles around the bleachers.

Nobody cared. This was our life now. Running map exercises all day, chopping our way through swamp with slippery machetes. Sitting in those bleachers at Benning had been a holiday.

62
Drinking a Chicken

The instructor reappeared and talked about the importance
of being able to live off the land. His poncho periodically
twitched. He emphasized how important it was to eat all parts
of an animal. We could see this one coming, too, but weren't
quite sure how it would play out. We knew the instructors
were all frustrated actors.

A different Ranger now stood at the edge of the jungle, arms
crossed, no poncho for him, being a Ranger and all. He was
wearing sunglasses on a rainy day, the spitting image of Jack
Nicholson. The instructor finally lifted his poncho and
produced a live chicken. He stroked its head, telling it how all
parts of a chicken could be eaten except for its beak. Then he
carefully handed the chicken to the Ranger.

The Ranger nonchalantly took the chicken by its head, gave it
a swift twirl or two and popped off its head and put it in his
pocket. Then he stuck the chicken's neck into his mouth and
drank its blood, rhythmically squeezing its body to make sure
it all came out. He drank until the chicken was dry.

We immediately gave him and the chicken a standing ovation,
just for the pure theater of it. He handed the limp chicken to
the instructor and disappeared into the jungle. The instructor
turned to the bleachers and said, "Now all you have to do is
pluck it, cook it and eat it. 165 degrees is recommended. Any
questions? Class dismissed."

63
Liberty Train

How humid was it in Panama? We kept our civvies dry by the light bulb in the closet.

A few days before our last weekend in Panama, the Navy showed up and beach-landed the Marines. On Friday all the Navy, Marine, and Army guys got liberty and leave.

We hopped on the first transcontinental railroad ever built, to cross the isthmus to Panama City. Along the way, we stared at all the ships lifting in the Canal, which had been built along the railway 50 years later. Original train coaches, polished wood seats, locomotive smoke blowing into the windows, I expected Pancho Villa to swagger down the aisle any minute.

The consensus was booze first, then food, then women. One of the Ranger's last farewells was, "I hope you all go to Vietnam and die!" We did not intend to go out softly.

Unkind soldiers refer to Navy guys as squids. Squids call Marines jarheads and yep, they don't like each other unless there are some Army guys in the bar, then they lock up back-to-back and take on all comers.

Screw that. Six of us had it all mapped out. Me and Darryl and the others crammed into a '58 Pontiac cab at the depot, had some great seafood at a place overlooking the Pacific, then dropped by the Blue Goose.

You may know it. That high class whorehouse with gaudy antique black iron fencing surrounding it? Blue stone walls shimmering in the spotlights while Panamanian Army guards carrying machine guns walk the perimeter?

I can't recommend it enough, if you're ever in Panama City, Panama, in 1970, on your way to Vietnam to die. Follow me.

64
Travis

I landed at San Francisco International Airport late one night, preparing to take a shuttle to Travis Air Force Base with a First Sergeant I'd met on the flight.

He was returning for a third tour and carried a briefcase full of scotch miniatures. A veteran.

We were on our way to Vietnam and we watched a newscast of President Nixon talking about how he was pulling troops out of Vietnam.

My Travis flight would be a month behind my Benning pals. A Pentagon rule stated that siblings could not serve in combat, simultaneously. At the behest of my mother, I'd requested a delay in my arrival in Vietnam until my brother could repatriate.

My orders were changed.

My brother landed at Travis at 7:30 a.m., and I left an hour later.

Mom was tormented, with one son coming home safe as her other son was sent to replace him.

I loaded onto a stretch 707 filled with hundreds of other soldiers in brand new jungle fatigues and boots, officers in front in our Class A's.

When we landed in Anchorage to refuel, four or five soldiers grabbed blankets and left the plane, deserting. I've always wondered what happened to them.

Where would you go if you're wearing a blanket on an Air Force Base in Alaska in March when desertion is a capital offense?

We left for Tokyo without them.

The flight took forever. We played a lot of rummy. We refueled in Tokyo and by the time we were on our final approach to Tan Son Nhut Air Force Base near Saigon it was dark, timed to keep us from being an easy target.

On final approach, the captain announced that the plane's lights were off and we were to do the same in the cabin. One soldier took too long and a hundred guys hissed, "Turn that... light off!"

I couldn't tell our altitude in the blackness. We flew over a few fires then we were wheels down, rolling to a stop, the door opening at last, admitting the first smells of Vietnam: humidity, heat, the smell of jet fuel and something burning.

65
Tan Son Nhut airbase

We walked into a giant building, dead tired from 20 hours on a
plane. A loudspeaker was blasting, "All personnel manifested
on Flight R2B3 will be seated in the empty seats immediately."

We moved towards empty wooden benches polished smooth
by the butts of tens of thousands of GIs, Marines and airmen
who'd flown into Vietnam. As the noise increased the
loudspeaker would say, "At ease in the building!"

We started paying attention to the guys sitting in the other
half of the building on identical benches. They looked nothing
like us and they looked at us like we were specimens in a petri
dish. Smiling, pointing, laughing. The loudspeaker would
again issue "At ease!" Those guys had been sitting on our
benches 365 days earlier. They'd once been "new meat," too,
just like us.

Now their faces were burnt leather. Boonie hats decorated
with pins from grenades were raked up in the back, their
fatigues were sun faded, monsoon washed and hung out to
dry on sweaty men for an entire year. Their boots were not
only not polished, but had been scraped skin thin. I remember
wondering what I would look like in 365 days. Or not.

The loudspeaker said, "All personnel manifested on Flight
R2B4, ON YOUR FEET!" The sudden cheering from their side
was deafening.

162

"OFFICERS AND VIPS MAKE YOUR WAY ONTO THE AIR-CRAFT, AT EASE IN THE BUILDING, ENLISTED PERSON-NEL LOAD FOLLOWING! AT EASE IN THE BUILDING!!"

The group didn't care, they were going home, laughing, smiling, giving us the finger, you couldn't help but laugh, too, they were having such a great time. Refrains of "You're all gonna die!" came our way.

We loaded onto buses with steel grates over the windows to keep grenades from being tossed in. We stopped at a depot and were issued fatigues, helmets, poncho liners, everything we'd need in the bush and then mercifully were allowed to sleep on our duffels until sunup.

Just before dawn, helicopters began flying overhead, and within the next hour the sky virtually filled with them. Not like cabs in NYC condemned to the streets. Think of a dank swamp in Louisiana and swarms of mosquitoes.

Choppers, everywhere.

I came to love them.

66
Mommy!

That afternoon, I was in a cargo plane heading "up country" to Chu Lai and the Americal Division. After a few days of orientation to the unique combat environment surrounding Chu Lai, I flew in a smaller twin prop Caribou, down to LZ Bronco.

Long, gentle, low altitude landing patterns don't work in war zones, where Viet Cong with AKs fill fuselages with tracers. The pilot came in high, then dropped gear and flaps, and aimed the nose at the perforated steel runway far below. We weren't exactly vertical but it felt like it.

He flared the plane level at the last minute, and we bounced and rolled to a stop.

The pilot and I shared a jeep into the brigade's Operations Center, and I asked him how he knew when to flare the plane at the last minute.

He told me he waited for the moment when his copilot yelled, "MOMMY!"

The Army is full of comics. Don't let anyone tell you different.

Snake Eyes

1st Lieutenant Ron Sorter, Charlie Company Commander
(1970)

67

A Roll of the Dice, Part I

Who won and who lost is not a question. In war no one wins or loses.
There is only destruction. Only those who have never fought like to
argue about who won and who lost.
— Bao Nihn, North Vietnamese Army

Each day in Vietnam was two bone-white dice with blood-red
dots bouncing lazily through the air. They'd land, slowly
rolling to a stop on jungle green felt. If you were still alive at
the change of watch at midnight, the number of days you had
left were reduced by one. As the sun rose, the stakes did, too.

Back in the 1950's, Truman decided that a split Vietnam was
preferable, just like the Koreas: democracy in the south,
communist menace contained in the north. Eisenhower,
Kennedy and Johnson all reluctantly agreed.

Nobody at our platoon level cared about demarcation lines.
Not down here on the bloody ground. Each of us was just trying to keep a heartbeat for 365 days. And the best way to do
that was to kill as many of the other guys as we could because
they saw it the same way.

The indifference back in "the world," was obvious to
everybody. We saw it in the newspapers we got. We knew
America wasn't with us. We only had our buddies and a hope
that the number of days we thought we had left was really correct. We hung tight with our platoons and did our duty. Screw
the world.

68
Dust Off

*Once the United States began to withdraw...this last and most trying
period of the American experience in Vietnam severely tested the
courage and dedication of the U.S. Army's combat troops...*
— Army Aeromedical Evacuation In Vietnam

The next few months, that summer of 1970, were reduced to
ambushes in the dark. We popped them at the VC and NVA.
They threw booby traps at us.

We'd often kill them and send the enemy body count to the ea-
ger division commander's board of grease-penciled numbers.

When someone's wounded, we didn't lose it, get excited or
emotional.

We'd just call a medevac chopper for a Dust Off.

It's not even stoic, because stoic would mean putting too much
attention on it. There are no tears outside the wire.

I also did that four times for those of my men who'd died and
once, in the dark, for a squad leader who'd, an hour earlier,
seen his best buddy disintegrate in front of him.

And once for a 10-year old Vietnamese boy who'd been shot in
the chest by one of my machine gunners. From five feet away
with a .45 automatic.

His imploring eyes looked at me as my medic sealed his back with a large piece of vaselined poncho so he could breathe.

He was terrified. He died en route to Chu Lai.

The machine gunner ended up in Long Binh Jail for shooting the kid with his .45 in cold blood.

As the commanding officer, I was responsible for every death. There is no asterisk, explaining the circumstances.

There is no passing the buck out there, or when you are state-side or when you're a 72-year-old man writing these words.

The kid died inside my perimeter at the hand of one of my guys, who I should have taught better. A day doesn't pass...

After every skirmish I'd ask Sgt Jones for a headcount. I could breath when he said "All accounted for."

Whenever we'd lager up for some chow, to maybe get our resupply chopper in, Sgt. Jones would set his helmet out.

After the guys put their letters home in there, he'd get them in the next resupply chopper going back to the rear.

It seemed like everybody carried an extra grenade pouch holding a camera. I wrote a letter to Bob once and took a picture of the letter, sitting in the helmet.

Then the stampless letter was off, back to the world via chopper, airliner, mail trucks and postal employees to Bob at the DKE house, while we mounted up and walked back into the jungle.

After each three-week stint in the bush, we'd rotate back to Liz, our battalion LZ, to guard its perimeter, guard the access road and refit.

69
"What Do We Do, Sir?"

"Sorry, guys, the mine detectors aren't here yet," the road guard said.

The driver hung his arm out and looked down at the road guard.

"Aren't here yet? I can't wait, I got a shitload of ammo on here."

The road guard said, "Don't know, man, they're late. It might take awhile. Our radio is toast so I don't know anything."

Vietnamese people streamed by on both sides of the truck, casting careful, disdainful looks at us as they passed. Living their daily lives, while we waited for our mine detectors. The river of Vietnamese had other worries.

Troopers riding on top of the trucks kept one eye on the nearby bamboo forest and their M-16s pointed in the direction of the trucks' gas caps. All it would take is one grenade in a fuel tank.

Our convoy of deuce-and-a-halfs (two-and-a-half ton supply trucks) sat idling on the only highway in Vietnam.

I'd been wounded two weeks prior and had been sent to a MASH unit in the rear to be stitched up.

I was making my way back to Liz to join up with Charlie Company, who would be arriving that afternoon to guard its perimeter.

Our convoy had driven the resupply route between LZ Bronco and LZ Liz. Liz was a mile up this access road off Highway 1 and we wouldn't be safe until we were inside its perimeter. We all knew the risks of just sitting out here in the open.

You might say I was seasoned by then. I'd survived five months as a combat platoon leader with just some recent minor wounds; 32 stitches was all it took.

After ten days at the Chu Lai military tent hospital, I looked forward to rejoining 1st Platoon when Charlie company rotated back to Liz that afternoon. Our CO, 1st Lt. Nelson, was a Ranger, a good officer and we worked well together. I was looking forward to seeing Sgt. Jones and the rest of the guys in my platoon.

The driver shook his head. "Shit." He turned to me and asked, "What do we do, sir?" Yep, I knew this was coming. I was the ranking officer even though I was just hitching a ride.

I lit a cigarette to have a few seconds to think. Liz' access road was guarded by a half dozen pairs of road guards every minute of every day. The road had never been mined. I doubted any truck had ever driven over it before the mine team had cleared it.

Every morning, two guys with mine detectors scanned every inch of it. They worked behind a dump truck, its bed tilted and loaded with dirt. It rolled the entire length of the road, to trigger any pressure mines. The driver ran it in reverse so any explosion would be deflected by the tilted truck bed.

There were rice paddies on either side of the road. Metal culverts ran under the road to balance the water in the paddies. Stowed inside a metal culvert, the metal in an improvised bomb would never be detected.

Every four hours, the road guards would be changed, and they would check each one of the culverts. Supposedly.

I had history with this road. Last month, after I'd posted the first pair of my platoon's road guards and began moving to the second position, one of my men, Bobby Harris, as he was chambering a round in his M-16, accidently shot his best friend Marshall right in the heart.

There was never a safe day. I was responsible for Marshall's death. Today was just more history. We were an easy sniper shot from that bamboo forest over there. We were surrounded by a flowing river of Vietnamese.

In addition to pulling water buffaloes, (400 gallon tanks of drinking water), every truck was carrying food, materiel and ammo. Claymores, grenades, crates of 5.56 and 7.62 caliber ammo. A few quick tracer rounds through any of these trucks would be a disaster.

"Let's go up the road," I said. I tossed my butt out the window and in the mirror I saw a few kids fighting over it.

The dice rolled and we rolled safely up the access road to Liz.

70
Lt. Nelson

I was happy to be back at Liz. I inspected the defenses in front of my platoon's sector of Liz' perimeter.

The tanglefoot (criss-crossed barbed wire in the grass) had to be taut. The wiring from my command hooch to the fougasse (pronounced "foo gas") barrels and claymores had to be electrically sound. I checked everything.

I had 32 healing stitches on my upper body, but I was happy to be alive since several rounds had impacted my M-16 and not me. I was sorry to lose that rifle, but it had saved my life. I'll take the shrapnel damage over death any day.

I kept thinking, "Lt. Nelson and the company's convoy should have arrived by now." The trucks were probably late picking them up. That happened all the time.

It was hot. I waited. I was tired and I slept.

I woke and nobody had arrived yet. I walked down to the company's headquarters to see what was up.

71
A Roll of the Dice, Part II

The lead truck turned off Highway 1 for the 1-mile ride to Liz. To the side, a couple of Vietnamese kids played in the fields that lined the road. A village lay nearby in a stand of bamboo and banana trees. The two and a half ton truck picked up speed.

With a half-mile to go, the truck hit a mine and was thrown high into the air. The engine and back wheels were blown off and went flying. The truck landed 50 feet from a 5-foot crater in the access road. Lieutenant Nelson was dead...27 other soldiers, who were riding in the back of the truck, were injured.

The two Vietnamese kids ran toward the village. They were caught and later admitted that the Viet Cong who lived in the village had shown them how to detonate the mine when the truck reached a point marked on the road.

— Gary W. Bray *After My Lai: My Year Commanding First Platoon, Charlie Company,* (2010), OU Press

(Editor Note: Lt. Ron Sorter took over First Platoon, Charlie Company, from Lt. Bray. in May, 1970)

72
Checkmarks

As I walked up to the Command Post, I heard the battalion
commander ask Lt. Poule, "Are the checkmarks our KIA?"

Killed In Action? What the hell? Poule was platoon leader
of 3rd platoon and they were both looking at a clipboard.
I looked over their shoulders. Lt. Nelson's name and Arm-
strong, from my platoon, had checkmarks on the roster. They
were gone.

Poule saw me and filled me in. He and his platoon had been in
the second truck. My platoon was unscathed except for Arm-
strong, who'd been in the lead truck with Nelson.

We spent the rest of the afternoon policing up the bomb
site before any of it could be scavenged by the VC and used
against us. Broken weapons, ammo, grenades with bent pins,
broken claymores and every kind of bloody clothing was
strewn around the site.

The next day we affixed bayonets onto M-16's, shoved them
into the dirt, hung their helmets on top, placed a pair of
combat boots on the ground in front of each, everyone gathered around, taps played through a tinny tape recorder, a few
words...

It was a brutal loss. There's a distance one keeps, ready to lose
one's friends, one's compatriots, without it destroying you. It's
a cold, necessary part of infantry life. But brutal.

73
Fourth in Line

For me, I'd always thought of courage as charging enemy bunkers or standing under enemy fire. But just to walk every day, from village to village, and through the paddies and up in the mountains. Just to get up every morning and look out the land and think, "in a few minutes I'll be walking there." Just to walk was incredibly brave.

— Tim O'Brien, author of *The Things They Carried*

Normally, you didn't walk on a trail. A trail might be an easier route, but it was a quick road to your death.

Six weeks later, my point man led our platoon onto a faint trail (that he hadn't noticed). I watched as the man in front of me, Gary Lister, exploded in pieces in a black geyser of gunpowder. He was there one moment, and then he wasn't.

Every man who ever served in Vietnam secretly wondered how many rolls of the dice he'd survive. I'd survived more than my share, I was sure of it.

Here's what I mean by a roll of the dice.

My first day in the bush, I took over my platoon late one afternoon.

Ten of us walked over the same patch of earth, as we separated into squads to set up ambushes.

Nine members of my platoon walked over a spot on the ground and nothing happened. I stepped near that same patch. Later, the eleventh man, Oren Hammstein, stepped on a number-10 can filled with gunpowder, killing him instantly. That's how close it was, and how completely random.

I had just taken over the platoon that afternoon, but Oren Hammstein's death was my responsibility, forever.

I was their platoon leader. Choices I made or did not make made me responsible for all their deaths.

That's why I decided to drive the access road to Liz before it was mineswept, when the VC in the neighboring village didn't expect any traffic. I'd saved our lives, but it was a dice roll.

Following the truck mining, Lt. Poule became the new Charlie company commander, replacing Lt. Nelson. Two months later, Poule, grinning like a wild man, rode a chopper out of the bush for the last time and I was the new CO, "the old man" at age 23. Commanding Officer, Charlie Company, 1st of the 20th.

Make sure you read that number correctly, "age 23." But in Vietnam years, I was an old man.

I'd been a Platoon Leader, leading from the front.

Now as Company Commander, I'd lead from the rear. Or, in the Vietnam parlance of perimeters, I'd lead from the center.

178

74
Vietnam. This....

Take an empty number -10 can of tomatoes, fill it to the top with gunpowder, insert an electric blasting cap into the gunpowder, run one of the wires from it to a battery, do not connect yet, run the second blasting cap wire to a piece of aluminum juicy fruit gum wrapper laid out flat on a small, flat piece of bamboo, attach a second gum wrapper to a curved piece of bamboo, run another wire from that foil to the battery, place the curved piece atop the flat piece. Make sure the two foil pieces of foil don't touch each other.

Connect the circuit, seal the can in plastic and duct tape, place the bamboo trigger on top of the can, bury it all shallow so that if anyone steps on the top curved piece it snaps in two lengthwise forcing the two pieces of conductive aluminum foil together, completing a circuit, triggering the blasting cap, exploding the gunpowder disintegrating whoever steps on it. Don't mark or monitor it, in violation of the Geneva Convention.

75
...or this

Take a claymore explosive device filled with C4 and ball bearings, stick it in the ground aimed at a kill zone. Lay the electric blasting cap next to it. In the kill zone take a plastic spoon from any C ration box with a hole bored in the spoon and tie clear monofilament fishing line to it through the hole. Insert the stem of the spoon into a wooden clothespin separating a metal thumbtack pinned into each jaw, tie the other end of the line to any natural feature on the other side of the path, assure the line is taut.

Connect a wire from one thumbtack to the blasting cap. Connect another wire to the other thumbtack and run it to the battery and insert the blasting cap. Run the other wire from the blasting cap to the battery. Camouflage everything so that if anyone walks through the monofilament line it pulls the spoon out, completing a circuit, triggering the blasting cap, which explodes the C4, which blasts the ball bearings into whoever tripped it. Don't mark it but monitor it, in accordance with the Geneva Convention.

76
Skirmishes

If I wanted to add a personal touch to this story I could insert a combat flourish like the rush of flying my company of killers in helos at 1,000 feet, one foot on the skid, all of us armed to the teeth, looking forward to killing lots of similarly armed enemy in the jungles ahead. But that'd be overkill.

By 1970, the War in Vietnam, from an infantry point of view, had devolved into those first two skirmishes, playing out between us and them, every day and night. I've witnessed the first scenario twice and the second often.

"Vietnam, the only war we lost," or, "Vietnam, the war the protestors won," is an illusion.

Humans are predators. Infantry training centers are finishing schools. Geneva Convention aside, there was no difference between us except for the medevac chopper which allowed me to sit here at my desk and write this.

77
Typhoon

My scrambler RTO handed me the secure handset and said, "LT, it's the S-3." The battalion operations officer and I could talk on the scrambler in uncoded language for speed.

I pressed the handset's button and said, "Brick 3, this is Blue 6, over."

All of us in my command group heard him respond on the speaker, "Roger, Blue 6, a typhoon crossed the Philippines this AM with winds of one five zero knots, I repeat, one five zero knots. It's headed straight for us. Get your company to the following location. Ready to copy, over?"

I said, "Wait one, over," grabbing my grease pencil and map.

"Brick 3, go ahead, over."

"Map reference 81643596, how do you copy, over?"

"Brick 3, I copy 81643596, over."

"That's a good copy, Blue 6. Make all good speed, we're notifying any other unattached units on your route to attach themselves to your company. Notify us when you're on top. Go fast, be safe. Any questions, over?"

"Roger, Brick 3, can we be resupplied today, over?"

"Roger, Blue 6, we'll arrange it on Highway 1 somewhere. Contact me when you have an ETA there, over."

"Roger, Brick 3, add two dozen entrenching tools to the supply chopper, over."

"Wilco, Blue 6, but resupply will be via truck, they're moving all the choppers they can to the safer revetments at Chu Lai. Brick 3, out."

My Field First, Sergeant Traynor and I worked out the wrinkles of arranging the supplies, then I called each platoon leader on the radio and ordered them in code to safely haul ass to the Mo Duc village on Highway 1, and said, "Double your point men, razor sharp."

Traynor lit a fire under everybody as we donned our 60-pound packs and began slogging east. My troops were used to working squad sized, so we'd have to be careful moving all 74 of us at once.

Plus, the monsoons had arrived and we lived in mud. Thankfully, the rain shorted out most of the booby trap batteries.

Six kilometers later we found our resupply and continued east. No enemy contact. Good. The objective was on the coast of the South China Sea, maybe fifty meters higher than ocean.

Nobody wanted to be out here in the open, especially in a typhoon.

78
At the Base of Big Red

Three teams of mine dogs and an ARVN Ranger platoon had joined us by the time we reached the base of Big Red. The hill was mostly bare but laced with hedgerows.

I found the name of the place interesting because Big Red was what they called Oklahoma University.

I set the mine dogs to work on the few gaps available in the hedgerows. When any of them smelled even a little bit dicey, I rolled the dice and had my guys chop holes in pristine hedgerow with their machetes.

It was slow, hot work. As dusk approached, we arrived on top. One last sniff by the dogs, who came up with nothing. We'd done it. Everybody had stayed sharp, combat ready.

No injuries. I assigned sectors of the hill's crest to my platoon leaders, inviting the Rangers to remain in the middle with me.

I didn't want my guys hearing Vietnamese spoken near them in the dark and mistaking them for VC.

The ARVN Ranger platoon leader had a man whose sole job was carrying both his and his own rucksack for him while he carried his swagger stick. The swagger stick was ceremonial so everyone would know he was in charge.

In contrast, I lit my cigarettes with an engraved Zippo lighter my men had given me for my birthday a few weeks before. I still have it, bent and dented, and it works perfectly.

Over the ocean, the setting sun was trying to illuminate the blackness that filled the sky from the approaching typhoon. Lightning stitched it all together. I ordered everybody to dig foxholes and get in them wearing their rucksacks and ponchos.

The wind was picking up as it got dark but everything was proceeding well, considering. We'd accomplished the day's mission. I'd finished digging my foxhole.

I put all of my weight on my right foot to step out of the foxhole. It would have been an ordinary step anywhere else, but here in Vietnam, a simple step was not always what it appeared.

In my digging, I had inadvertently uncovered an 81mm mortar round with a Chinese grenade in its fuse well.

79
Snake Eyes

I was thrown. Ten. Feet. Into the air.

It was if I was looking down on myself, in the silence.

It was like touching an electric fence.

My RTO (Radio Telephone Operator) shifted his head toward the noise, gradually moving his eyes towards me.

I crashed face-first into the ground next to him.

He grabbed my collar and pulled me into his hole.

All was quiet.

"Medic!!"

There were no more explosions.

This was no mortar attack. It dawned on everyone that I'd been blasted by a gigantic booby trap.

The company medics descended on me.

They pulled me out of the hole and began cutting my clothes off. They started an IV.

I'd been wounded before, and I'd felt the electric buzzing before. In the darkness, I knew nothing of the severity of my wounds.

With clarity of mind, I reminded them to get all the Commanding Officer documents and scrambler codes out of my pockets.

Moments later, a medevac chopper evacuating to Chu Lai took a detour and I was thrown on. We lifted and tore into the darkness.

Chu Lai to Christmas

80
Medevac

For the second time in Vietnam, I was being Dusted Off.

It was dark, but the interior light in the Huey was on. I hadn't been on a helicopter very often at night.

I was looking into the eyes of one of the ARVN Rangers across the floor from me. He was looking at me, puzzled, trying to say something. He had a piece of shrapnel the size of a stapler lodged in his forehead.

We were lying on ponchos on the floor of the chopper.

There were no doors, so blood poured across the floor, out to door edge, whipping into the slipstream, and into the air, falling into the jungle below.

I hoped it was his blood and immediately felt regret for thinking that.

Minutes passed. The medic yelled over the din, "Hold on, we're almost there!"

I just wanted to sleep. I was so tired. Blood loss.

The blood falling into the jungle was mostly mine.

190

81
Lizard brain

When I began to shut my eyes, the primordial lizard inside my brain vetoed that whole scenario:

It screamed, ""If you sleep, you'll die! Stay awake, goddamnit, we're gonna live!"

And we did, me and the lizard.

82
Eye of the Needle

When the medevac landed at the M.A.S.H. unit in Chu Lai, the typhoon had arrived in full force.

If that typhoon had arrived even one hour earlier, that medevac chopper would have already been moved to save it, and it would not have saved me.

I had a million dollar wound.

I was not going to die in Vietnam.

I was being pulled through the eye of a needle.

What was on the other side, I had no idea.

83
Chu Lai

As the chopper found its footing the rain blew through the doors onto my face. Two guys jerked my poncho with me on it onto a gurney and raced me through the darkness into a lighted building.

Several nurses grabbed me, "OK, on three we slide him over. Ready? One, two, three," and I was onto a table.

Doctors clustered around me, "Blood type!" A mad scramble for my dog tags, "A-positive!"

"Start a unit, stat, get the docs for OR 2 ready."

A nurse's face looked into mine, urgent, unconcerned, "Can you tell me your name?"

"Ron Sorter...Lieutenant..."

"Do you know the date, Lieutenant?"

"October...23rd, 1970."

"Where are you?"

"Chu Lai...hospital."

It felt like the typhoon was spinning the building.

"He's oriented times three," she said, as she patted me on the shoulder.

"BP 70 over 40," another said, then "Blood I.V. rolling."

A nurse lifted my left hand and gripped a 5" piece of shrapnel with some huge hemostats. It was stuck in the joint between my left thumb and hand.

She couldn't move it. Damn. It was the same electric fence feeling, but it must be worse than I thought because this one hurt!

A doctor leaned in, "We'll have you sedated soon, we just need some Xrays to see if there's anything internal then you'll go to the OR and they'll put you under. You have no head wounds, that's great. Don't worry, you're gonna live." Then into another room, X rays, and then another room.

"Count backwards from ten."

Another life was beginning.

"Ten...Nine..."

84
Ball of Confusion

People all over the world
are shouting, "end the war,"
and the band played on.
— The Temptations "Ball of Confusion"

When I awoke, I was dressed like a mummy. Similar mummies lay in beds to my left and right.

Female nurses in fatigues were moving from bed to bed in what appeared to be a temporary building.

A nurse came over and said, "Good morning. I'm giving you a shot of Demerol. You can have another in four hours. Are you doing OK?" I don't remember saying anything.

The last five minutes of every four-hour period waiting for the nurse with the needle I needed became a distinct kind of pain.

My surgeon came by later. "You still have your right leg, but your blood pressure was so low we couldn't debride the back of it so we'll just have to see. Some major shrapnel wounds, lots of rock but nothing internal. Broken left femur, your left ulna is missing a 2 inch piece. But all in all, you're good.

"We'll see in a couple days if your body wants to keep your leg. Any questions?"

195

Well, here are some questions:

My ulna? What's that?

"The Vietnamese Ranger I arrived with?"

He said, "Severe head wound but he'll make it," and he walked away.

I began living my next four hour shift. A few days later they changed my dressings and that was painful. I saw what was left of my right leg and I knew it was toast.

That night I called for a blanket. I was freezing. Minutes later I needed it off because I was burning up.

The surgeon arrived. "You're having chills and fever, classic infection signals. We'll have a look under anesthesia tomorrow morning."

"We may need to amputate your right leg."

85
Tokyo (One Set of Toes)

I'd healed enough for them to move me to an Army hospital in Tokyo.

I'm on the tarmac next to the plane, laying under a blanket on a stretcher. An Air Force guy, with his hat on sideways, looked at me. Then he saw I had only one set of toes sticking up.

He recoiled and looked away. It was the beginning of my homecoming and the reaction to my new life: recoil and look away. So, that's how it's going to be, eh?

Then I remembered the nurses at Chu Lai. They saw this every day and had never looked away. Extraordinary women.

In Tokyo, I and another guy were placed in adjoining beds, the only occupants of a forty-bed intensive care unit built after World War Two. It was like a private room, but a very large room with no one else in it.

Every four hours, two nurses would arrive with demerol and, for whoever's turn it was to go first, they'd put a leather clinch between our teeth then change our dressings.

This time he'd talk me through my dressing change, the next time I'd talk him through his. "OK, she's got the gauze all off, she's going for the Xeroform…"

A week later, I was on a C-130 aeroevac plane over the Pacific, on a stretcher arranged bunk bed style along the center of the entire fuselage. We landed first at Travis. I barely noticed.

Next, Buckley Air Field in Denver. When the huge rear hatch opened the most awesome cold air rushed inside. It was the first cold air I had felt in nine months.

It was two weeks until Thanksgiving.

86

The Five East Brotherhood

Fitzsimmons Army Hospital in Denver, Colorado is where they sent military patients with orthopedic wounds.

I was back in Colorado. I was happy for that at least.

Every four hours, some more demerol.

They put me in a circle electric bed, two rings holding me on a padded surface. A foam-covered frame with an opening for my face was periodically strapped over my body. They'd flip me 180 head over heels. Change the dressings on my back. Relax for a while, maybe read the comics on Sunday which the nurses would place on the floor and come by to turn periodically. Flip back. Go unconcious over the top.

I was in my new home with forty other guys, Ward Five East, Fitzsimmons Army Hospital, Aurora CO 80045. Five East was for lower extremity wounds. Five West held the upper extremity amputees. It cost an arm and a leg to get into that place. Rimshot.

My new doctor was pulling all the steel stitches out of my body, including the mess of limb where my right leg ended. The deep wounds needed to heal. I was stoic, saying nothing.

I had landed in the dirt, but had no infections at all. That was huge.

199

Doc said, "It will be easier if you let it all out. There's no reason to keep it inside anymore."

My Dad and his wife were waiting out in the hallway. I wish somebody had told me.

Finally, just before lights-out a guy missing both legs rolled up wearing his dark blue hospital gear. He smiled at me and said, "So, do I gotta salute?" Humor. It lets one survive.

I said, "I'd lock your heels but I can see that would be a waste of time." He laughed. Then I did. It had been a long time since I'd felt like laughing at anything. We would become good-friends, Glen and I.

87
Fitzsimmons: Family

A nurse carried a phone up to my bed, plugged it in, put it to her ear and said, "Are you still there? Yes, I can hear you, hold on, he's right here," and handed me the phone.

What the hell? She was already gone. I struggled to lift the receiver. My left arm was plaster from shoulder to fingertip and my right arm was wrapped with gauze and I had new wire stitches that caught on the sheets. I finally got it to my ear and said, "Hello?"

"Hi, Ron, it's Matt."

Matt? Damn, I needed a second.

"Wait a sec," I said, and got it back together.

"Hey, Matt, how are you?"

He said, "We're fine. I just wanted to make sure that it's OK with you if Vi and Marvin and I and the family come up and spend Thanksgiving with you."

That took me some time to process. "Of course," I said, "that sounds great."

"Good," he said, "let me put Vi on, she wants to talk to you."

88
The Tierno Factor

What an emotional conversation with Mom. But we did pretty good and she eventually said, "Do you remember Bob Tierno?"

I said I did. He was a good friend and fraternity brother with whom I'd kept in touch by mail when I was in Vietnam.

"Well, when they told me you'd been wounded that's all they told me. I was beside myself with worry. Anyway, Bob's dad Rocky is a colonel in the Army, with a friend at the Pentagon.

"When Bob told Rocky you'd been wounded, Rocky found out where you were, and how you were doing, and Bob's kept me up to date on you the whole time. I'll tell you all about it when we get up there, OK? Don't go anywhere. Here's Matt."

Mom, she was such a card.

89

Thanksgiving, 1970: Colorado Snowflakes

My family arrived a week later en masse and it was wonderful
to see them. It's difficult to explain the powerlessness of
having to always look up from a bed to interact with other
healthy humans. To force Mom to see me like that made it
especially hard for her.

But we coped and she enjoyed telling me how happy she was
that I was alive. Matt then mentioned the difficulty in driving
in the snow and I said, "Snow?" He looked around and saw
that I didn't have a window view then disappeared.

He returned with a nurse and they all rolled me, my bed with
all the traction clamps, the IVs and everything else down the
hallway, took a turn and pushed me up to a window.

Huge flakes, my favorite Colorado kind, gently sifted down
outside the window.

It was my first realization that the other side of the eye of the
needle hadn't changed at all. But I had.

We had a wonderful Thanksgiving. My family departed too
soon, saying how sad it would be to have Christmas without
me, but they understood.

My doctor was a great guy. I told him he had a month to get
me healthy enough to fly home for Christmas.

90
Sticks and Legs

Mike Quinn was going home

Mike was a "baloney," a below-knee amputee.

We all went to a bar, the closest one to the hospital. Twenty of us jammed into booths. We made a pile in the corner, a comical tangle of crutches, canes, artificial legs and wheelchairs.

We were Knights of the Round Table, downing large flagons of ale. We toasted the guys who hadn't made it back. They were already in Valhalla, at the great Banquet Hall.

We handed Mike's leg around, as a chalice.

We were wounded. We were a Brotherhood. And we were alive.

91
The Brotherhood of the Purple Heart

Ten Bears: *There is iron in your word of death for all Comanche to see. And so there is iron in your words of life. No signed paper can hold the iron, it must come from men.*
— *The Outlaw Josey Wales* (1976)

The Brotherhood of the Purple Heart began to do its work, too. This particular brotherhood is one in which all its members are initiated against their will. But once one is a proud member of that crew, the bonds are iron. There are no war stories that can match those shared after lights out with these brothers.

And there is no one better to help a brother deal with the rejection of a wife who refuses to even come see her "crippled husband." Or the rage of another as he sees his peers on television happily cursing him and all soldiers. The therapy provided by that brotherhood over the ensuing year and a half helped me heal my mind.

The Brotherhood came to realize that we were the wounded detritus of a war everyone despised and wanted to forget. We knew our futures would have to go in a different direction so we helped each other get onto that different path.

In the process, we learned how to become the type of man who can, repeatedly, stumble, fall, get up off the floor and thrive. In essence, how to become a different kind of man. The kind of man with a Purple Heart.

92
Brown Suede Pants

I rarely got out of the field, except for a few days at a time. But when I did, I made the most of it.

In Chu Lai, I went to a Vietnamese tailor on the base there. The shop was next to the PX where all the REMF (rear area MF's) went to buy the whatnots they needed to live in their fancy hooches with their nice hooch maids "in the combat zone of Vietnam."

The ladies from the local town were a nice REMF perk I would never have. Resentment? Naw.

Everything then was about your DEROS (date effective return from overseas).

Bell bottoms were just the thing in 1970. And not just any bell bottoms, no. When I landed back in the world, I was going to buy a Harley and take an epic road trip before going to jump school. For that I'd need some suede bells.

The tailor recommended they be lined with silk, too. Sure, sounds good. "You pay now, GI, you keep ticket. No ticket, no pants." Sure, sounds good. I stuffed the ticket in my pants and went back to the bush.

A month later I was laying in my new home, a hospital bed in Fitzsimmons and I remembered. "I never picked up my bell bottoms!"

I had a couple of camo shirts that'd been sent home with me, along with that small canvas backpack with a bullet hole through it I'd taken as a souvenir. Those suede bell bottoms, I'd be needing them so I wrote a letter to my First Sergeant saying something like:

"Hey, Top, wish I was there, but the food is better here, so I think I'll stay. I need a favor. Can you have somebody go by that Vietnamese tailor's sometime, the one just west of the Chu Lai PX? He was making me some brown suede bell bottoms and I never got a chance to pick them up." I tossed the letter in the mail and it was flown to the other side of the world."

A month later, I got a box. Inside were the absolute coolest, tailor-made brown suede bell bottoms. Double buttons up top, covered in the same suede. Quality zipper. Heavy-gauge maroon silk lining. Great workmanship. Exactly what I'd ordered. There was a letter in the box.

"Dear Lt. Sorter,

I'm glad to hear you're doing well. A different life, I imagine, with a different future but we're all glad you lived. I just have to live another 27 days, then I DEROS.

Remember Charlie, our resupply driver? I sent him up to the tailor's and he told the owner you'd been wounded and were back in the States. The guy gave Corporal Charlie some grief, something about him not having your ticket. He probably figured he'd keep the pants and sell them to somebody else.

207

You know Charlie. That's why he's my main scrounger, he gets things done. He stuck his weapon up the guy's nose and told him, 'Give me the pants or it's gonna get ugly.' Wear them in good health, SIR. We're glad you're alive.

Sincerely, First Sergeant Yates"

93
Over the River and Through the Woods

"LT, are you sure you want to do this?"

Tommy was the coolest orderly in the hospital. He handled everything we couldn't do ourselves. He was holding my Class A's, freshly shipped to me from Vietnam. My Zippo lighter was in one of the pockets.

"I'm flying home for Christmas, Tommy. What's the worst that could happen? Will they send me to Vietnam?"

He laughed and said, "OK, you want these dry cleaned?"

"Yeah, and could you locate some shoe polish for me? These shoes need some polish."

"Roger that," he said.

I was doing great. I now lived in a normal hospital bed, I'd graduated to solid food and could eat by myself. And, at long last, I'd even met the bed pan. And I'd met a civilian nurse from 4 West who arrived to play chinese checkers with me at that precise moment. Timing, it's all timing.

Glen hollered, "Hey, LT, you gonna polish those shoes with your face?"

"You wanna do what with your face?" I replied.

I'd also learned there was no rank in the hospital. We were all just patients so we talked constant smack. I swear, it was just like the Deke house.

But Glen was right, I only had the fingers on my right hand to work with, my left arm was still in plaster.

I had a temporary right leg, basically a length a pipe with a shoe at the end, and a simple hinge at the knee. My permanent prosthesis was still months away.

They'd issued me a wheelchair with an extension for my plastered left leg and it had two rims so I could maneuver it using only my right hand. I was doing great, damnit, and I was going home for Christmas.

A couple days before Christmas Eve two volunteers from the local Elks lodge showed up, got me into my wheelchair and to the airport. One even, God bless him, helped me to the john when the need arose.

The easiest place to put me was the front row aisle seat. I was wearing my uniform with all its regalia so, mostly, everybody just tried their best to ignore me. I proudly wore my shoes that Glen had spit-shined for me.

94
Gravy

I took a Continental flight from Denver's Stapleton airport to Oklahoma City. I was used to jungles, rice paddies, and hospitals. This was my very first foray into the world since leaving it.

I had some painful moments, but thankfully didn't need to use any of the meds in my pocket. This airplane ride today was off the map. I have to say, the stewardesses were nice to me.

They waited until everyone was off the plane then put me in my wheelchair and rolled me to the gate.

The welcome I got from Mom, my brother and his wife was warm and ecstatic. Apparently I'd gotten some huge boxes from Japan. Christmas!

We headed for baggage claim where I was amazed to see Bob Tierno and a few other Dekes. I looked like a man from a concentration camp but that didn't matter. I was alive.

This was all gravy.

Bob leaned over and shook my hand. "Welcome back to the world," he said and my hand came away with a joint, wrapped in stars and stripes paper.

The bonds of brotherhood are iron.

The shrapnel from the Chinese mortar missed my heart. As brutal as my wounds were, I had no interior injuries. I had not been spared to become some example of courage and inspiration.

I'd been spared for something else entirely. What that thing was, I had no idea.

Despite everything that had changed, the brotherhood had remained rock solid and unchanging. It will always be there.

95

A High-Fidelity Christmas, 1970

At Mom's apartment, I lay on the couch while my brother put together the sound system I'd received from Pioneer. I'd ordered it on the other side of the world under a snapped-together poncho crawl space in a jungle monsoon, using a flashlight with a red lens. It was the biggest amp they made, giant speakers, tape deck, turntable. It didn't disappoint.

Mom had a small Christmas tree on the table by the couch, covered with pictures in little wooden frames of our previous Christmases together. We had a wonderful time. I was home.

We also spent an evening at Matt's with every relative that could fit in his house. Marvin asked me if I could drink and I had to think. "I guess so," I said, "You got any bourbon in a square bottle?" He did.

The last drink I'd had was six months prior in the Officer's Club in Chu Lai. I'd gotten a day to be pay officer and sat that night in a huge room with a thatched roof overlooking the South China Sea.

I and three others in filthy worn fatigues and matching boots were drinking straight Jack Daniels in a sea of polished officer REMFs. Vietnam and America constantly overlapped in my mind. The doctors said it was normal. Marvin's bourbon was nice. Inside the buzz, I was surprised and happy to discover it made my phantom pains disappear.

96
"He's Flying with Me"

I was again seated on an airplane. Matt was helping me get situated on my return flight to Fitzsimmons.

A ticket agent arrived and said, "In your condition you need someone to fly with you. You'll have to get off the airplane."

What the hell?

"Wait," I said, "I flew down here and nobody said I needed anybody to fly with."

"It doesn't matter, those are our rules."

"This is insane," said Matt, "I'm going to find your boss," and bolted out the door. There was confused conversation for a few minutes then the cockpit door opened and the captain came out.

The pilot looked at the agent and said, "I'm supposed to be airborne, what's the holdup?"

The agent pointed at me. "He can't fly unless someone's with him. Look at him."

The captain looked at me. He knew how to read a uniform.

He turned to the agent and said, "Get off my airplane, he's flying with me."

We landed in Kansas City on the way to Denver. The pilot and the copilot came out to shoot the breeze with me. They'd both been combat pilots, the captain with the Navy, the copilot with the Marines.

We shared some funny stories, from my viewpoint on the ground and from theirs in the air. Combat is a bloody brotherhood, but the bonds are iron.

Once you've had a brotherhood, you realize how priceless it is.

V. Bob
Corrections

97
Rocky Mountain High

In the early summer of 1971, I returned to Denver. Ron wanted
to head to the mountains and go camping. We had no gear,
so we went to a Dick's Sporting Goods and bought a tent,
sleeping bags, backpacks and mess kits. We headed off to the
mountains. We bought a case of beer and some food as well.

We camped above Evergreen under the stars, with a campfire
and quite a bit of beer, as you might imagine.

In the middle of the night, Ron woke up screaming, which
nearly sent me through the roof of the tent: the demons of war.
He rolled over and went back to sleep.

Ron handled his situation with dignity.

I set a goal of moving to Denver one day. Each day at 5:00
p.m., during rush hour, there was a ritual that sealed it for me.
A salute to Colorado, with a recording of John Denver singing
"Rocky Mountain High".

98
Playboy Bunnies

In order to take this trip to Denver, I had to negotiate with an OU history professor to delay my taking a final exam. Surprisingly, he was very sympathetic to the situation. He told me to go take care of my friend and upon return, take the test open book. I will be forever grateful.

One of Ron's benefits as an amputee was a grant to help purchase a car outfitted with pedals so he could drive without any trouble. Ron bought a new 455 Trans Am and had it painted black. He moved into an apartment during my visit and I helped him out.

One evening we joined a group of his fellow amputees from Fitzsimmons at the Playboy Club in Denver. It was quite a sight with Playboy Bunnies and drinks for all.

By the end of the night, we were all dancing with the bunnies.

99
The War Winds Down

Ron and I kept in touch by mail and the occasional phone
call. Ron attempted to make a go of it in real estate, but it was
difficult physically to get around in the winter. He accepted a
position at the VA Hospital in the Prosthetics Service.

In 1972, I was discharged into the Army Reserves following
91 days of active duty. The Democrats voted to end funding
for the War and Nixon pressed for negotiating the peace (after
carpet bombing the landscape along with leveling the jungles
with Agent Orange which continues to impact veterans with
prostate and colon cancer).

I had cut the cord with OU and didn't really want to go back.
My Deke Sweetheart Karen wouldn't move east. I moved back
to Vienna, Virginia where I had high school friends. Turns out,
most of them had left the area.

100
Virginia

I left for Fort Eustis, VA in March of 1972 to attend my Transportation Officers Basic Course knowing in ninety one days I'd be returned to civilian life, unemployed. The Vietnam War was winding down and nobody was hiring anybody in uniform. I didn't want to go back to Oklahoma although I had offers from companies who had serviced the student store.

My sense is that it was time to conquer the world. What a rude awakening! While on active duty, I was assigned to a landing craft company as the U.S. Army has the second largest fleet in the world.

As a boat platoon leader, I had an odd assortment of troops who had been "river rats" on the Mekong Delta and had already seen the worst of war. Most had drug problems and were constantly getting into trouble.

Once we took the landing craft out on the bay, they would settle down and do their job. It was like a switch was turned on and they were at home on the water. Frankly, the movie Apocalypse Now accurately described some of the river rats in my platoon.

I bought a pure-bred Irish Setter I named Caesar. Irish setters were very popular but overbred. Caesar was hyperactive and a handful. Over the next five years he was a great companion. We lost him to a strange ailment while in North Carolina. No more dogs for us.

I was introduced to ocean-going tug boats. What a life! I put in for an assignment on them hoping for a two or three year tour. As much as the Post Commander tried, there were no billets (slots) to be found in the Army, a real disappointment.

101
"Of Course, I'll Marry You"

I flew Karen out to Virginia during my assignment. She met my dog Caesar, a handsome, crazy Irish Setter puppy. When I asked Karen to marry me, she said "What took you so long? Of course, I'll marry you."

Karen returned to OU. Upon my discharge I returned to the Washington D.C. area. I took a job working at a classmate's dad's store selling jeans. I found it boring and quit after two weeks. I got a job at Hechinger's Lumber Store (think Home Depot or Lowes) selling paint. The majority of men working there were enlisted veterans of the war and didn't take to me as a young 2nd Lieutenant in the Army Reserves.

The president of the company interviewed me for a management trainee position. I had to take a test then complete the interview process. I aced the test and was offered a position making $125 per week. I turned it down, while searching for a teaching position in local public schools.

I rented an apartment in Gaithersburg, MD and accepted a job as an aide in school for special needs kids. I worked with a teacher, Bill Melvin, who was so dedicated to the kids that I enjoyed the work. However, the principal and I didn't hit it off, so I began planning for a move.

I rented a nearby apartment that would accept pets. The apartment was a one bedroom, one bath.

Karen graduated and agreed to move in with me, eloping in October of 1972, unbeknownst to our parents. Karen's brother Jim was our best man at the civil wedding at city hall in Rockville, MD. We had formal wedding announcements printed and sent them out. I think my mother in Bolivia almost had a stroke when they received theirs.

It was an act of rebellion, as Karen wasn't too keen on being married in the Catholic Church. So we were "legal" in our parents' eyes, so we thought. This turns out to be a blunder because our parents were never given the chance to meet each other until fifteen years later after a separation and our agreement to renew our vows in a Catholic Church.

While stranded in Gaithersburg, MD. Karen put her interior-design degree to work at a store in Georgetown. It became obvious that teaching in Montgomery County was not going to happen.

I got a lead on a civil-service position with the U.S. Department of Justice, Federal Bureau of Prisons. They were hiring four-year college graduates to work as correctional officers and teachers. The Correctional Officer (guard, hack, bull, you get the picture) position paid more, so I focused on that opportunity. I was qualified according to Bureau of Prisons, so once I was rated as a GS-06 I waited for interviews. Karen was supportive, as it meant more income.

I interviewed at the reformatory in Petersburg, VA. This place was scary to say the least. The Warden and Chief Correctional Officer offered me a job starting immediately. I told them my goal was to move to Denver to work at the Federal Youth Center.

I had the naive notion that working with youth, I could make a difference. The Warden understood and committed to let the Warden at Englewood, Colorado know of my interest. I was excited and encouraged. Karen and I decided to pull up stakes and head to Denver.

I called Ron and asked him if we could stay with him briefly upon our arrival in Denver.

Karen and I quit our jobs and packed up our personal goods. We gave Caesar tranquilizers and headed west in our fully loaded VW Bug.

This was a big risk, as President Nixon had just declared a hiring freeze. I figured this would not last long so it was worth the risk to get to Denver, prepared to work. The hiring freeze went on forever, it seemed, so I wrote a letter to President Nixon, which was referred to the Director of the Bureau of Prisons, Norm Carlson (see Appendix) who routed it to the Warden at the Federal Youth Center in Englewood.

I got hired, and we rented a small bungalow with a fenced back yard for Caesar in Aurora. Karen got a job as a painter for a contractor for some time as I started this new adventure working in a federal prison.

We did not talk about it much. We were a young couple starting out in life.

103
Reserves and Ron Time

I was required to join an Army Reserve Unit. Most everybody assigned in my unit were Rep 66s or, like myself, a draft dodger. The post-Vietnam-era military was a mess and I quickly observed that soldiers were treated worse than inmates when we were sent to Fort Leonard Wood, MO, and Fort Ord, CA to fulfill our annual two weeks training requirement. I was a range officer.

I bought a wig to avoid hair cuts. That worked for monthly weekend drills, but when I went to summer camp I had to cut my hair.

My job as a correctional officer went well. Double shifts meant more money. I toed the line with the veterans, most of whom served in World War II and the Korean War. They taught me to be fair but firm. Inmates had 24 hours a day to screw with you and plan escapes. It wasn't my job to screw with them. I could write an hysterical book filled with stories about my prison experiences; but that's another book.

Karen got hired as the first female car salesman for John Poppell Toyota/Oldsmobile in Denver. She got a demo car which was nice and Toyotas were flying off the lot. I was working shifts so it was hard to schedule socializing. We moved from Aurora to a rental in Northglenn. I bought my first motorcycle, a Honda 350-4 cylinder (thanks to *Easy Rider*), now that I could afford the payments.

Meanwhile I talked my way into the record office. I could type and Joe Summers the manager wanted to create a new concept for taking over the receiving and discharge function.

Hiring me (a correctional officer) offered him the opportunity to sell the concept. The bureau was on the cusp of the computer era. Batch processing of data was still done every night, we still had a teletype machine (no email yet), and manually computed every inmate's sentence upon arrival. On the outside, we didn't socialize with any prison employees.

We partied with Ron and his girlfriend who was a flight attendant for Frontier Airlines. Karen was a trooper, putting up with the moves, adapting to new environs and supporting my career.

We decided to buy our first house which was a classic old brick home in old north Denver near Sloan's Lake and Elitch's Amusement Park.

104
Tobacco Road

We knew that my position was a trainee slot, and that I would be assigned to an institution at the discretion of the Bureau of Prisons. No sooner did we get accustomed to our new home than, in late, 1975, I was informed that I would be transferred to the new Federal Correctional Institution in Butner, NC (near Durham).

I would receive a promotion and be a department head at age 26. I would "own" receiving and discharge, the mail room, and the record office all under the new name Administrative Systems Department.

Karen and I approached this move as a new adventure. However, we did not take into account the brutal humidity of the south, nor the attitudes.

We bought a small home in Durham, about 20 minutes from the prison. Imagine the culture shock of moving from Denver to Durham. The closest Taco Bell was in Greensboro. This was tobacco country and our neighbors were career Liggett-Meyers employees. I swear they all had a cigarette sewn inside their lips.

Karen adapted by getting hired selling Mercedes Benz' and was a top salesperson. She won a sales contest and bought our first pieces of nice furniture, manufactured in North Carolina.

Caesar Dog finally settled down but he passed away after turning five. We decided to not have pets for a while. We had taken him to see my parents in Carlisle, PA where he almost ate their small dog.

Karen was really taken aback by Mom T's loud voice and frankly she was scared. She hung in there, though, and years later she was Mom's best friend.

The job at Butner was interesting but pressure packed for a 26-year-old guy and I nearly had a nervous breakdown. A doctor prescribed a mild sedative and I was able to manage the stress after talks with the Associate Warden who turned out to be a great mentor.

105
San Diego (Temporarily)

At the end of 1976, I jumped at the opportunity to transfer to the Metropolitan Correctional Center (MCC) in San Diego, CA as a booking supervisor in the bureau's first online booking environment. Since I had the administrative systems background, I fit right in working for a terrific manager, Donna Stratman.

Karen and I sold our house, packed up once again and jumped in our Toyota Station Wagon. The trip was fun and we rolled into San Diego renting a hotel room right on the beach!

"Hotel California" by the Eagles played on the radio. We took a few days, and drove to Ensenada, Mexico with Ron, who had moved to San Diego. Coronas were a quarter, margaritas were a buck. The Mexican food was real too! Adios, Taco Bell, at last.

Karen was hired by Glaser Brothers, installing and stocking shelves in grocery and drug stores. I worked graveyard shifts at the MCC, which was midnight to eight a.m. I would head home, pull on my swim trunks and hit the condo complex pool or go to Pacific Beach. We decided to rent a condo because, even in 1977, real estate was off the charts.

106
San Francisco

While working full-time, I took a course at the University of San Diego to become a legal assistant or paralegal. There was a rumor that the regional offices were hiring paralegals to assist regional attorneys. Since I understood legality of confinement issues, sentence computation, and prison operations I was a natural for this new position.

Karen and I took advantage of every opportunity to hit the beach, sail, and explore Southern California. We were both conflicted about the possibility of this move because we loved the Southern California lifestyle. I was eventually selected to be the legal assistant in the regional office in Burlingame, CA south of San Francisco.

The Bureau paid for the move so we packed up a 28-foot U-Haul truck and headed north. We planned every detail including one stop off I-5 after nine hours of driving. The next day we motored into the Bay Area, located our hotel, and I called the office.

The good news is there was a two-bedroom apartment in San Mateo above where a fellow regional office administrator, Buck Samples lived. I had worked for Buck in Colorado. We unloaded the truck, moved in and enjoyed the cooler weather, with fog rolling in in the evenings.

We spent practically every weekend in Napa wine country or San Francisco.

Karen kept her job with Glaser Bros so it was just new territory. We discussed buying a house in the North Bay but it was out of reach on our income.

We headed across the bay to Fremont and found a brand new condo development was being built. It was about a 40-minute commute with several fellow administrators. One of them bought there and another lived in Hayward on the way to work. We enjoyed gourmet cooking and hanging out at the pool with our resident friends.

We met newlyweds Tom and Jean Bolger, who moved to Fremont from Cal Poly. Tom was a CFO at a Redwood City Hospital and earning an MBA. We treated Tom and Jean to homemade pasta, sausage, meatballs and tomato sauce one Sunday evening. Tom and Jean announced that they were expecting their first child and asked me to be their child's Godfather.

What an honor and, of course, I told them I would be honored. Kelly was born and from the time we met her in her onesie under the Christmas tree she stole our hearts. A wonderful relationship to this day. Kelly and her husband Aaron have two beautiful children, Josie and Bode.

Having moved around all my life I thought that maybe we'd have a chance of establishing roots with our friends, only to have them move away. Karen and I were both a bit confused by all of this and then it happened again so we decided that we'd manage our life and not tie it to anybody except the Bolgers.

We attended Kelly's baptism, confirmation, and even hosted her in Ohio when she turned twelve, her first time travelling out of state on her own.

We sold the condo and bought a home in Fremont. I pursued an MBA at Pepperdine University instead of a law degree. In the meantime the regional director fired the Records Administrator and promoted me on the spot. The next two years I spent on the road turning over managers and converting record offices to administrative systems management offices.

Once I completed this goal at ten federal prisons in the Western Region I asked to be considered for a Federal Prison Industries Management Position in Pleasanton, CA.

I got passed over and through my student connections met an Intel manager who got me an interview with her manager. I was offered a position in marketing/manufacturing planning which I immediately accepted. I gave my notice, and went to work at Intel's headquarters in Santa Clara. Karen knew my goal was to work in private industry focused on marketing/sales. Karen was still working at Glaser Brothers.

Leaving the security of a government job was a big risk. Karen was worried but supported the move because the money and health benefits were equal but the upside was greater. I was on a warden track at the Bureau of Prisons. That would have meant another move back to Washington, D.C. and then to at least a couple of institutions. With every move we lost money up front.

VI. Ron
Captain Ahab and the VA

107
The Car That Became My Legs

Things were looking up. Jenny, the nurse from the fourth floor was visiting more often, and one afternoon she said, "Your eyes are yellow." I thought that might be one of her Portuguese come ons, so when she stared deep into my eyes I held her gaze, ready for anything. She turned on her heel and left. Damn.

Then she returned with the head nurse.

Yup. Hepatitis. Cripes, what else? Being put in a private room was better than living in the open ward. Jenny and I made the best of the privacy, which was really nice.

I recovered from the curse of hepatitis only to meet the nice Occupational Therapy lady. On my first visit to her lair, she tried to flex my left distal phalanx. I sat, grimacing, in a comfy chair in her bright room in spring, polished linoleum floors glistening with the morning sun. My full arm cast was off and I could see it in all its glory. Under my skin, my palms and forearms were peppered with shrapnel; tattoos by Blast.

I was sweating a magazine of bullets, trying to let her do her worst without a peep. After four months in that cast, every joint in my arm and fingers were frozen into a backward curl.

She smiled at me, "I know it hurts. These tiny finger muscles will hurt the worst. It just takes time." It did, every day.

236

My broken left leg, the sound one, had healed. They used skin grafts from it to close the open wound at the end of my amputated femur. The day arrived when all of the skin on my body was, as they say, "fully enclosed."

My gnarled left hand had improved, so I graduated to a two-handed wheelchair. It took only a few days for me to perfect the Follies move, balancing on the rear wheels while whirling the front wheels, and then in opposite directions. The nurses would throw their underwear at me, or maybe I just dreamed that.

This coincided with the springtime opening of the wheelchair-accessible rooftop balcony where patients could smoke the various types of tobacco being donated to we poor disabled veterans by our brotherhoods.

After more weeks of daily OT pain, I could finally handle fore-arm crutches, which allowed me to stand up. Imagine your-self, after sitting in a wheelchair for months, finally standing up again. Looking eye to eye with the rest of the world. It's motivational, that I'll tell you.

To celebrate, I bought a different wheeled vehicle, a brand new 1971 Pontiac Trans Am, white with blue racing stripes, 455 cubic inches under the hood. I had them strip it, paint it black and added chrome mag wheels.

One day I rolled down my window with my left hand and, amazed, looked at my hand. It worked!

I rolled the window up and down a few times. Let's hear it for the OT lady! That car became my legs: fill 'er up, drive in movies, Jack In The Box.

It was an empty life but man, every second was gravy.

108
Captain's Bars

A bunch of guys was in this bar room,
Most of them had been there half the day.
They'd been telling jokes and fairy tales,
Lying, just to pass the time away…
— Chuck Berry, "Dutchman"

Then it was fraternity brother season. Bob Tierno came up for a visit that spring. We bought some C rations for old time's sake and went camping up in the mountains. Apparently I wasn't ready for the inside of pitchblack tents yet but, hell, I could roll down a car window. I was crawling out of the hole.

A few weeks later in the ward I heard, "Hey, Sorter, wanna do some shots?" Fred Streb, another Deke, had walked up to my bed unannounced, holding a fifth of scotch. All the guys within hearing chimed in, "Hey, buddy, over here!"

I shook his hand, grabbed the bottle and hid it under my pillow. I was amazed he'd gotten this far without somebody stopping him, considering all the guys on Demerol. The nurses were always on the watch for smuggled booze.

But Streb's a genius. He returned in an hour with a couple of pink and blue plastic baby bottles with rubber nipples. Like two POW's digging a tunnel, Glen acting as lookout, we emptied the scotch into the baby bottles and hid them in the bottom of my kleenex box. Let's hear it for the brotherhood!

239

It kept getting better. The Holiday Inn across from the main gate had a limo and they'd begun giving rides to any willing patient who wanted to have a civilian dinner, listen to some music and have a few drinks.

The Holiday Inn became The Brotherhood's new chapter room, with its own bartendresses and barmaids. I'd go there to drink my phantom pains away.

I celebrated my new captain's bars there, with the guys, combat vets all, lowering, folding and presenting me with the American flag out in front of the building. I still have this prized possession.

Now all Captain Ahab needed was a pegleg made from whalebone, but first, the dreaded (gasp of horror) revision.

109
Don't Come All this Way to Die On the Operating Table

I couldn't merely wear an artificial limb, technically known as a prosthesis. It had to be perfectly crafted to my residual limb and become a part of me.

But first, in a fashion, I had to be fitted to it. Surgically they call these operations "a revision."

For the record, "stump" is a descriptive enough word for a residual limb, but no one who has one uses it.

Fitzsimmons, because of the number of amputees it treated, had orthopedic surgeons who were masters of surgery. I've benefited from that my entire life.

So imagine this: you're blasted through the air, you land in the dirt, your body has had dirt and gravel blown into it, later causing hepatitis, a medevac flies you to a field emergency room, your blood pressure is 70 over 40.

Jagged pieces of metal stick out of your limbs looking like needles. They pull out a few but the others are just stuck inside. They eventually cut off your leg and you're shipped home.

After many months your wounds heal from the inside out and when you're finally healthy enough, your first operation is designed to "debride" you, to remove much of the "troublesome debris."

Your anesthesiologist that day uses oxygenated pentothal to knock you out, and curare (the "poison arrow" stuff) to paralyze you so you don't move around under anesthesia.

It's important to use the pentothal first. (I found out all this much later). Nevertheless, as you lay on the operating table, waiting to count back from ten, you realize you've become completely paralyzed.

You try to say, "Hey..." and nothing comes out. You can see and hear the nurses and doctors chatting, laughing, the blue sky out the window, you feel the chill in the room, and your last thought as you lose consciousness is, "Crap. After all this, I die on an operating table."

The next morning, I met with the Command Sergeant Major and the Chief of Staff of the hospital, explaining how *that* shit was unacceptable. They all apologized for the "sequencing glitch."

110
I Am Revised

That's the reason, a month later, yet another revision was done under a spinal to paralyze me, with a relaxant to make me nap. I wasn't looking forward to waking up during my operation and see them sculpting my femur. But of course, I did.

I think it was the rocking back-and-forth action of the saw on my femur that woke me. I saw one of my favorite people, the chief of the orthopedic service. He was a nice guy, full Colonel and a great surgeon. He saw that I was awake and said, "How are you doing?"

I said fine, and he told me he'd taped the shrapnel he'd removed from my knee joint to my chest for a keepsake.

A (different) anesthetist, seeing that I needed a bit more juice, tuned me up. Sharp edges were then removed from my femur, my rubbery femoral nerve was located, pulled out a little, trimmed and allowed to retract, then I was sewn up and sent back to 5 East. I was put back on the four-hour demerol schedule because bone ache, I'm telling you, was painful.

The Colonel told me later that, as I drifted off, I told him to, "Be careful with the sharp saw, you might cut my leg off." He said the comedy showed I was healed. It's great to have your 'sawbones' think you're a nice guy. I took it as a compliment.

243

111
Bennie

One summer evening in 1972, I walked into a Denver restaurant with Bennie. The Colorado Mine Company had just opened and it was the latest thing. Native stone, deep carpet, nary a sign outside to identify the place. It looked like an old mine outside but inside it was filled with celebrities, the nefarious and, most importantly to a single me, beautiful women. It was the kind of place your mother warned you about. Of course, Bennie and I hung out there a lot. It was Mom's favorite place, too, at least early in the evening. She just loved Bennie, but he had that effect on women.

I saw Mom sitting at a table. She got up as we approached, hugged Bennie and patted him on his cheek. "Ben, it's so nice to see you. How are you?" she asked.

"I'm doing great, I guess. But it's a full time job keeping your son out of trouble."

She smiled at me and patted my hand as I sat down. "You're being nice to Bennie, aren't you?" she asked with a smile.

"Nope", I said. "Besides, he can take it, he's all legs."

"Hey!" said Bennie.

"Legs" are what the airborne call the non-airborne. I wasn't airborne but Bennie was. He had his legs on.

112
Montana Smoke

Bennie's trademark was his innocent look. He looked like Shirley Temple's boyfriend all grown up but he was an ex-smokejumper from Montana. He routinely told every airborne guy he met that in jump school he'd had the most fun imaginable making fun of the airborne DIs for making them jump out of airplanes into LZs that weren't even on fire.

He'd lost both his legs leading a 101st Airborne platoon west of Phu Bai. Fortunately, he still had both his knees so he was already walking around fairly well. He claimed he was the best dancer in Montana.

I'd met him when I'd healed enough to be moved to Fitzsimmons' outpatient building where he and I had been roommates. His and my families became close over the next few months and after we were discharged we rented a townhouse bachelor pad.

His girlfriend, Jan, was a schoolteacher in a town up in the mountains and he'd stay with her a lot, leaving his Dalmatian, Hobo, with me. That dog and I had a ball in my Trans Am. I'd roll his window down and he'd stick his entire body out of the car as we drove around town, front feet on the window sill, him barking, "Where's the fire?" at the other cars at stop lights. A great ice breaker. I loved that dog.

245

113
Dancing with a Bunny

Tierno was in Denver later that summer, so we talked Bennie into showing us his dance moves at the new Playboy Club where I was a member. We spent some time drinking and reminiscing about the various members of the brotherhoods we all belonged to.

A Bunny delivered a new tray of drinks and Bennie, ever the charmer, asked her, "Do you mind if I dance you back to the bar? My friends here think I don't have the requisite moves."

She said, in her sultry way, "Well, we'll show them, won't we?"

This was gonna be good. He'd only been walking a couple months but nobody here knew that. He was dressed in a tailored western suit, matching boots, and his trademark grin. As they moved across the dance floor, Tierno and I were amazed. The guy, surprisingly, had some seriously cool moves.

Damn, in cowboy boots, he was up on his toes, people were making room, and then, oooops, a little balance problem, uh, oh, he slammed onto the floor and one off his legs, complete with boot, shot out of his pants, skidded across the floor and everybody just...froze.

Bennie was laughing hard, so everybody else did, too, then they started cheering.

Bob and I grabbed his leg, he put it back on, stood up, yelled, "God bless the Airborne!" and came back to the table. We drank free for the rest of the night. The guy was fearless.

A few months later he and Jan learned she had a condition that would make it wise to have children sooner rather than later. They quickly moved to Montana, got married and started a family. Bennie had a glorious life, worked as an engineer for the U.S. Forest Service, was loved by everyone and died in 2012. His son Ron lives in San Antonio.

Did you notice we were both walking? Here's how that happened...

114

From Belt Level to Eye Level

The front door of Dwayne's prosthetic establishment had a hydraulic closing mechanism that was acting like a bouncer. I'd only been using these forearm crutches for a few days. I wasn't yet adept, so I made a gamble, shoved it wide with one crutch and swung inside before it could slam on me.

I had an appointment to pick up my first leg, but he place looked empty. There were a few chairs, some parallel bars, a mirror, that's it.

"Anybody here?" I said into the silence. I took another few steps.

"Hello?" Silence. I scanned the floor for booby traps as I slowly made my way to some curtains. I lifted a crutch, using it to slowly separate the curtains and looked inside.

On the walls hung old artificial arms, legs, braces, all dangling from hooks and nails, like so much excess mechanical anatomy. Plastic foam, frozen in midboil, was attached in broken piles to tables and vises with canisters of plastic and sheets of polyurethane cluttering every flat surface. I expected to see Edgar Allen Poe smiling in a corner.

Clamped at the ankle into one huge vise was a perfectly vertical, finished above knee prosthesis. A voice behind me said, "That's you." OK, I jumped.

Dwayne was wiping his hands, saying, "Sorry, I was in the john, I didn't hear you come in."

I turned to him, then looked back at "my leg." I'd been without one for almost a year, so I guess it was time for us to finally get acquainted. Dwayne had taken a cast of my residual limb at Fitzsimmons. This prosthesis was the result.

Prosthesis: An artificial body part (noun).

Prosthetic: Denoting an artificial body part (adjective).

That's all the lingo you'll ever need to know.

You can see the fabrication on YouTube. It all starts with a shoe. Or more precisely, a particular shoe's heel height, which affects the forward lean (and stability) of the leg.

Want to wear flip flops? Want to wear cowboy boots? Got an Allen wrench? You can adjust the ankle angle sometimes, otherwise you'll need to buy another foot.

It's every person's dream: a body part goes bad, just buy another one off the shelf. Plus, you'll save a bundle on laundry since you'll hardly ever need to wash the sock on your prosthesis.

Of course, today prostheses are all made using carbon fiber, aluminum and microprocessors. The prosthetic facilities now resemble pristine, high-end BMW service facilities.

Fifty years ago, after having one's residual limb cast in plaster, a model was made of it, over which some fabric, then a clear plastic sleeve was pulled. The fabric was infused with liquid acrylic plastic. After it dried, it was the perfect shape of your limb.

Now, attach this "socket" to whatever knee you can afford. Add a tibial shin attached to an ankle/foot, align it all, get dressed and go dancing. In theory.

Dwayne was a wonderful guy and the prosthesis he made for me allowed me to walk but not well or comfortably. His artwork wasn't da Vincian.

If I wanted a masterpiece, a prosthesis with which I could fly, I realized I'd need someone different. I'd need to find a perfect blend of master engineer and phenomenal sculptor. A perfect marriage of da Vinci and...da Vinci.

Those kinds of prosthetists were, and still are, extremely rare. Their work is alchemy, a form of magic, of transformation.

115
A Moment of Truth

The Park Lane was a swanky tower at the north edge of Washington Park in Denver. I had a corner apartment on the sixth floor overlooking the park south of me, with a view west over the tops of the trees that was sensational. Orange sunsets over azure mountains were routine from the balcony. I was also the youngest person in the joint so at night I had the pool and pool table all to myself.

One afternoon I answered the phone and a voice said, "Hello, my name is Richard Gabriel, I'm returning a call from Ron Sorter. I work with the Fitzsimmons Liaison Office."

"Oh, hi, this is Ron. I had a conversation with you when I was discharged from Fitz last December."

"I remember you," he said, "did you ever get your real estate license?"

"Yes," I replied, "I've apprenticed with several firms, two here in Denver and one developing a ski area up in Marble."

"Well, that sounds like you don't need my help finding employment. Why did you call?" That was what the Liaison office did. They helped dischargees get "settled" into the World.

"Well," I said, "do you have a minute?"

"I do" he said.

"I guess Fitz taught me how to look truth in the face," I said. "I have to admit I hate being off balance, trying to go up and down stairs showing houses. I can't maneuver worth a damn in the snow anymore. The truth is, I keep stumbling over my own disability."

"And there's something else. My social life is on the nefarious side of the street and I'm enjoying that way too much. There are days when I don't see the sun. I need a change. I need something that will force me to regulate my hours, maybe somewhere I can work on a flat surface. That's why I called."

He said, "Well, it sounds like you're looking it in the face, alright. Let me see what I can come up with. I'll get back to you."

I thanked him and hung up. I didn't tell him commission work was great only when I was selling. I knew how to cold call but my difficulties navigating the real estate world was really tripping me up. It was a major concession for me to admit I was having difficulty with my new life. But I was. And my new prosthesis wasn't helping. It was barely wearable.

Gabriel called me back a few days later. "Would you be interested in a position in a hospital where you deal with disabled people and soon-to-be disabled people?"

"Well," I laughed, "I do know the field."

He said, "Here's a man's number. His name is Bruce and he's expecting your call."

I hung up and stared out the window at the Park. People were biking around the flower gardens, the lake was filled with scores of canoers having a race. Everybody was so able bodied.

They lived their own lives. In mine, these were the kinds of choices I had to make. I called Bruce.

116
The VA Just Like That

I dialed the number that Gabriel had given me.

"Hello, this is Bruce."

"Hi," I said, "my name is Ron Sorter and I'm calling about the position you have open for someone to deal with disabled people."

"Yes," he said, "Richard said you'd call. Can you come in this Monday at seven for an interview?"

"7:00 p.m.?" I asked.

"No," he laughed, "a.m."

Damn, of course it was a.m.. "OK, where's your office?"

He said, "We're on the first floor just off the lobby."

"I mean, what's your address?"

He said, "Sorry, I thought you knew. I'm the Chief of Prosthetics at the VA Medical Center."

I was stunned. The VA? I didn't want a government job, especially not the VA.

I swallowed my doubts. I met him in a suit and tie, and we traded war stories. He'd been a machine gunner in WWII and, after having his weapon and the arm holding it blown off while he was hosing down some Nazis, they'd taken him prisoner somewhere in Belgium. I told him about my own injuries and a little about my college days.

Bruce and I talked the same language.

He hired me and said, "I'm severely understaffed. I have to attend a meeting this morning but someone needs to see a diabetic in the orthopedic ward who's going to have his leg amputated tomorrow. Can you go up and talk to him?"

Just like that.

117
I Make a Difference

I found the nurse's station on the orthopedic ward. A young nurse with her dark hair in a bun looked up at me and said, "You must be Ron. Bruce called and asked me to take you to Mr. Beal's room. His family is there, too, is that all right?" I was busy encountering this beautiful nurse and said, "Yes. Sure. Of course."

I followed her at a discreet distance to the room. It was still morning and the warm sun shone through the windows, lighting up the faces of Mr. Beal and his desperately worried family.

The nurse introduced me and left. I pulled up the only empty chair and sat at eye level with him. I asked his first name, and told him I'd like to hear a little about his life. He told me his family were very close.

He described their life as, "Great, until all this diabetic stuff happened..." He was having trouble speaking about it. Understandable.

His wife took his hand and looked at me, saying, "He...we just want somebody to tell us what's going to happen to him. His vascular doctor said the orthopedic surgeons were going to have to take his left leg below the knee but that's all. The nurses said the surgeon is supposed to see us this afternoon. But..."

She looked at her husband. They both were completely distraught. I'd seen this so many times at Fitzsimmons, so I said, "How about if I lay it all out for you?"

His wife said, "That would be wonderful!"

Certainty is as valuable as money. I told him what the amputation would be like. Exactly. One of his kids left the room. I told him what his tomorrows would be like. And his next few days, and weeks. I answered some questions from his wife, who obviously loved him.

I took half an hour to say, in the kindest way I could, "It's not going to be easy but you'll get over the surgery. It's going to save your life. You'll feel frustrated. Many people will shun you. You'll find out who your real friends are. You'll make new friends, new connections. Your family will stay tight, and you'll be fine. I work here, call me anytime. About anything, and I'll come and see you after your surgery, OK?"

I used my arms to help lift myself off the chair and his wife noticed. "Are you disabled, too?" she asked.

"I lost a leg in Vietnam," I said. I'm an above-knee amputee."

She was completely surprised, "My goodness, I didn't even notice." I was completely surprised I'd said it so easily.

I said, "Your husband will have his left leg amputated below the knee tomorrow to save his life. He'll..."

257

I remembered to look at him.

I hated when people would stand by my bed and talk about me in the third person, without making eye contact. "You'll still have your knee so when you get your prosthesis, you'll walk even better than I do."

They thanked me and I left the room.

I got on the elevator and, I have to say, I thought I'd just made a difference. There was the ease with which I'd told his wife, without a qualm, that I was, in fact, disabled. The truth stared me in the face and I was fine with it.

118
A New Corvette

Tierno and Streb visited for a few days. We drove up to Vail.
I was bummed to see all the people skiing so effortlessly. Bob
and Fred rented cross country skis. I rented snowshoes and
poles. We explored a remote snowy valley and had some fun.
It's always a blast to reconnect with the brotherhood no matter
the place or circumstance.

I was re-entering the world. I was flush, so I sold my Trans Am
and, at long last, bought a brand new 1973 Corvette, loaded, a
454-cubic-inch big block. Forest green, gold metal flake.

My hair was down to my shoulders by then. I bought hats to
keep the wind from whipping it into my eyes when I took the
tops off. I kept the hats that didn't blow off my head at speed.

My social life became more normal. I enjoyed the contact with
the patients. It felt like I was helping my own men, in a way.
I put the VA's government ethos to one side, along with the
internal pathos created by their perpetual underfundedness.

I kept my focus on the patients. America's attention was
focused elsewhere. I was a handicapped Vietnam veteran
working at the VA. I began living my life to the hilt. Then,
several months later, the newly-eloped happy couple, Bob and
Karen moved to town with their Irish setter, Caesar, who was
a hoot and a handful. I'm sure he chilled out sometimes, I just
never happened to be there when it happened. He was just
happy, always.

119
An Award

In 1974 the Denver Fleet Reserve, a philanthropic group of
Navy retirees, gave me an award for "...serving as an example
of courage and inspiration." Each year, one of their paralyzed
members who'd learned to carve as therapy carved a small
wooden statue of the awardee.

My award is a carving of me in fly fishing gear pulling a huge
fish out of a carved wooden river. I hold a tiny bamboo pole
which arcs under tension, complete with monofilament line
running through tiny eyelets.

It's beautiful and it's sitting here on my desk.

My social life had moved from the dark side to the fun side.
I met Jerry Bingham, who ran a western nightclub down on
Colfax. He was an ex-artillery officer with the Big Red One
and together we invaded the stewardess world.

Bingham and I soon were dating two best friends, Carol and
Judy, both Frontier "stews." We threw parties at my place in
the Park Lane where, I swear, the stews could outdrink any
man alive. I hired a maid to keep the place spit-shined.

Judy and I lived alternately at each of our apartments, and Bob
and Karen had a new place over on Havana Street. Judy and I
had a lot of fun attending barbeques in their backyard.

I still had a Playboy key and one night a comedian friend of Bob's was performing there so we went by and, bad decision, smoked some weed with him. You know, when you partake, how a bug crawling on the floor is funny? Imagine trying to breathe as a professional comedian is trying out his new material on you.

We were catatonic from laughing. He'd tell a joke, set up the punchline, then he'd wait and just when we could breathe again he'd pound us with the punchline. I've never laughed so hard in my life. The guy had great timing. I have no idea how we got home. I blame Tierno for forcing me to go.

120
Ivan Long

New 'Vettes are nice but they're no match for a finely crafted prosthesis. The finest ones are fitted so perfectly that one no longer needs to tell it where and how to move. One can just... walk. Naturally.

Sadly, great prosthetists don't live in every village, as I could attest in 1975. I'd had several artificial limbs by then and they'd been adequate but neither got along very well with my residual limb and it complained, every night. That year, my luck allowed me to discover a da Vinci living right in Denver.

I met him like this. I shook a man's hand and said, "Hi, my name is Ron Sorter, I understand you're being seen in the Amputee Clinic today to have us approve your new limb?"

"Yes, I just picked it up last week."

"How does it fit?" I asked him.

"It's perfect."

Let me repeat that. He said, "It's perfect."

Usually, every new limb needs time for small adjustments to be made to it, to refine its fit.

This man walked effortlessly into the clinic, and was seen by several physical therapists and doctors who congratulated him on his "ambulation."

He kept saying, "I just put it on, walked through the parallel bars a few times and walked out with it. It's the best."

His prosthetist's name was Ivan Long.

I'd met Ivan previously at Fitzsimmons, where the limb facility fitted military patients and also did quite a bit of research. I learned that Ivan had used their large X-ray capability to discover the exact causes of the perennial alignment mis-marriage between above knee amputees and their prostheses.

He'd gone into private practice, called his method Natural Shape, Natural Alignment, and had become a transformer of lives. I was his very next client.

Ivan transformed me. He wrapped my residual limb in plaster and, while I stood, he held it in a certain shape with his hands. None of the usual clamps, tape measures and paraphernalia. Just his hands.

Once it was set up, he removed the plaster and I left, returning the next week to have him fine tune the precise height and alignment then I left again as he finished it.

I returned later, put it on and walked out the door. It was like flying. It was perfect.

263

I paid attention to it for a while but quickly forgot about it, it was so intuitive. When I met him, I was an amputee but when I put on the limb he'd made for me I could forget about falling at last. No more teetering back and forth, my shoulders stayed perfectly level. No more catching myself, my balance now was perfect. Effortless. Natural. I didn't even have to think about it.

I just walked out.

He made many limbs for me over the years as my weight changed or newer knee components became available. We even began laminating them in wild cloth patterns, they being so ugly laminated in pink plastic. The red plaid one was popular on the Idaho float trips Judy and I would make.

I even had an engraved blade from a sword cane cut down to fit into the shin of one of them, with a handy leather loop at the knee. I practiced a quick draw with it, and could throw and sink it in anything. That may sound ridiculous but I still carried a concern that I be prepared somehow, because I was now a man who, even if a measured retreat was a sound tactical move, couldn't.

Other amputees around the country can be equally thankful for Ivan's contribution to this obscure niche of medicine. An amputee's life is dictated by his remaining limb joints. His or her life must be spent at belt level in a wheelchair or perhaps limping everywhere in discomfort. Or walking effortlessly one's entire life, thanks to Ivan.

I couldn't legally direct amputees to him versus the many other prosthetists who contracted with the VA, but I could legally answer who my prosthetist was when I was asked. And as Ivan's ideas caught fire nationally, his technique was adopted, and spread to the benefit of above-knee amputees everywhere.

Current sports figures and those they inspire have Ivan and his disciples to thank for their success in track and field, downhill skiing, hockey and the rest. Their successes have helped spawn the long overdue removal of disgust for the handicapped.

Judy and I had a Halloween party at my new place across town. Keystone Cop Bob and wife, belly dancer Karen were the first customers at my bar. I made their cocktails using ice cubes, each with an artificial eye inside. I had an artificial hand clasping the toilet lid in the lady's room.

Hey, it was Halloween.

121
Chuck Brix: Best Man

Chuck and I have been friends for 46 years. I first met him when I went to the Colorado Mine Company in Denver one night in 1973. I walked up to the bar and had a conversation with Bartender Brix that went something like this:

"What are you drinking tonight, my man?"

"Jack Daniels, neat, ice on the side."

"I'd like to serve you some Jack, but the only whiskey we pour is Wild Turkey. Want some gin? We only serve Boodles."

"Wild Turkey, it is," I said.

He brought a filled glass for each of us. "There you go, for new customers it's on the house."

Classy place. I don't remember ever paying for a drink there, but I'm sure I must have. I tipped Chuck and the valets, too, big time, so no matter the crowd of people waiting for cars, they'd always get mine first, hold the door for the lady I was with, and we'd head out for the open road.

We both have a love of fine firearms but as much as I like to think I'm a crack shot, Chuck is, for real.

He has a silver concho on the back of his gun belt,
showing his award in 2015, using historic single-action pistols,
as the Florida State Black Powder Champion, Senior Duelist.

Chuck and I had this in common, too: he'd served in the Navy
in submarines, but drew the line at jungles. I loved the jungle
but no way could I ever get in a sub. Chuck served in a diesel
sub during the Cuban Missile Blockade, standing off Russian
ships filled with nuclear missiles, and I had some interesting
stories from Vietnam.

He described the chaos at the Norfolk marine yard as they'd
prepared the boat for combat, then steamed out of the bay in
a line of subs heading into the Atlantic to stop the Russians on
the high seas.

"I was the last man on deck before we submerged," he said. It
was my job to make sure everything was tight, battened down
so we could dive.

"I stopped long enough to wrap my arms into the rigging
around the exhausts, and leaned back, feeling their power.
They were roaring, blasting fire out of their exhausts, ready
for anything. I felt like Neptune, taking my trident to sea to do
battle with the dastardly Commies."

He married his longtime-girlfriend Debbie, and a few years
later he was my best man when I married Jean, arriving with a
coal scuttle filled with iced champagne.

I was offered a promotion to San Diego. I bought a new Corvette and we moved there in January 1978, while Chuck, a real artist with Harleys, got a job with them through an uncle of Debbie's.

We had a couple of drinks at a San Diego hotel once when he was visiting Harley dealerships in his new SoCal region. The guy was a natural, so he was doing well. What wasn't to like about a job with Harley Davidson? They eventually made him a Vice President.

His bonus each year included his choice of any bike he wanted off the assembly line. And this: "When I show up at Sturgis on our latest bike wearing manufacturer's plates, the whole town treats me like a rock star."

122
Jean and Hope, San Diego

Jean Berry, her daughter Hope and I lived in San Diego in '77 and we flew back to her sister Donna's house in Denver to get married, with Chuck as my best man.

Hope had long blond hair, was three and a half, and cute as a button. It took awhile for us to adapt to each other but it was a fun time for us, living in San Diego, to do that. We had a nice house with a pool, good schools and year-round perfect weather.

I enjoyed working at the VA Medical Center where, like all companies in San Diego, they could choose from a large group of talented people who would accept less salary in order to live there. I wasn't at the top of the heap, but I was working on it.

Bob and Karen had arrived from Durham in 1977, so we had fun in the sun for awhile before they moved up to San Francisco.

Two years later I received another promotion back to Denver. Before leaving the San Diego VA Medical Center, I was surprised to receive the hospital's first Hand And Heart Award. The award is given to the person chosen from the thousands of other employees by the employees themselves. It was a huge honor.

The Director of the Medical Center, soon to become the Chief of Staff for the entire VA system in D.C., called my new boss in Denver telling him that he'd "stolen" one of his best employees.

I hated leaving San Diego, but the Denver facility had a larger treatment center and I felt I could have a bigger impact. Yes, the fly fishing was better there, too.

123
Jean and Hope, Denver

Midlife in Denver in the early eighties was the everyday
business of life, getting Hope to school, finding her a nice
family with kids to walk home from school and hang out with
until I could pick her up after school.

We bought a CJ Jeep for Jean since driving in snowy traffic wasn't her thing. We spent a lot of time in the mountains
enjoying life. I fly fished all the local Gold Medal water and
family life was good. Plus, poker with the guys, fishing trips
for the stonefly hatch, shooting at Perry Park.

Hope's cat, who'd gotten the kitten name Scoofer, was my
nemesis. We owned an Arts and Crafts pitch-roofed bungalow
and it had a southeast room with multi-paned windows on the
east and south, double glass doors with glass door knobs on
the north.

The single wall I mirrored, added a jute rug and hanging
bamboo chair and enough hanging plants and potted bushes
to remind me of Vietnam.

In the corner I made a yard-square pool with water pumped
into it from a stone lion's mouth. I added black mollies and
neon fish, rippling the water with my fingers to clue them it
was feeding time.

I'd sit there in the dark of night, waiting for the cat.

271

He'd slink in, put his head up over the edge of the pond and look at the water. Then he'd climb up and lean down for a drink. His lapping tongue on the water clued the fish so they'd swim up, mouths on the surface looking for food.

He'd see them, want them, extend a paw to grab them but he was too afraid of getting his paw wet. There he was, king of the jungle, fierce predator, a little eccentric letting a fish kiss him full on the lips. I told all his cat pals about it.

In 1984, we attended my 20th high school reunion in Grand Junction. My best friend Owen talked to me for five minutes. Then, looking at my name tag, doubled over in shock. "Oh, my God. Ronnie, it's you!"

Later that evening, my graduating class voted me The Most Changed Man.

124
A Few Thoughts on Shrapnel

One week in 1982 I was in bed, sicker than a dog, hacking, sneezing, feeling like the world owed me some entertainment. Then I remembered the Rubik's cube someone had given me for Christmas. Realizing I wasn't brainy enough to solve it, I'd bought a book, "How to Solve a Rubik's Cube." Jean had tossed them both on the bed before leaving for work.

Simple enough algorithms. Twist this face this way, that one that way, and soon it's solved. What could be easier?

It's not that easy. I spent all day working on it and that night, Eureka! The next time it took me half as long. I slowly got better at it. And faster, twisting the cube like a dervish.

I showed my daughter Hope what a smart Daddy she had. After a couple minutes, she said, "That's GREAT, Daddy!" and went back to her Barbies. Sweet kid. She knew her priorities.

A few days later I noticed a red bump on the inside of my right forearm. Nothing unusual. I've got a bunch of shrapnel and rock in me and sometimes they decide to edge their way to the surface. I was sure that was what was happening.

There's some fun to be had with shrapnel when Hope's young friends would have sleepovers in our living room. Tents and flashlights and horror stories, sure, but Daddy had...shrapnel.

Hope would shine a flashlight through my hand and, visible to everyone, was a blood-red hand splattered with black shrapnel. "EEWWWWWWW!!!" they'd scream in unison.

Each morning, I'd pull off the Band-Aid from my forearm, slosh it with peroxide and put on a new Band-Aid. One day, as I slowly peeled it, it seemed to not want to come off. I pulled harder and it felt like something was holding on, deeper inside my arm. What the…? I pulled harder and it suddenly came loose.

It wasn't the little piece of stone or metal that I'd expected. It was this slender green and black wormlike thing. It was stuck to the bandaid. I couldn't believe it. I had a worm in me?! I studied it more closely and I finally recognized it.

It was a thread from my camos. That night in Vietnam a piece of shrapnel had dragged part of my camo fatigues into my body with it and it had lain there undisturbed for a dozen years, until my expertise with a Rubik's cube had dragged it, gasping for air, to the surface.

I threw it away, got out of bed and had a beer. I was alive. It's all gravy.

125
Toreador Red

"What color do you think it should be?" I asked Hope.

She put her chin in her hand and thought for a moment. "I like the green color but I really, really like the red one, Daddy."

"Hmm, I said, "Red is a popular color, you see a lot of red Corvettes. I've had a green one already, so maybe that red is the color we want."

Hope and I had been looking at a huge book of DuPont auto paint samples and had landed on a color Saab had used in 1974: Toreador Red. I was having the anemic small block in my '78 Vette rebuilt into a beast and we hated the stock color. Hence, Toreador Red.

It was a great choice. After the car was painted it was drop-dead red in the sun and orange under the street lights at night. My leg and my car allowed me to be free. My legs were always being laminated with wild fabrics now under a clear lacquer finish and the car needed to hold its own.

Toreador Red wasn't a true Corvette color but I didn't care. Little Hopie loved red.

We'd had enough of the snow by 1985 so when the San Diego office became open I returned. My job required me to be on my feet most of the day, and I also needed to visit my clients in their homes.

The snow and ice in Denver were taking an increasing toll on my ambulatory life. A move to San Diego made sense.

I was doing more consulting work then for the service's Director in D.C., too, and I could do that in San Diego so it worked out well. We bought another house with a pool and palm trees and enjoyed the return to warm Januaries in Southern California.

126

The Zippo Lighter

My wife's sister, Donna, also moved to Santa Barbara, and soon began to talk about this guy Bill that she'd met at her 30th high school reunion. Apparently, he was quite the deal. She brought him down so we could meet him.

"Did you get this Zippo in 'Nam?" he asked.

I turned and looked at the lighter I had framed on the wall, next to my Purple Heart and Bronze Star.

He read the words engraved on it, "To a Great Bushmaster. Happy Birthday, October 4, 1970."

It was deeply dented. He looked at me. "Your men gave you that?"

"Yeah," I said. Bill was an ex-Artillery staff sergeant. We looked at each other. He got it.

"That's unheard of," he said.

He called Donna into the living room and pointed at it. "Ron's men gave him that lighter as a birthday present. Enlisted guys just don't do that."

I told him, "I had it in my pocket when I got blasted. That's why it's so bent out of shape. Kind of like me."

"But I've worked on it, got it open, filled it with fluid and it works like a charm. It's my most treasured possession."

Hope was at school so we sat out by the pool, filled a pipe with weed and lit it with my Zippo. This peace pipe was shared between two military friends. Over the years, we've become brothers.

We speak the language of howitzers, Brasso, fine bourbon and the exquisite personalities of first sergeants we've known.

A few months later, Bill and Donna got married in our house and that night we treated them to a party on one of the old sailing ships that cruise San Diego Bay at night.

There was a band in the hold and Donna and Bill did The Bebop as if they'd been doing it since high school. Which, they kinda had. Everybody knew it was their honeymoon and let them clear the floor. It was zoot suit cool.

127
I Join the Private Sector

By 1987, my "good" left knee, so damaged by shrapnel, was no longer painless to walk on. I'd finally been forced to work out of a wheelchair. More arthroscopic surgery didn't help, I was "too young" to get a total knee replacement and my left knee condyles, after years of walking at work, were shot. So I quit.

I was happy to learn I was still entitled to Vocational Rehab through the VA. I could have picked any school but Jean had a great job at a law firm and Hope liked her school so I matriculated at San Diego State.

It wasn't Stanford, but they offered a really good Master of Science degree in their Business school. It included the new field of artificial Intelligence and robotics and, since I was partly a mechanical creation, that was right up my alley.

Those three years were a blast. I didn't have to simultaneously work and go to school and I had the maturity at age 40 to realize the gift I'd been given, so it wasn't hard to make all A's.

128
Hope Moves to Grandma's

Hope, now a teenager, sat next to me on the couch one afternoon and said, "Daddy, you know you're my real daddy, don't you?"

I said, "Yes, and I'm so happy you think that."

"I've been talking to Grandma Sammy and she thinks it would be fun for me to visit her and stay for awhile to meet my real dad." I was conflicted. She'd never heard from her biological father in any way. But she'd become curious about him and I knew that these thoughts of hers were normal.

Jean wanted Hope's father to have a relationship with her so we let her visit her grandmother's for a while to see if a bond with him might be possible. She was fifteen and smart. We agreed to a train ride and off she went. We'd call her often and her adventure there was a happy one.

As I was finishing my last year at SDSU, I and two other graduate students developed AI coding language to help a local top-secret, non-nuclear pulse generator analyze itself.

According to the physicist who ran it, who was also a student on our team, a DoD satellite's armored componentry had to be electromagnetic pulse (EMP) proof, as in surviving a close blast of a nuclear weapon while in orbit and still function.

The "Black Jack 5" was one of the few machines in the U.S. which could generate sufficient power to test those components before launching them into space. That's all we were told. We weren't allowed to see the classified machine, "somewhere out near Pt. Loma."

Downtime cost tens of thousands of dollars a day so if the machine had been damaged by the capacitor's final, gigantic release of energy, it had be diagnosed and repaired immediately. Our coding used the machine's metadata to do that automatically after each shot, using predicate calculus logic and primitive machine learning. It was cutting edge at the time, extremely rewarding work.

In 1990 I finished my master's thesis (a Knowledge Engineering program) designed to facilitate unusual cash flows and sold it for $14,000 to a San Diego company which also hired me to run it for them. It didn't require much walking so it was perfect for me.

The Director of Prosthetics was hired as the new Director of Marketing, and the CEO asked if I'd take over the prosthetic's department. It involved working with prosthetic facilities in North America who used our products.

The R&D department was furiously developing computerized joints, using artificial intelligence to predict the most efficient gait traits synced to its wearer. Our Marketing department used me as the actor in a professionally produced video for sale to hospitals and other caregivers to show to their patients who'd had amputations.

It was my VA local work writ nationwide. I enjoyed it immensely.

The next year a Christmas bonus for me was a trip with Jean to Kauai. A chopper ride over the Na Pali Coast triggered this response from Jean when we landed, "I want a divorce. A separation. Anything."

I was surprised at that and also at my instant feeling of release.

Hope had decided that living with Sammy was delightful and Jean agreed to let her stay for a while. I'm sure the rules were more lax at Sammy's.

Jean had never let me adopt Hope, fearing the response from her biological father, so I had no say in that decision. The last few years had been empty. I agreed, and after a six month separation we divorced.

VII. Bob
Intel Inside

129
Thanks for the Memory, Intel

Intel was a terrific experience, but also a challenge to our marriage. After a year or so in Santa Clara, the Programmable Memories Operation (PMO) was being moved to the new plant in Folsom, CA. Karen wasn't excited about yet another move but Intel paid us incentives to move and the $5,000 bonus went to the dining room set she desired.

We bought a new home in Roseville, including a pool. We did our own landscaping. We made friends with a number of new graduates who pitched in to help us move dirt, roll out grass.

The pool and hot tub were great relief in the hot summers. We partied, I partied, engineers who ran into Karen at the bank told her she was a saint! They were right.

I was managing the Ford Taurus/Sable custom memory program for Chrysler and GM. I spent almost every week in Detroit. Trips to Japan, Motorola in Seguin, Texas and NCR in Colorado Springs were the norm until we finally beat Toshiba and Motorola (by a year), to convince Ford to buy erasable programmable memory.

Meanwhile Karen was offered a promotion to regional sales manager based in Dallas. We weren't doing well as a marriage so we thought a change of scenery would be a good thing. I was able to secure a position as a field sales engineer (FSE). Karen's company was paying for the move.

We bought a townhouse in Carollton a suburb of Dallas. I was given a company car as was Karen although she was flying all over the region. My first year was account development.

Texas is a great place to start a sales career. Customers no matter how mad they were at Intel still were friendly and, trust me, Intel had screwed many OEMs over recent years.

My second year, I was a systems sales engineer supporting an Army program with our hardware and service. It was a launch of the personal computer and development systems through-out the U.S. Army. Lots of travel, lots of drinking, culminating in Karen and I separating.

Karen moved back to Northern California. I accepted a district manager position in Cleveland, OH. It is there that I learned what was really important in a marriage: integrity. Especially after seeing what had happened to several women in a church support group I attended.

We agreed to counseling when I travelled to the west coast. We discovered that we are both opposites. I'm an extroverted driver and Karen's more introverted. We would talk right by each other. We decided that we would talk from the heart about emotional issues and from our head about business issues. They were completely different conversations.

130
Renewed Vows

After a couple of trips to Cleveland and me to the Bay Area, we later agreed to renew our vows in the Catholic Church. We also decided that we would arrange for our parents to finally meet in Cleveland.

This was an important step in rebuilding our marriage. We flew Karen's parents into Cleveland and my parents drove in from Carlisle, PA. We had a great dinner, asked for their support and we sealed the deal. We renewed our vows in California, then Karen made the move to Cleveland. In Dallas we had "decided" not to have children.

We gave it a try in Cleveland, but to no avail. We are happy as Aunt and Uncle as well as being the Godfather to Kelly! Oh, by the way, I bought a 25-foot sailboat we named Hapikat, after the rescue cat who adopted us in Dallas. Many days and evenings were spent on Lake Erie!

In 1991, the Intel Field Sales Organization executed a massive redeployment effort . My office was reduced to me and several FSEs plus the service department. This really impacted me a great deal because of how it impacted so many good people.

Once the dust settled, I was offered a business development manager position for the Intel Inside ® Program covering the east coast out of our home in Chagrin Falls, Ohio. This was a great opportunity and we had a successful run for a year.

The winters in Ohio were brutal and when offered the opportunity to move back to Northern California in 1993 to manage U.S. Distribution for Intel's Semiconductor Products Group based in Folsom, California. I accepted.

131
Sutter Creek

Over the next few years, we discussed exit strategies from Intel. One idea was to buy a bed and breakfast. This was my idea all the way and Karen finally agreed to buy it in 1995. We took a course on how to run a bed and breakfast. We both had spent many nights in all kinds of hotels (mostly Marriott) so how hard can this be? Well, very hard!

We bought the Hanford House B&B Inn in Sutter Creek, CA in December of 1995. It was owned by a couple who were both retired and the inn was due for a makeover. The 850-square-foot conference room would be perfect for business retreats.

We have been asked many times "would you do it over again?" The obvious answer would be, "No," but over the course of thirteen years the inn grew in stature and value. We were granted the coveted Four Diamond AAA Award four years running.

We positively impacted many employees' lives and have several close friends today. We experienced everything including, a fire, flooding, and theft. I kept working at Intel until 1999, but was at the inn every weekend. I spent many nights there when our innkeeper couldn't make it.

Karen was the detail person. She worked tirelessly to insure that our housekeepers had the inn ready for check in by 3 p.m. every day.

Over the years, the inn took a toll on her health. My parent's health was failing too.

In 1999, I retired from Intel.

Over the next five to six years, I would be spending time flying back east, to look in on Rocky and my mother, whose mind was failing. In 2004, we put the inn on the market and had a failed sale the day of closing.

The next four years, we hired full-time on-site innkeepers and in late 2007 accepted an offer from a young enterprising couple from the area. Despite SBA delays and a changing lending environment, the inn changed hands in May 2008.

Talk about timing. While this ended a chapter in our life, the great recession hit and we took a bath financially. Over the next seven years I had a successful business coaching practice while Karen managed a successful home staging business.

In July, 2012, Rocky Tierno passed away from congestive heart failure. I was named executor of his estate. Following his burial at West Point we had to address Mom T's dementia/ Alzheimers.

I remained at their home in Carlisle until Skip, my brother, could fly in and escort Mom to Houston where she was checked into a memory care center. She died fourteen months later.

Karen spent over 90 days working with my parent's housekeepers shipping goods , donating items, and disposing of items at their house. A great deal of personal property was sent to auction and all proceeds went to support Mom T's care. The house was sold at a loss but the books were finally closed on this chapter.

132
And on to Texas

Following my mother's burial with Rocky at West Point, we
flew to Oklahoma to attend my first Deke Reunion. It was
great to see everybody. I asked about Ron, knowing he had
been in Redstone, CO. I learned he and Michelle had moved to
Sequim, WA.

As costs continued to escalate in California, we did things like
add solar to reduce our electricity bills, and conserved water.
Everywhere we turned expenses kept growing.

We decided to move to Texas once I secured a job, which I did
in July of 2015 as an area manager for 1-800-Got Junk?. We
sold our home of fifteen years and moved to Denton, TX.

Karen and I faced a major detour in 2018 as I was diagnosed
with prostate cancer. On the day of my surgery, August 30th,
Karen fell down a flight of stairs at the hospital and
shattered her elbow, sprained her wrist, shoulder and had a
mild concussion. Three surgeries and many hours of
physical therapy later, Karen is almost back to 90%. My
surgery to remove my prostate was successful and so far no
cancer is detectable.

We are two patients who are also caregivers. We are a team.
Integrity is a key word in my life and our relationship.

133
Dovelet Rose

How did Karen get the nickname "Dovelet Rose"?

DISC Drive

Albert Camus, the French philosopher, author, understood that our behavioral styles were polar opposites, which actually makes for a good marriage as long as we acknowledge our differences.

For years we sensed our differences, but I never addressed them. When I started business coaching I got very proficient in interpreting DISC Styles. Karen did, also, since she taught Meyers-Briggs team building to groups at Intel and Motorola. I guess I didn't listen. Number one characteristic of a D.

My behavioral style is what's known as a DISC, based upon Marston's Theory about behavior, which states that we all communicate/behave with at least two characteristics.

DISC stands for Dominant, Influence, Steadiness, and Compliant.

D - In the wild kingdom, the eagle represents Dominant, leaving carnage in its wake. The D needs to win, and is so competitive it walks all over you with combat boots. The D personality keeps on trucking. If you haven't guessed, eagles are very competitive often leaving carnage in their wake.

292

I am an off-the-charts D, thus my nickname, according to Karen, is Eagle.

I-Influential is represented by a peacock who wants to be liked. I'm an off- the-charts Dominant Influential. I want you to like me but if you don't, I'll make you, and soon.

S- Steadiness is represented by a dove; not wanting to upset the applecart or offend anybody. Resisting change, not in an overt way, but quietly hiding in plain sight. Said another way, Karen is risk averse. Although she married me!

C-Compliant is represented by an owl or Dove, who requires rules, data, and detail before attempting to move forward. Very analytical, risk averse: bankers, accountants, engineers, PGA golf professionals. (Yes, PGA golf professionals-Fore!)

Yes, you guessed right! Karen is a DOVE, ergo Dovelet and her love of roses over the years earned her the name Dovelet Rose.

VIII. Ron
A Fabulous Woman

134

The Tao of Michelle

TAO, Inc. had an unusual, matrix-like organizational structure with a CEO, CFO and four Directors, of which I was one.

All the remaining staff, approximately one hundred people, all worked for the Director of Operations, a gifted woman with a great sense of humor. Her name was Michelle Struve, and she always seemed to be just on the verge of laughing.

Gayle Terry was the Director of Marketing and I'd worked with him when I was at SDSU designing my thesis AI software.

On my first day at TAO, he introduced me to Michelle. We had a seat in her office and she reached over to shake my hand. "Hi," she said, "I'm Michelle and if you have any problems with the staff, let me know. And as far as Dale goes, just do the opposite of everything he tells you and you'll be fine."

She smiled at him and he acted wounded. Apparently, the culture here had a lot of laughter built into it. This could be fun. I knew the CEO, Claude. He was the scion of a French family who'd started the business in Europe. When he visited Europe, which was often, Michelle served as the acting CEO. Under her direction, the company ran like a Swiss watch.

"Are you settling in to your office," she asked as she sat down, "do you need anything?".

"No," I said, "well, actually, I've met all the staff but I have no secretary."

"Oh?" She frowned at me. "Don't tell me you're going to need a secretary, too?"

I looked at Dale, I looked at her. She smiled at me, "I have a few women I'll be interviewing this morning and I'll send them to your office one at a time. You can choose whichever one you prefer, OK?"

I said fine and Dale and I left her office to continue my orientation. I decided to never play poker with Michelle.

My time at TAO was filled with travel to conventions and seminars where I taught our leading-edge fabrication techniques and the most effective uses of our research to attendees from all over the world.

When we moved into a new, larger building, I received an increase in staff but regretted the fact that I now had insufficient time to implement my AI software. Without the time to sell it to our clients, it lay fallow.

A year and a half passed. My personal life was becoming complicated again. At work, I watched my AI dreams fade, as the CEO reorganized the firm. It was too much.

By then, I knew that I could live anywhere and work by phone. I began looking for the perfect place.

135
Looking for an LZ

I left TAO and departed San Diego on a two-month long
Corvette road trip, a long-held and finally-realized dream.

It was time for Ivan to make me a new leg so I included a
swing through Colorado.

Along the way, I searched for a place to land.

My brother Chuck and I had moved Mom to San Diego when she'd been diagnosed with cancer. She'd alternated living with each of us. After being in remission for over a year, her cancer had returned. My sister-in-law Jackie, lovingly cared for her until she had to be hospitalized.

I visited Mom every day, and read her well-worn Bible to her. I hung my first painting on her nursing home wall. Mom finally passed away that December. I arranged her funeral, and we buried with her family in Oklahoma. A niece sang "Amazing Grace" inside the stone chapel. It was transcendent.

Dad passed away soon after that, but the impact was minimal.

I'd long envied the relationship Bob had with Rocky. Mom will always be the kind of mother they write devotional books about. She moved us to Oklahoma, not only for her to be with family, but for me to have a male mentor in Uncle Matt. Her steady toughness inspired me every day she was alive.

She'd teed me up to be able to recognize the fabulous woman when she appeared. Michelle and Mom spoke only once, by phone, for a few moments before she passed away.

Mom's love, plus all the brotherhoods I'd been a part of, had prepared me for one realization: the remainder of my life would be a love story, with a woman who wanted to spend the afternoon of her life with me.

137
Crystal Clear: Revelation in Redstone

Michelle and I sat outside on the deck of a terrific restaurant and bar in Redstone, CO called the Crystal Club. It was a beautiful June afternoon in 1993. We sat at a table having lemonade, overlooking the town's only street, known to locals as "The Boulevard."

She'd quit working at TAO and we were on a road trip, searching the West for that place, that perfect place to live. Idaho, no. Montana's nice, but the winters. Santa Fe or Taos? No.

Michelle suggested, "We could go by Redstone on the way back to San Diego."

She'd meant Marble, so when we arrived in Redstone she realized she'd never seen it before. It was easy to get confused. Colorado, understandably, has countless towns named after rocks, including Basalt, Leadville, Golden, Silverton and countless others.

"Ron?"

"Hmm?" I replied. I'd been staring at her, she was so gorgeous.

"I mean, yes?" I smiled at her. She smiled at me. She was always smiling at me.

"I think this is the place," she said. We'd been there ten minutes.

I was surprised, but as I looked at the historic houses, the Permian maroon cliffs, soaring mountains and deep, deep blue sky, I understood.

"I think you're right," I said.

Discovering the perfect place is more powerful after an intense search. It is exponentially overpowering, because the search is fused with love. We'd found the perfect place. Together.

I looked across the Boulevard at a weathered one-story log house surrounded by aspens. An enormous blue spruce anchored one corner of the lawn.

Luck favors the prepared. We'd agreed I'd build a log house for us wherever we landed. I noticed a For Sale sign on the fence, half hidden by blooming lupine.

"Over there," I said pointing to the log house.

She gazed at the house, turned back to me and smiled.

We finished our lemonade and located the realtor.

Michelle gave it a quick inspection and we put an offer on it. Two other offers made before ours fell through and a week later we owned it. I hadn't even gone inside.

301

They originally called the river "Rock Creek," but they changed the name to Crystal River to reflect (no pun) the crystal-clear quality of the water. It's so clear, you can't even see it if it weren't moving.

92 souls inhabit Redsone, on Colorado's Western Slope. You can only catch a glimpse of it from the highway, since it's hidden by the Crystal River and its trees.

Redstone is a gem, a Brigadoon. In winter, it's the twinkling village under the Christmas tree and, like Xanadu, it is surprisingly difficult to find.

The town was an anomaly, built in the 1890's by an absurdly rich coal baron, to aid the men who worked the coke ovens by the river, where they cooked local coal into coke for his blast furnaces in Pueblo.

The men and their families benefitted from his patronage. Their houses were, and still are, wonderful cottages.

Considering the Colorado mountain wilderness of the times, building a 35,000-square-foot mansion there, complete with red Chinese marble and his own railroad would, in retrospect, be like me building a mansion on the moon.

The Snowmass/Maroon Bells Wilderness Area started at our back door. Just a few steps, and you were in true Colorado.

Everything fell together. It was like magic.

138
The Apple Pie Welcome

We moved from San Diego, arriving Thanksgiving Day at dusk.

It was snowing, as we pulled into Redstone. We only had an apple and some carrots left in our cooler.

We parked our U-Haul at our snow-covered motel. In the frigid darkness, we wandered down the Boulevard, lit only by antique street lamps, to visit our cabin. Across the street, we were excited to see the Crystal Club's lighted windows. Food!

But a sign on the door said," Private Party." Damn. So, we peered into our new (old) log house, then walked back to our motel and split our supper of carrots and an apple.

We learned the next day that the party had been for locals who had no place else to celebrate Thanksgiving. Had we known, and walked in, we would have been welcomed by our new Boulevard neighbors.

The hostess of that party was the first lady to bring us a just-made apple pie the next morning as we were moving in. It was all we could do to keep from face planting right into it.

The sugar crystals glittered in the morning light. Bruce and Parker Lemire, soon to become lifelong friends, were helping us move in, so we split it with them.

The house was November cold, so we made a fire. The coffee pot was found and we welcomed more people. We were happy to meet so many wonderful, open neighbors.

The denizens were protective of their hidden paradise and since it also included some very interesting characters, we were being examined. We found out later we'd passed with interesting colors.

That night, Michelle and I toasted the first of thousands of sunsets we'd see from our very own forest. As it turned pitch black and temperatures dropped into the teens, we were looking at the brightest stars in the blackest skies we'd ever seen.

We'd found the perfect LZ, and we adored each other.

A few weeks later, at the annual Christmas Ball, we met the other residents, all dressed to the nines, and discovered our arrival story was no different than everyone else's: "We arrived by accident and never left," was a common song we heard that night and constantly for the next 25 years.

As a retired New York actress and I watched Michelle socializing with her new friends, she remarked, "Every woman here would kill for Michelle's hair."

I had to agree.

139
Michelle's Smile

She had eyes like Cleopatra
And a head of luxurious hair,
With the brilliance of her beauty
None other could compare.
— Chuck Berry

Michelle had a wonderful smile. We played lots of poker with lots of friends in Redstone. She had as much fun beating you with a royal flush as she did bluffing you out of your shorts with a pair of twos. She was impossible to read.

At Thanksgiving at my brother's house the next year, he asked her if she knew how to play poker. She said she wasn't very good. Rubbing his hands together, he smiled and said, "So, can we play a game?" and she said, "Sure."

Later, after she had all his money, he said, "I thought you didn't know how to play poker."

"I don't," she said. "But I know how to bet."

She said that with such a sweet smile.

140

From Michelle to Ron

This is the true measure of love.
When we believe that we alone can love.
That no one could ever have loved so before us.
And that no one will ever love in the same way after us.
— Goethe

Here's a card Michelle sent me while visiting her mother:

"Dear Ron,

June 28, 1998

Oh, my love,

I have been thinking about you all day, all evening. It is so hard for me to be away from you - you are my breath, my nourishment, my joy, my life. We are meant to be together, we have to be together.

I feel like I've cut a little slice out of the middle of our lives and set it aside, put it on hold for a while. And I don't like it – I want to be living our life and I can't while we are apart. How can I live when I can't even breathe?

The times we're apart only reinforce the amazing "us-ness" we share. I think when we're together we flow so intimately and vibrantly that it begins to be status quo for us.

When we are apart I feel at odds, half alive, not vibrant at all and I realize, once again, what a gift we share in our joyful life.

So, my love, I want to tell you what an amazing, wonderful, wise man you are. You have brought such tenderness, such wildness, such depth to my life. You have truly awakened my deepest, truest self and have given me the greatest gift of all: unconditional love.

So I give this most precious of all gifts back to you, back to us, because I love everything you are – even the stuff back in the corner in the dark. You are always safe with me, I promise.

I love you with my whole heart, my whole self, my whole life.

— Michelle"

141
Parades

The Fourth of July Parade: tourists lined both sides of the Boulevard and kids from everywhere brought their bikes and we 'Stoners helped them decorate their bikes so there'd be an army of happy kids (and most of the town) in the parade.

The parade wound from one end of town to the other, fire engines' sirens and horns blasting, kids on the back throwing candy. At the other end, the parade turned around and came all the way back. Two parades for the price of one.

One year Michelle got drafted onto an ad hoc baton-twirling team. She confided in me that she'd never perfected that skill, so I bought her a suicide knob (a rotating knob for steering wheels), attached it to her new baton and she amazed her compatriots with her talent, twirling it unseen with one little finger, around her head, between her legs, cheers, huzzahs...

Later, the Redstone and Marble fire crews would string a cable between two trees, attach a soccer ball to it with a sliding carabiner and help the kids into fire gear.

Two teams of five tiny people were given a firehose and, with a fireperson's help, they'd try to spray the soccer ball to the far end of the cable, while the opposing team of five tiny people tried to do the same in the opposite direction. The crowd went wild and got totally soaked by the kids whenever they did.

142
Puppies

Redstone held the Sleddog Races in February. They were the only races on the mushers' winter schedule where they didn't have to help build the trails, get insurance, time the races, find places for their dogs, or find a place to camp for two days.

Redstone did all of that for them. The turnout was large and happy. The mushers brought their families and their puppies to this family event. There's nothing like an armful of snow-white Samoyed puppies in a little girl's arms to bring out Michelle's smile.

We loved Redstone and naturally became involved in everything. We'd lay in bed at night in our loft, talking about our fortune to have found Redstone and its people. I installed skylights above the bed, tuned to the ecliptic, so we could enjoy the moonlight and admire the photon display.

We were delighted to receive a Christmas card from Bob and Karen, from their new address, a B&B in the Sierras. It was great to see them moving their chess pieces with such style.

Redstone had an art scene, so I got pulled into that, too. I sent Bob a painting I did of an Indian chief, which he sold for millions on eBay, I'll bet. After a few years I only painted big bears and sold them for prices that surprised me. I kept the last one, to inspire the grandkids whenever they arrived.

Our life was bliss.

143
Blueprints

"So, it's official?" I asked.

"It is," the lady at the Building Department in Aspen replied, as she added her approval signature to my building permit.

She handed it to me and said, "Just be sure to get some work done, and call for an inspection within six months."

I was looking at my now-official building permit and the blueprints Steve, our architect neighbor, had drawn up to double the size of our 1,200 sf cabin in Redstone.

It was at the limit of what I thought I could build.

I rolled up the blueprints and left. I couldn't wait to get started.

When I got home I told Michelle, "I'll do this as fast as I can, but it's gonna take years."

She said, "I don't care. We'll love each other no matter what and when it's done it will be amazing." And she was right.

I began digging the footers two days later.

144
Juggling Elephants

To think I did all that
And may I say - not in a shy way
Oh no, oh no, not me
I did it my way.
— Frank Sinatra, "My Way"

Picture me, a "100% service-connected, totally and
permanently disabled" veteran, remodeling a 1,200 sf aging
log house and turning it into a 2,421 sf dream home, while also
chairing Master Plan meetings at the county level, *and* leading
a million-dollar purchase and renovation of the historic
Redstone coke ovens.

It was a complicated balancing act, but thanks to Ivan Long's
perfect prothesis, I pulled it off.

My Redstone brotherhood included Chuck Downey, a retired
rocket scientist. He and his wife, Doris, a retired Dean at
Colorado University, travelled the world, ice climbing.

While remodeling the house, I'd built a trolley to pull shingle
bundles up from the ground, so I wouldn't have to haul them,
one at a time, up the ladder to the roof.

Chuck showed up one day, watched me using the trolley, and
announced: "Doris and I are going to be climbing in Peru next
month. I need to build up my arm strength - can I carry your
shingles up there?"

I told him to have at it.

Chuck and I were soon running the local Crystal River Caucus as co-moderators. I'd convinced the County Commissioners to, instead of imposing a Master Plan on our valley, give us the funds to create one ourselves.

They did and, at the end of three years, including some of the most contentious meetings I've ever chaired between ranchers, Redstoners and everybody else, it was adopted.

Michelle and I were good at finding friends and fellow believers, and then the projects found us. For example, the restoration of the coke ovens.

The coking process was integral to the settlement and development of the West. Throw a pile of metallurgical-grade coal into a beehive oven and cook it for 48 hours to burn off the impurities. The coal transforms into pure carbon, known as coke, lighter than balsa and stronger than steel.

In a blast furnace, the carbon atoms join with the oxygen atoms in the iron ore, blowing off as carbon monoxide and carbon dioxide. Voila, pure iron, the most valuable material in the West: locomotives and rails, barbed wire and carbines.

I was President of the local historical society, when we decided to restore over 100 historic Redstone coke ovens that Michelle and I had purchased with grants we'd obtained from the state.

We wrote more grants and, with the county, persuaded state and county groups to give us even more funding. We helped design the project with the engineers the county had hired.

Our work took fifteen years. In recognition, Michelle and I received an Outstanding Community Award at a Redstone celebration held just for us.

145
The Torch

In 2002 the Salt Lake Winter Olympics were a popular topic.

At a party I told Chuck, "You won't believe this. I got a scam email telling me I only had a few days left to receive my Official Torch Carrier clothing. What a rip off..." and in mid sentence he hugged me like a long lost brother.

"They picked Ron!" he yelled to the room.

"No, no," I protested, "it was a scam to get me to buy Olympic Torch clothes."

"No, it wasn't!" he said. "We nominated you a couple months ago. They picked you!"

Everybody was shaking my hand, and slapping me on my back as I thought, "Wait, I deleted the email. Today's Sunday. I was supposed to respond no later than last Friday."

As soon as we could leave we did, I told Michelle what had happened on the way home and as I checked the computer, I saw I'd missed the deadline. Damn.

I made a call. "Hello, Peter?"

"Hi, Ron, What's up?"

"I feel ridiculous calling you, but…" I told him what had happened. He laughed. "Don't worry about it," he said. "I'll call them tomorrow morning and straighten it all out. And congratulations."

I hung up and kissed Michelle. "Sweetie, you are my lucky star." Peter was a principal in the firm which oversaw the biennial Olympic torch run and he and his wife just so happened to be Redstone friends of ours. How's that for luck?

A few months later, in Official Torch Carrier clothing I, with Michelle and a crowd of friends walking alongside me, carried a flaming torch down the center of an empty highway, traffic blocked off for a half mile in each direction.

My entourage and I had free food and pitchers of margaritas at a local joint and that night Michelle put on a Torch party for the whole town which packed the Redstone Inn until lights out. What a day that was.

The Olympic Torch Relay clothing I received would clothe a small army. One vest, replete with embroidered logos, fit Michelle perfectly so she'd often wear it in winter.

When someone would ask, "Did you carry the Olympic Torch?" she'd smile and say, "No, but I slept with a guy that did."

146

Requiem For My Little Sweetie (June, 1998)

The phone rang. It was Bill, calling from Eureka Springs, AR.

"Hope is in a coma, Ron. She's terminal." I was stunned.

Jean had decided to remove Hope from life support and after learning more about her condition, I agreed. I composed a eulogy in my head as I drove from Colorado to Eureka Springs. An awful road trip. Cathartic. Brutal.

At Hope's life celebration, I was amazed at the number of people of every age who had gathered, under a huge magnolia. Her death and our harmonies singing "Amazing Grace" haunts me to this very day.

My eulogy:

I first met Hope when she was three. She was wearing a red dress, a little white blouse and her blonde hair pulled up into a ponytail. I always called her My Little Sweetie.

I'd put her up on my shoulder and walk around at night, showing her the constellations. Orion, Andromeda. Pegasus was her favorite. She loved the idea of a horse with wings big enough to fly across the entire night sky.

She brought a cat home once. It wouldn't let anyone within ten feet of it, but it would let Hope carry it around like a ragdoll.

She must of had 1000 Barbies. Her favorite, and this is so like Hope, her favorite Barbie was a Malibu Barbie, you know, the one with the tan lines? But with its head popped off and the head of the then-named Black Barbie, put back in its place.

She didn't have a Ken doll. So she used a monkey doll made out of an old sock. With Velcro on its paws so it could hug stuff.

One Christmas I bought her a remote-control pink plastic Barbie Corvette. She put that Barbie in the driver's seat, lashed her monkey across the hood like a deer and off down the sidewalk they'd go.

She later moved to Arkansas for a while when she was a teenager. I'd write her letters about philosophy, living in truth, life. She told me just last month that she still had every one.

She wasn't without her challenges in life. At the end of one particularly trying period for her I gave her my Purple Heart. When she married Jon and gave birth to Lulamae I was living on a cloud.

Hope, losing you is like losing my other leg.

I'm going to go home now, back up to that log house in the mountains of Colorado. There's going to come a hummingbird to the feeder on the front porch. It's going to look at me in just a certain way. I'm going to know that's you.

A cloud is going to come across our mountain and the wind is going to blow through the big blue spruce next to the house in just a certain way. I'm going to know that's you.

317

And the eagle that lives across the river… She's going to leave her nest and fly up into those mountains so high… So high she looks like an angel. I'm going to say, "Look. There's Hope."

Vaya con Dios, my Little Sweetie. I will see you in Paradise.

On the way home, I bought some flowers in OKC and stopped by Mom's grave. We talked about Hope.

They were both gone now.

I was consoled by my visit.

147
It All Comes Together

I returned to Redstone filled with heartache, from which Michelle helped me recover. I dove into The Master Plan and it was adopted by the entire Caucus and the county in 2003. The restoration of the coke ovens was finally completed in 2006.

And our house? It took ten years of sweat equity, roofing in the snow, squirrels in the attic, wiring in cramped crawl spaces and I forget what else. Ivan had died, so it was not easy.

With the help of my pal Bruce and others, we finally got our coveted Certificate Of Occupancy in 2011. Let me tell you about Bruce.

Bruce met all the requirements for brotherhood. He could do just about anything with a chainsaw, he was an expert with a chop saw and, like me, had a ridiculous sense of humor.

No better guy to help me build a palace for Michelle. He became one of her and my closest friends, the only one who, forever after, could walk into the house unannounced through the glass front door he'd helped me install.

We stripped the old kitchen/living room back to the logs and built an Edwardian library for Michelle's collection of books, now arranged in floor to ceiling shelves. The new soapstone stove sat on a slate hearth from India. It crackled with warmth. Flakes of Christmas snow floated down outside the windows.

319

Michelle's grandmother, in the early 1900's on their farm, had made and sold cottage cheese. With the proceeds, over decades, she'd bought a huge collection of Fostoria faceted-glass dinnerware. It had been handed down through Michelle's mother to her and it needed a space to be displayed.

I made glass-fronted lighted cabinets on the side of the kitchen island, which faced into our new Great Room. Its glass shelves now held the entire collection.

One evening,I turned off every light in the house, save for the ones in that cabinet. It was like looking at piles of diamonds. If Michelle is to be believed, "It's the most beautiful thing I've ever seen."

The grandboys arrived in Sequim, WA; Billy in 2010, and Paco in 2012. I became "Gramps," a new brotherhood.

I heard from Bob that his dad had become ill. I wrote a long letter to Rocky from our library, describing my wife, my life, and thanking him for the great gift he'd given my family after I was wounded.

IX. Bob
The Detour

Dealing with a diagnosis of prostate cancer is like threading the eye of the needle, as in being pulled through it. The view on the other side, after a bunch of "I'm still alive!" is amazing and life-changing. To write an ode to the journey is cool, too, including all the lessons on how to slip through the eye while holding a Pickleball racket. That'll help other guys.

— Ron Sorter, back cover blurb on *The Prostate Chronicles: A Medical Memoir by Bob Tierno.* (2019)

148

The Prostate Detour (Musings of a Prostate Cancer Survivor)

On August 30, 2018, a da Vinci robot, guided by my urologist, Dr. Rich Bevan-Thomas, extracted my cancerous prostate, culminating the detour of a lifetime. Three PSA tests later and my cancer is undetectable, including a one-year PSA test conducted in September, 2019 (Prostate Cancer Awareness month).

At the time of the surgery, I wondered whether I'd see my 70th birthday and my bucket list goal of attending the U.S. Open at Pebble Beach in June with a close friend. We'd attended the Open at Pebble Beach nine years prior, at the Olympic Club in San Francisco.

The cancer diagnosis meant I had a 95% chance of living for ten years (80), and slightly less to an older age. Of course, I'll never be cancer free and something else may terminate my time on this earth. Regardless, I don't walk outside in thunderstorms, and I always check my side mirror when changing lanes on I-35.

Seventy is quite a milestone! It did not sink in until the week of July 20th, a vivid reminder of the first moon landing fifty years ago.

I was 20 years old and a basic trainee at Fort Benning , GA.

The Summer of Love was the "Summer of Wasn't," as I "volunteered" for a two-year Army ROTC program to evade the draft notice I had received after dropping a class in college. I figured I would play the odds of potentially being shipped off to South Vietnam. Time flies whether you are having fun or not.

A number of my Pickleball peeps are in their seventies. Cody, who ran me ragged around the court, is 80. There is hope!

There must be more as this ride isn't over.

I have emerged from my detour and the da Vinci surgery as a strong advocate for Prostate Cancer patients. Numerous people have called me about their brother who was just diagnosed or the gentleman who had stomach pains and checked into the hospital only to be diagnosed with prostate cancer. Oh, he also has to have his appendix removed first. He was so overwhelmed that he did not know what questions to ask or what his PSA or Gleason Score was after a biopsy.

Another sent me a note with his PSA score thanking me for writing *The Prostate Chronicles: A Medical Memoir* published in June, 2019 (Cancer Month). This irreverent view of my life's detour is aimed at men forty and above. My advocacy includes writing for ProstateCancer.net and serving as one of the moderators of their Facebook Forums

So what's next?

I'm teaching marketing and other courses at a local community college, as an adjunct professor. Another way of giving back, sharing my life's experience.

I'm playing Pickleball, cycling to the courts, and working on my golf game (or lack thereof).

Karen is about 85% recovered from two surgeries for a fall shattering her elbow while I was recovering from surgery. She couldn't make the trip in June to California to celebrate my birthday but baked the Italian Cream Cake that my mother used to bake for me every year keeping the streak alive!

We are booked to fly out to California in late September to visit old friends and enjoy fine California wines. Our first trip together in over eighteen months. Now that the detour has been successfully navigated, we are back on the express lanes of life and looking towards the future.

149
Building Your Army of Support, Deke-style

No Man is a Failure Who has Friends.
— Clarence Oddbody, *It's a Wonderful Life*

A diagnosis of prostate cancer can put a man into a dark place emotionally. My number one priority was to enroll and enlist family, friends, professional connections developed over decades, my parish priest, my fellow Knights of Columbus Knights, and my Deke fraternity brothers to take this detour with me.

No One Fights Alone
— Prostate Cancer Foundation mantra

I was surprised by the number of prostate cancer survivors I have met through this army of support. All around the world I connected with over a dozen survivors to understand how their experiences would help my journey. Each helped fill in the questions I should be asking and assuring me that da Vinci Robotic Surgery was successful in every instant.

Enroll College Fraternity Brothers: Delta Kappa Epsilon

Friends From the Heart, Forever
— DKE motto

Some of the most influential associations I have made in life have been with my Deke fraternity brothers. As you have read in this book, Ron Sorter, Fred Streb, Bill Nation, have been the stalwarts. For some of the other Deke brother, it took over 40 years to reconnect, but every day I get a text, email, or Facebook comment from one of my brothers.

If you have read this far, you know that in the spring of 1968 I pledged at the Rho Lambda Chapter of Delta Kappa Epsilon at Oklahoma University, and moved into the fraternity house the fall semester.

I studied intently my freshman year, forgoing beer, women, and song. The result was a 2.5 GPA . Fraternity life was like the movie *Animal House*, but experiencing the friendships and bonds that last a lifetime is priceless. My roommate Bill Nation met his late wife Karleen through our Deke sweetheart group and I married my Deke sweetheart Karen.

Fast forward 47 years. I admit that I didn't keep in touch with more of my brothers over the years. In 2014, a core group of Oklahoma University Rho Lambda Chapter Deke alumni brothers started hosting a reunion
during the University of Oklahoma homecoming weekend.

Keep in mind that it had been over 40 years since we tipped a beer together. Some things never change. The tales of years past get larger in scope, funnier by the word, and yes we've all put on some poundage.

Maybe it's the timing, but it was great to have my brother Dekes supporting my cancer fight. It's been said that there are good friends and there are fast friends. A fraternity brother is a great friend because as we met again it was almost like yesterday.

When I was diagnosed with prostate cancer in 2018, I reached out to all of my Deke brothers for support. Of course I got needled (versus a rectal), but everyone rallied to my "cause."

I was determined to make the 2018 reunion aka "The DKE Roundup" in late October. Bill Nation made his annual trek from Memphis to Dallas to spend several days with us drinking very good scotch and playing golf. We motored to the roundup and had a terrific time.

Several of the guys shared their brothers' experience with prostate cancer and everybody shared their age-driven maladies. We were still jolly good fellows, albeit technology-assisted with hip and knee replacements, shoulder surgeries and heart monitors. Reenergizing these relationships has been awesome. Friends from the heart, forever.

Bob Tierno, speaking at the launch of his medical memoir, *The Prostate Chronicles*, May 31, 2019, Denton, TX

X.Ron
Leaving Redstone, Sequim Lullaby
(2012-2019)

150

A Clump of Dandelions

Michelle and I loved road trips. We wandered as much as we traveled. Seeing Monument Valley in a convertible at sunset is a memory we cherished. Michelle looked forward to being a grandmother and I looked forward to teaching Billy and Paco how to belch. It's a talent every young man needs.

After twenty years, our house was beautiful and Michelle's gardens were award-winning.

One day, I came in and there on the kitchen counter I saw clusters of dandelions, dirt still attached. Michelle, wearing gardener's gloves, was sitting on the couch looking at me.

I sat next to her on the couch and asked, "Are you ok?"

It took her a moment to give me an answer. She said, finally, "I don't know."

She looked at me, her face filled with confusion.

I asked her, "Are you having a problem saying words or you just can't think of words to say?"

The house was all glass, with no curtains. Behind us was a beautiful backdrop of green aspen trees.

She looked at me and said after a longer pause, "I don't know."

"C'mon," I said, "we're going to the ER in Glenwood."

I safely broke every law getting us o Glenwood Springs. Michelle's BP was through the roof and a CT scan showed a significant brain bleed.

Outside, it had started to snow. The doctor said, "You need to get to Swedish in Denver. You could die from this."

I was instantly on the phone to Mike and Chelle, her kids.

A blizzard in the darkness meant no helicopter could fly through the Rockies so we had to wait for a special plane to be flown to a runway downvalley in Rifle.

We loaded Michelle onto the Lear jet and soon she was in the ICU in Swedish Hospital. I rode in the jump seat for the half-hour flight over the Rockies.

Michelle loved airplanes. Here was her chance to fly in a Lear jet, but she was lying supine with IV lines and monitors, not knowing what would come next.

Mike and Chelle joined us there.

In Denver, it took them three days to give us a final diagnosis: Cerebral Amyloid Angiopathy (CAA). CAA is another name for blood vessels acting like a colander, leaking blood and drowning the surrounding brain tissue. She'd always been in perfect health. This was cataclysmic.

331

151
Getting to Know Billy and Paco

History doesn't repeat itself, but it often rhymes.
— perhaps, Mark Twain

Four days later we were home from Denver, no worse for wear, except for a few memory issues and an inability to think of the right word. CAA survivors often have few immediate after effects but the occurrence itself can often be more fatal than strokes. She'd been lucky.

We'd been told how this would play out. The amyloid proteins, even with blood pressure medicines, would continue collecting, slowly causing more and more problems.

By the time we got back home, our friend Bruce had put a huge bouquet of mountain wildflowers in a pristine picklejar atop the kitchen island where the dandelions had lain. A new life was beginning for us. We called our broker pal Jeff. We put our Redstone house on the market. If time was short, we needed to know our grandkids.

We'd visited Mike and Ilsa (daughter-in-law, parents of Billy and Paco) in their Sequim house many times and had always admired the town and especially the house next door to them. Shortly before the sale of our Redstone house closed, Mike called and told us that the house next door in Sequim (pronounced "Squim") had just come on the market.

We had Mike inspect it, we made an offer and after another offer fell through, we owned it. Neither of us had been inside it, and the house was ours.

Somehow, Michelle and I have a talent for jumping out of the airplane, and a parachute appears.

152
Goodbye Redstone

Redstone gave us a sendoff for the ages. What a party that was.

It was heartbreaking. We loaded our U-Haul van in another blizzard, with seven helpers in high winds.

Overnight it froze to the lawn, as if trying to not let us leave. A neighbor hooked up his power wagon to our U-Haul and jerked the van from its frozen slumber. He was a pal, a member of my military brotherhood.

And leave we did. Bruce and his son Parker drove the U-Haul straight through to Sequim, while Michelle and I followed in our Jeep at our own pace.

It was reassuring that Bruce and Parker, the same guys who had unloaded our moving van on our first day in Redstone, would unload this van on our first day in Sequim. I was beginning to see connections and full circles everywhere.

153
Sunny Sequim

Sequim is a lovely place in the rain shadow of the Olympic mountains. The sun shines when it's overcast and raining everywhere else. I had given my snow blower to my pal Rawley. Our new house at sea level had a huge garage and a 1,000 sf workshop.

I installed a gate between our new house and the grandkids' house and we began a new life here. I traded carpet for a new hardwood floor.

I built raised flower planters for Michelle, so she wouldn't have to get up and down anymore.

I completely remodeled the old kitchen and learned how to make our food in a new place.

Over the next several years, Sweet Michelle always asked, "Can I help?" so I'd give her something easy to do. Her brain issues had slowly begun to affect not only her memory of words but her rationality so I began putting dangerous tools away.

Dementia is a horrible thing to endure.

Cruelest of all, was her inability to read her books. She carried them and held them close but the words were now lost to her.

Her doctors, therapists, and everyone we dealt with in Sequim's wonderful medical environment told me, "You are so lucky, it's unusual for anyone with this disease to still be so happy. She always has such a beautiful smile."

And to my endless joy they often said, "She is so lucky to have you."

We made as many road trips as time would allow. Her mother's death affected her deeply but her Iowa family, friends she hadn't seen in decades, filled her with the sweetest kind of happiness.

We took the long way back to Sequim. We deeply drank every drop of each other.

154
The Pace Quickens

Four happy years passed, with wonderful holidays spent with family. Our daily trips to favorite places helped us enjoy our life immensely. I eventually needed to hire caregivers to come in and help me. I attended my own caregiver groups to help give me context for what was ahead.

I finally had to make some steps for her to be able to get into our Jeep. One day, after trying so valiantly, in vain, to get in, she finally said, in such a sad voice, "I can't."

Soon afterwards she lost the ability to walk well, and we learned how to use rolling walkers, then wheelchairs and, finally, a hydraulic lifter. I'm so happy I had one ready the day she simply lost the ability to even stand with my help.

Being bedridden added complexity to my care. Every morning I'd wake and when she was awake, I'd see her smile at me.

"Hello," I'd say. "I'm Ron, your husband. We've been married for twenty-five years. We live in Sequim, WA, next to your son Mike and his wife Ilsa. Our grand boys Billy and Paco visit us all the time and they just love you to death. As do I."

She would smile at me. Every morning. Then I would feed her breakfast, spoonful by spoonful. I bought her a formal black bib with embroidered pearl necklace and brooch.

155
The Magnitude of Michelle

My life had always been leading me to her and her ultimate gift was allowing me to be a part of her incredible family.

Before I knew her, Michelle worked at the Pentagon, the youngest person there with a Top Secret, For Your Eyes Only clearance. She worked on projects involving the M-16 and the C-130 airplane.

I used the M-16 in Vietnam and I flew home on a C-130. Michelle's influence was with me even before I knew her.

At the end, my life became majestic.

I had been revised, yet again. By Michelle.

156
"Angel on My Shoulder"

One Friday in March of 2019, I, Mike, Ilsa and Chelle (on Face-Time) were at our dining table. The new visiting nurse, Claudia said, "I'm filling in for Trish who can't be here today. I've reviewed everyone's notes in Michelle's file and, Ron, you're to be commended.

"Trish said she's been doing this work for twenty years and she's never seen such an accomplished caregiver as you."

To say that in front of Michelle's kids was...I can't describe it.

We have a wonderful volunteer hospice group in Sequim. They were called and three days later I, Chelle and Mike were on the bed, holding Michelle in our arms.

She was mostly unresponsive now and Chelle turned to Mike and said, "Mike, do you remember when Mom would hold us in her arms, in her rocker and sing lullabies to us?"

She turned to Michelle. "Mom? You remember that, don't you? My favorite lullaby was, 'There's An Angel On My Shoulder.'" In the softest voice possible Chelle began singing her lullaby to her mother,

"Got an angel on my shoulder
Got a penny in my pocket
And I found a four leaf clover
And I put it in my locket..."

339

A smile slowly appeared on Michelle's lips and as Chelle continued singing she struggled to open her eyes and finally they locked, overjoyed, on Chelle's as her daughter sang to her the very last lullaby she would ever hear, the same, very first lullaby she had sung to Chelle when she was a tiny baby. When the lullaby was done, Michelle shut her smiling eyes and slept and, a few hours later, she passed from this Earth.

What a great gift she gave the three of us, that last smile in her final, sweet moment of awareness.

We loved each other so deeply, there was never a need for actual words in those last months she was alive. And there's the final awareness of not truly knowing how valuable something is until you've lost it forever. (You can find the obituary that I composed for Michelle in the Appendix.)

One of her best friends recently sent me a condolence saying, "Michelle told me often how much she adored you." Reading those words was like finding a bottle on a beach with a note to me inside, from Michelle, telling me that she loves me.

Someday I'll pass away, be cremated and my ashes will be joined with hers. The Old Guard at Arlington will then place our urn in their marble wall where we'll eventually become one, atomically.

My military brotherhood will play Taps. They will give my last folded flag to Paco and Billy, the two brothers whom I love the most.

340

XI. Brothers
DKE Interviews

157
Gestalt and the Deke Diaspora

August 6, 2019

Bob:

Here are the rest of the Deke interviews. I don't know how or
if they'll fit together. They're a bit disjointed, but maybe that's
the point. Time passes, we all change and remember events
differently.

But there's a certain Gestalt in there, certain commonalities,
especially the refrain of regret that no one kept as much in
contact as they would have wished.

Doug Mistler had an interesting point: The metaphorical
"closed" sign on the house after '73 might have helped infuse
an ending to the connections many brothers felt they had with
the other brothers.

The recent re-establishment of connections by Fred, Bob,
Burnsie and others rhymes with a book I reference somewhere
in my part, written by a guy with clinical depression. About
the unanchoredness of life he experienced as his connections
were lost and his reprieve when they were regained.

Enough philosophy.

Ron

August 7, 2019, 5:17 a.m.

Ron,

My drill sergeant at Fort Benning told us pukes that the only words he wanted to hear in the mess hall was "pass the #*@ gestalt!!".

I tend to look at the diaspora that occurred upon graduation and ultimately the closure of the house as a result of so many brothers from out of state as well as a lack of undergraduate leadership and alumni support.

George Otey fought to keep the Deke Fraternity alive after closing the house but times changed in 1972. OU went from slightly left of moderate to far right and took aim at the fraternity/sorority system, buying up houses and instituting new "rules."

Students became students again, apathetic to the outside world and wore their Harold's clothes and focused on OU Football.

In talking to Bill Nation over the last couple of years there was a core group that kept in touch over the years, including Fred Streb, and Bob Pickup, who grew up in Bolivar, NY and had a natural connection regardless of Deke.

Bill Nation was from Tulsa, so he kept in touch with Tulsa and pledge brothers from Oklahoma.

I adopted the same gypsy life as my folks. Karen and I saw the country on the government and private industry's dime. If we were in the same grid square, I'd get in touch (Fred on the east coast, Bill Nation in Dallas).

It was a Deke Diaspora!

Bob

158
The Questionnaire

Dear Brother PΛ Deke,

 We're writing a book (don't laugh) about Fraternity and the brotherhood adventure which began for us in the OU Deke House. We're illustrating our tale using descriptions of our intersections over the last fifty years.

We're wondering if you'd be interested in helping us. It would enrich our book immensely to have some thoughts from our brotherhood on this theme.

Perhaps these questions will prompt some memories from you:

1. Looking back over 50 years, what are your longest running relationships from the house?

2. What are your top three memories?

3. When did we first meet each other?

4. How have your DKE relationships sustained and supported you in general?

5. If you were talking to any DKE chapter members today, what wisdom would you share with them, that crosses the generations?

345

6. What guidance would you provide for today's Deke, ie making life decisions, balancing the modern rules of fraternity life with the inevitable trade-offs and social opportunities?

7. Can we use your name in our book? Would you mind us contacting you if we do?

We plan to have our book complete by October, 2019, so we'd like to receive your contribution by July 31st.

Thank you very much.

Kerothen,

Ron and Bob

George Otey
Tulsa, OK

Author Note:
George Otey fought hard to save the chapter. In recent years he drove the founding of a chapter at Oklahoma State, received awards from DKE Headquarters and is a legal adviser for DKE investigating potential violations.

1. Looking back over 50 years, what are your longest running relationships from the house?

One of the most engaging and fulfilling experiences of my life has been the emerging relationships, while at the house, after graduation, and throughout life.

Through the years I have kept in close contact with various brothers from my pledge class (Mike Brooks, Alan Bauman, Orin Piepho, and others) and older and newer brothers (Mike Shipman, Mike Bromiley, Mike Hall, Bill Millar, Bill Nation).

One of the most rewarding experiences has been rekindling older friendships because of the Rho Lambda Roundups and developing closer bonds with those for which time or other relationships did not offer an opportunity.

2. What are your top three memories?

Assisting Fred Streb in building the skull for the 1969 Graveyard Party and making "Rum Runs" with Tom Vizard.

Continual "debates" in 2W among Mike Brooks, Ed Balikov, Wes Owens, John Whipple, John Deupree, Randy Baumgarten, Bill Millar, and Lee Kilpatrick regarding war/peace, social change, religion, literature, philosophy

Listening to and sharing the latest albums (Moody Blues, Firesign Theater, Rolling Stones, Janis Joplin, Cream, Neil Young) with various brothers and playing days-long board games like Blitzkreig between classes.

3. When did we first meet each other?

Although I already knew Wes Owens and Mark Coe from high school days, pledgeship introduced me to a number of my now close friends and older brothers (Dennis Clowers, Rob Stites, Bill Nation, Bob Tierno).

As a member I also developed close relationships with newer members (Randy Jenkins, Ramsey Cantrell, Mike Campbell, and Jimmy Rubenstein).

4. How have your DKE relationships sustained and supported you in general?

Throughout the years my Deke relationships provided me with a sort of grounding where I can not only reminisce, but move forward with strength knowing I have close friends who encourage my personal growth through the sustained relationship.

5. If you were talking to any DKE chapter members today, what wisdom would you share with them, that crosses the generations?

One of the greatest opportunities I have had has been to meet with Rho Lambda Dekes from earlier days like Dave Johnson and George Patterson and exchange stories with them. From these encounters comes the knowledge there is a commonality of experience that transcends the "eras" giving us a unity that bonds and ultimately strengthens us personally from being part of a unique group.

6. What guidance would you provide for today's Deke, ie making life decisions, balancing the modern rules of fraternity life with the inevitable trade-offs and social opportunities?

Staying true to yourself. Deke has always been a fraternity of individualists; don't try to be something else than who you are; don't try to fit the mold but learn moderation.

The Greek Golden Rule was moderation in everything, and as such, balance out the Gentleman, Scholar, and Jolly Good Fellow. Study hard (make your grades), party with temperance (limiting party hours to weekends), and maintain your dignity at all times (be in control of your body and tongue).

With social media, it becomes all important to avoid appearances of impropriety and "stupidity"; watch out for one another.

Dennis Clowers
Oklahoma City, OK

"I was shy coming out of high school. I had a close group of friends, but really not many outside that group. The only Dekes I had met before coming to OU were Jim Reed and Mark Hinshaw, who was the rush chairman in the summer of '66. They came to our house in OKC during my senior year to encourage me to go through rush and consider the Deke house.

"Jim's mother worked for my Dad at the time. There were 22 of us that pledged during rush week that fall and I knew none of them. We were, as most pledge classes are, a varied group from different backgrounds and interests.

"I recall the next summer that rush wasn't going well. I don't recall who rush chairman was that summer, but whoever it was had pretty much abandoned the job and, for various reasons, it appeared there were several upperclassmen who were not planning to move back into the house in the fall of '67.

"Dave Cooper, who had pledged during open rush in the fall of '66 hadn't made his grades in the fall, but did in the spring and was to be initiated in the fall. Dave took it upon himself to take over the duties of rush chairman, even though he wasn't a member yet.

"We didn't have a lot of guys back for rush week. But due to Dave's efforts, we had signed a good number to come through the house during rush week.

350

"Dave would have his issues with his brothers about two years later and was basically kicked out of the house. However, during rush week of '67 I recall we only had about 25 or so in the house and 35 to 45 coming through each of the first six rush sessions.

"Cooper would tell everyone to cram in the front foyer, shake hands with the rushees coming in the front door, then run through the living room to the back foyer, and then through the short hall back into the front foyer and greet them again, so it might appear there were twice as many of us as there really were. We were hopeful we'd get a sizeable class because we really needed the numbers.

"Reality set in on the last day of rush and we only signed nine pledges. From that nine came Fred Streb, Bob Pickup and Tom Norman, really good guys who turned out to be great members of our house."

Long Term Friendships

"From my pledge class I became close with Richard Burns and Rob Stites, and am still close with them to this day. From class the next year, I became close to the three I mentioned, Streb, Pickup and Norman, and am still to this day.

"I was honored to be asked to be the best man at Tom Norman's and Bob Pickup's weddings. Just to be clear, those were two separate weddings, they didn't marry each other!

351

"Rob, Tom and I shared an apartment in the spring of 1970 after we moved out of the house. I became even better friends with them during those few months.

"The next year, my last in engineering school, Rob had graduated and left for the Navy and Tom was going to work as a dorm counselor, so I had no one to room with.

I had become friendly with Mike Hall, who was two years behind me, so I asked if he'd be interested in sharing an apartment the next year, which would be my last in engineering school. He agreed and we also asked Steve Harrell, who was in Mike's class. Although Steve was a nice guy, it was Mike and I who became really good friends that year.

"I was fortunate to get accepted to the MBA graduate program the following year in the fall of '72, so I was going to be in school for another two years. Mike was, too, as he was getting another bachelor's degree. We ended up living together for three years.

"Living together for that long provides the opportunity to get to know someone extremely well. Mike and I were about as good friends as two could be during those three years. We stayed close for several years, but I haven't been able to contact Mike since about 2001.

"I would say those I mentioned, Burns, Stites, Norman, Streb, Pickup and Hall have been my longest running relationships from the house."

"Since the core group began putting the annual reunions together, it has been great to get back in touch with others that I considered good friends during my time at OU, such as George Otey, Bob Tierno, Bill Nation and Tom Vizard."

My Top Three Memories

"Initiation. Although I didn't particularly like being mentally and physically exhausted after five days, but looking back on it I think the whole process was well thought out and executed, and ultimately, very meaningful.

"The only break I recall was at dinner time on Saturday when we were allowed to go with our big brother and another member and his little brother to eat. My big brother was Larry Core, who was friends with Mike Tuttle and Mike's little brother was Richard Burns. The four of us went in Mike's '65 candy apple red GTO convertible. It was a nice day, and although we still couldn't speak without permission, I'll never forget going to the Boomerang on Lindsey that evening.

"Rich and I are sitting in the back seat eating our burgers and fries, and not yet knowing what lifelong friends we would become, taking family vacations together for years, attending each others' kid's wedding, etc. What a great friend Burnsie is. Even though the entire five and a half days was grueling, the lesson at the end, "you don't know how valuable and important something is to you until you lose it," is one of life's most valuable lessons, which most will experience many times in their life."

"Another strong memory is playing intramural sports with my Deke brothers. What a great time I had with the guys who played intramural football and softball. I had the opportunity to pitch for our softball team in the spring of '69, when we went undefeated, defeating the Sigma Chi's in the finals.

"The bastard sons turned us in shortly after the game for playing a pledge that didn't live in the house. So, the Sigma Chi's got the trophy, but they know they got their butts kicked by the Deke House.

"Then after losing about 35 pounds during the summer of '69 doing construction, coming back to school in the best shape of my life. I decided to quit the "Pride" after three years, and I was able to quarterback our intramural football team that fall. Although we didn't have a lot of really good athletes, not nearly what some of the larger houses had, we had guys that played really hard and held our own.

"Rich Burns may be the hardest playing competitor I've ever been around. I recall that fall playing the Delt's and Rich was taking an angle on their QB toward the sideline. Rich got there at about the same time as the QB and his momentum carried him right into a group of spectators. One was his wife of about 3 months, Bonnie who found herself on the ground.

"One of the Delt's watching the game asked if she was alright and helped her up, then commented that guy should be more careful. Rich had already gotten up and was back on the field. Bonnie simply said, "Oh that's ok, he's my husband."

"Another memorable occasion was when Hank Helton was rooming with his little brother, Randy Baumgarten on the third floor. Randy had been seeing Hank's sister and had taken her to Chicago for the weekend.

"Hank was pissed. He went into his room Friday afternoon after he learned of the trip to Chicago and by around 9:00 PM Saturday no one had seen or heard Hank.

"There were a few of us in the 3rd floor hallway outside Hank's door trying to decide if we should try to go in the room, or something else.

"About that time, the blade of Hank's Bowie knife came through the hollow core door. We decided Hank was ok and we left him alone.

"On another occasion, we had a couple of rushees over on a Wednesday night for dinner. After dinner, Burnsie and I had talked with one guy for a while, and we mentioned that we played 1 on 1 or 2 on 2 soccer in the 3rd floor hallway.

"He (I can't recall his name) said he played soccer and let's give it a try. We'd been after it for about 20 minutes (can't recall who the 4th player was), but we got into a heated battle for the ball and we ended up breaking the rushee's thumb.

"I think we got some ice on it and took him across the street to the infirmary, checked him in and wished him well. Probably not surprising, he didn't choose to pledge."

First Meetings

"I recall meeting Bob Tierno when he was going through open rush in the spring of '68. I think he was a freshman that year and was initiated the next fall and moved into the house.

"Bob always brought a lot of life to any situation. I recall he had a nice selection of neck ties, and although I seemed to have some decent threads, I borrowed a tie from Bob a couple of times. As I recall we only lived in the house together for a year and a half, as I moved out in the middle of the '69-'70 year with Rob and Tom.

"I recall having a great time playing intramural football and softball with Bob. I recently read Bob's book, *The Prostate Chronicles*. I enjoyed it and give Bob a lot of credit for making it through the ordeal he and Karen have had the past year.

"I met Ron Sorter during rush week the fall of '66. I didn't get to know Ron really well during the time I was a pledge. However, I admired the work he did as Brother X during our class's initiation. And I know those that still know the RMO by heart, Bob Pickup and I for sure, give a lot of "credit" to the authors who were, I believe, Ron, Jim Griffin and Mark Hinshaw.

"Someone can correct me if I'm wrong on that. Bobby and I recited it to the OSU Deke pledge class at the first two reunions, but after some encouragement from some of our brothers and critical thinking on our part, have chosen to keep it to ourselves from this point forward."

356

"My relationships with these guys has sustained me by knowing that I could call any of them at 2:00 AM, telling them I'm in trouble and need some help and they would be there for me.

Wisdom

"If I were to say anything to current Dekes in college today I would encourage them to please be mindful that it doesn't take much to turn a simple mistake in judgement into a life-long disaster.

"It is so difficult for someone at 18, 19 or 20 to be having fun with their buds and letting a simple situation get out of control.

"College is where guys grow up, get the basis for making decisions that will sustain them throughout their career and beyond. College can be so much fun, but at the same time one needs to be mindful of the end result, to get a great education that will enable you to reach all the goals in life that you want. At the same time, you can make friends and relationships that will stay with you forever."

Dave Butler
Santa Fe, NM

"My Deke friendships were impressive. The ones we make when we're younger are somehow more important, I think. I came from a small town, and was an only child, maybe a little naive. College was a wing-spreading eye opener. My friendships were no longer just in Enid but from all over the country. They expanded to different value systems. They were enlightening and not just my friendships on campus.

"It opened my eyes, helping me get over some of my inborn parochialism, and the belief that where you're from is the best. Travel itself helps eliminate bigotry and prejudice. I'm sure everybody's take is personal, as we meet different people.

"Political differences could be profound, but I discovered that brothers with diametrically opposing political views didn't have horns and fangs but could be decent and kind, even to the extent of standing up for others who disagree with them because of the bonds of brotherhood.

"The military is a brotherhood, for sure. In the Air Force, a Lt. Col. noticed I'd arrived late one morning and instead of criticizing me, he said, 'Lieutenant, I'd appreciate it if you could check around each morning and make sure everyone has arrived to work on time.'

"I remember that to this day: he let me know he knew I was late without needing to reprimand me."

358

"It inspired me to take a similar tack with people I dealt with in both my military and professional career. I approached that in a similar way with an airman taking advantage of sick time. I told him, 'You have to be responsible.' When you set an expectation directly to someone, people will usually live up to it."

Dave and Ron talked about witnessing decision-making in chapter meetings. They were usually the first experience we had of sitting in a room with fellow members, each with different ideas and, by using parliamentary rules, work out plans for dealing with matters of import. It is one of the keys to business success, which we learned early in that chapter room.

The Deke house had only a few local alumni to help when the house encountered serious financial conditions. Dave and Ron were drafted to return to the house to "right the ship" after a semester of spending that almost emptied its coffers. It taught them that things that appear to be obvious (ie that profligate spending is unwise) often aren't.

"Mother Harris helped give members a taste of a larger world, and lessons on how to socialize and live in it. She was persnickety and funny." We agreed that she adroitly helped keep a lid on many potential misdeeds.

"I've been in contact with Germond, Iseminger, Tom and Bob Bradford and Bullivant. The recent reunions and the email list put together by Burns (an enormous amount of work) has been very helpful in reconnecting with our brothers."

Ralph Duckworth
Noble, OK

"I lost track of everybody for 45 years. The brotherhood should be about being lifelong friends, so it's kind of nice that the reunions have made it happen again out of the blue.

"It's great to reconnect with my pledge class and Martin, Miller, Park, and the Buxtons. I saw Martin last year. Even though he's dealing with issues, he's still happy and having fun."

Ron and Ralph discussed Ron's wife, who'd recently died after a long struggle with dementia and what a wonderful wife Nancy, Vic's college sweetheart, is for Vic.

"I've had several jobs in my life, and retired from two of them. I have a husband. I was pretty much all alone in high school. I had a few friends and we played poker, but we didn't date girls, and didn't make friends very well. I went to my 30th high school reunion and realized I didn't know them at all.

"In college, after pledging Deke, I lived in the dorms for a few months, but soon moved into the frat house. It was my first experience of living like that. I became much more outgoing.

"Here's an example of brotherhood. One night preparing for initiation, out in the woods, Ted Burdett had taught me a little bit about cattle. One approached me, I reached out to let it know I was there, it was a bull and it tossed me. Ted threw rocks at it and distracted it. How was I to know bulls' dispositions are different than cows?"

360

Jim Griffin
Dallas, TX

"I retired as an Army Lt. Col. in 1992. During my military career, wife Karen and I spent several years overseas in Germany, Korea, and Belgium. My time in the military made it difficult to keep in contact with the brotherhood.

"We retired in Dallas after a second career with AT&T and kept apprised of chapter affairs through Mike Tuttle, a fellow OU Deke and president of the OU Club of Dallas. We attended many OU/Texas football games together.

"The reunions of today are a different world. The men we were in college with are different than who we are now. Some of the things we did aren't always the things we want most to remember, especially in front of our wives.

Ron and Jim agreed that OU Dekes had skill at marrying above our class, considering all our wives. Jim and Ron reminisced about a road trip they'd taken in the summer of '67, with Brother Mark Hinshaw through the wilds of Colorado and how Mark, after a stellar architecture career in Seattle, now lives in Italy.

The Gross Gift Parties at Christmas and the staid attendance of Mother Harris are still head-shakers to this day. We'd draw names, wrap up the most disgusting gift imaginable and open them with all the brothers in attendance. Their contents are barely printable.

Jim and Ron recalled their membership in Scabbard and Blade (a scholastic brotherhood) and that Ron's father-in-law was the only man he'd met who also was. We discussed the deeper meanings of the close-knit nature of the military and how the success of a brotherhood is the very foundation of military esprit de corps.

"My older brother Doug was an OU Deke, so that was my introduction to the brotherhood of the Deke house. Those of us serving overseas in Europe had the advantage of brotherhood, too. We'd have Hail and Farewells for those coming and leaving and it was sad to lose connections but good to always be making new ones, just like the Deke house.

"We had a deeper sub-brotherhood, Tau Chi, of myself, Martin, Reed and Duckworth, who'd watch TV in the basement." Ron remembered periodically attending their meetings just to listen when they'd turn off the TV and make up their own dialogue. They were all funny and it approached critical mass as they interacted around those old movies.

"My advice to younger people is to join brotherhoods and keep in touch. It's so easy for these valuable brotherhoods to get away. However, after fifty years, we're finding it easy to reconnect."

Howard Lee "Hank" Helton
Enterprise, AL

Regrettably, my post-graduate service of 28 years as an American Warrior, retiring in May 1999 with the rank of Lieutenant Colonel in the United States Army, made long-distance relationships virtually impossible to maintain.

I can report that except for answering a recent email from George Otey and sending him a bio for the history, I have had no active contact with any of my Deke Brothers. I devoted so much time and effort acquiring the skills of my trade and then applying those skills in exotic places, encountering interesting people, that I lost contact with almost everyone.

The only thing that could have made it worse was to have been single. However, I was extremely fortunate because Emily Garst (daughter of Elizabeth and John Garst of Healdton, OK) and I were married on our last Saturday at OU, and what a weekend it was!

I was commissioned a Second Lieutenant in the Army Infantry and we both graduated from OU on Sunday, 16 May 1971. I received orders on Monday to report to Fort Bragg on Wednesday. Impossible! (The President gave me a three-day delay in reporting.) Had it not been for Emily turning in and picking up my uniforms at the laundry, doing all the shopping, and handling correspondence with my parents, I would have lost the bubble and contact with the Home Front.

I am a lucky man.

My top memories of the fraternity include the Halloween "Hanging Until…" prank, as well as my on-campus law enforcement and chapter President stints:

Dekes were famous for the annual Halloween Party, especially the lawn decorations during the week leading to the All Saints Eve celebration of ghosts and goblins. A giant spider on a gigantic web and ghosts around the eaves of the house lured many sightseers. Of particularly special interest to me was on the front lawn where we created a "graveyard" of five graves, each with a headstone and a fresh mound of dirt.

In October 1968, I suggested we begin on Monday with a hanging at High Noon followed by the appearance of a grave and continue hangings until Friday Noon. I had devised a rather good harness for appropriate use with a Hangman's Noose, which we could tie to the sturdy oak tree in the front yard on Brooks Street. Each day at Noon, Deke Brothers would drag me out of the House and hang me. I mimicked the best I could the contortions one would experience if really hung.

One Thursday, a doctor from the Infirmary ran across the intersection with his doctor's bag in hand to render life-saving aid to what he had decided was a stunt gone wrong. After he got over his irritation of being fooled, he pronounced me dead, and another grave appeared on the front lawn soon thereafter.

The spectators seemed to think the doctor's participation was part of the act. He had so much fun that he participated with us the remainder of the week.

Circa 1968, O.U. quietly established a degree program in Criminal Justice and intended to use the police department as a laboratory; although, the laboratory part was never implemented. The Department staffed it with state police officers (reserve deputies from Cleveland County), becoming the 5th largest police force in the state.

The presence on Fraternity Row of a uniformed police patrolman equipped with a standard firearm and "a ticket book," and driving a Plymouth 440 Hemi Police Pursuit vehicle did not win the J.D. Power Award for Originality, but neither did it garner a "Darwin Award."

Fortunately for me, DKE interposed no objection to my employment or to my continued residence in the House. On several occasions — principally on Friday and Saturday nights — party guests would react with abject horror as a uniformed police officer entered and was welcomed into the House. No one ever questioned WHY our guests were so shocked — yeah, right.

In 1969, I was given the responsibility of leading the Chapter as its President. There were a heck-of-a–lot of things they didn't tell me when I hired-on with this outfit. Most challenging was leading underclassmen who were searching for an identity during the rise of recreational drugs and who rather often went against the flow.

One Sunday afternoon in Spring 1970, the Deke House was preparing for a reception to honor our new DKE Sweetheart.

With everyone in their "Sunday-best", my Little Brother descended the stairs into the Great Room dressed in shorts. We had a confrontation, which failed to produce the corrective reaction I intended.

He continued to refuse to dress appropriately. Everyone else vigorously defended him and the criticism was simply over-whelming. The realization set in that I had lost the ability to lead my Brothers in DKE.

They were heading in a direction I could not take; so consequently, I resigned, turned-over the reins to Don Burand, and moved out of the House.

Here's some wisdom to share with DKE chapter members:

1. Everything you need to know about how to act in public and get along with people you learned in Kindergarten.

2. You're the product of the choices and decisions you've made.

3. Your parents taught you how to treat women. "No" means "no" and there is no reason for further discussion.

4. Open and hold doors for a woman because you are a gentleman.

5. A gentleman does not comment about the gestational status of a woman unless he has played a participating part.

The true measure of a man is how he treats someone who can do him absolutely no good.
— Samuel Johnson, English writer, moralist, literary critic, biographer, and editor

God has given mankind only 10 rules.

Do the right thing, do it the right way, and do it now.

Don't interfere with something that ain't botherin' you none.

If it don't seem like it's worth the effort, it probably ain't.

Never miss a good chance to shut up.

Stan Germond

We began our discussion about brotherhood with Stan by reviewing those military memoirs we'd recommend to a fellow military man. We agreed the authenticity of the author, given Stan's service in the Navy and ours in the Army, is the key to the success of any such book.

"I've stayed in contact with Cole, Butler, Iseminger and Raleigh. As far as brotherhoods go, I guess I've been in several. Volunteering to coach high school sports is another kind of brotherhood.

"There are 25 million people living within 75 miles of me and even the richer towns are feeling the financial squeeze to build roads, repair infrastructure and field the school sports teams, and they need volunteers. Coaching is a way to bind the social fabric.

"'Why don't you coach soccer?' someone asked me. And my son played hockey so I coached that, too.

"Coaches are a brotherhood. They're all volunteer, they're the same guys doing the same things with mostly the same-age kids. The kids make the same mistakes, the context is the same, the jokes become the same, like any brotherhood. The strength of volunteerism helps create the bonds of community."

Stan and Ron compared notes about the close calls both their wives had had with medical issues. Stan's wife, Marilyn, almost died of a brain aneurysm 18 years ago when she was 57. Columbia Presbeterian Hospital saved her life and she recovered in the Helen Hayes Hospital, both in New York state. The medical episodes of Ron's wife are included previously, in Ron's section titled"Michelle: Redstone and Sequim."

They also discussed the potential contradiction of a book about male-only brotherhoods, in a world of amazing wives and the critical roles that females play in this world.

Richard Legatski
Dagsboro, DE

"I've stayed in contact with Terry Miller. He's been the best man at both of my weddings. We were roommates after Terry came back from the Navy and I was in law school. My first wife, Cathi, and I married when we were both too young and immature, and divorced a few years later.

"I married my second wife, Mary, in 1980 and we had an exceptionally happy marriage until she passed away in 2016. I have been dating a wonderful woman named Laurie with whom I have become very close. We are discussing marriage and probably extensive travel in the years ahead.

"There's a psychological closeness that begins with friendships and deepens to a real closeness in marriage. The bonds of brotherhood are similar, maybe not with everybody, but some of those bonds last a lifetime.

"The guys I met in the house were contemporaries for a time, and that experience helped me feel comfortable with a room full of strangers. I went to grad school, then law school. I got a job in D.C., and had several positions in federal employment. I retired at 56, built a second home in Delaware and that's where I live now. "

"I volunteer for Habitat for Humanity, Food Bank; whatever I can do to help. It's easy to find people in need. Staying constructively occupied is helpful emotionally."

"After Mary's death, talking and being in the company of others, provided the best release from the sense of isolation."

Richard and Ron had a deeper conversation regarding grief and the ways to deal with the death of a beloved wife. Richard's suggestions that Ron stay constructively occupied with volunteer work were welcome and apt.

"I was in ROTC during part of law school at OU, but joined the Army National Guard before I graduated and stayed with the ARNG as I moved to post-grad law school at the University of Washington in Seattle, where I specialized in international ocean and maritime law.

"I was hired after graduation as a direct commission Lieutenant in the Coast Guard, and moved to DC to work for four years in the CG Chief Counsel's office. After that I worked for a few years as a lobbyist on ocean environmental issues, and then moved to NOAA where I stayed until retirement.

"My advice for young men entering college? Look for true friends, not just a party place. True friends will last. But it takes emotional effort, and I worked at it.

"I'm talking to Laurie about visiting the Northwest, I loved the peninsula when I was in Washington state. Ron, maybe we'll come see you."

Gordon Bullivant
Calgary, AB

"I've stayed in contact with several brothers over the years, Butler, Raleigh, Germond and Tom Bradford before he died. I'm in contact with Harry Seck and was invited to his and Margo's (his college sweetheart) 50th wedding anniversary last year.

"Jim Bradford lived with my parents for a while. He took the Canadian bar but I haven't seen him for a long time. The story is that he died in Phoenix." Ron heard they found Jim's car and his arm prosthesis in Arizona, but never found him.

"I do remember Mother Harris. Living in the house was interesting and I remember that the food was good. Look at the skills we developed back then, how we learned as a group to function, and thrive as a community of brothers dedicated to the same ideals.

"I moved out third year. It seemed everyone moved out in the third year. We all enjoyed living in that crazy anthill for a few years but eventually needed some distance.

"In my career, I was a neuropsychologist helping children with learning disabilities. In 1979, I helped create a charity, Foothills Academy (https://www.foothillsacademy.org/about-foothills/our-history) which has raised over $50 million over 40 years for children with learning disabilities, children who are horribly failed in the public system."

"I retired from being the Executive Director and am now Director Emeritus." (Author note by Ron: The charity is elebrated all over the world.)

"I recommend that everyone read *The Lost Boys: Inside Mustafer Sherrif's Robbers Cave Experiment,* a book by Gina Perry, which explores how children find a way to work together. Sherrif was a professor at OU.

"I find that being a grandparent with grandkids ties into brotherhood. We immediately want to show everybody the videos of our wonderful grandkids. When children laugh, they feel relaxed. Then they bond."

Bill Iseminger
Collinsville, IL

"My memories are not just of the social camaraderie. As we matured, we saw how important the relationships were. I stayed in contact with Rich Cole for a while. I'm not a good communicator. I do better when I'm writing.

"Later, Rich was in Oklahoma City and was sent to Eastern Europe doing oil work, helping acquire oil companies for Kerr McGee. I just eventually lost contact, wish I hadn't. We had been roommates in the house and off campus for several years.

"I've kept the most contact with Stan Germond over the years. He visited me when I was in grad school at Southern Illinois University – Carbondale, and he was on his way to grad school at the university of Illinois. I visited him there and went to a football game with him and his new wife, who was pregnant at the time. I also visited him in New Jersey and in Florida when our families were vacationing near each other.

"I've kept in touch with Dave Butler, visiting him a couple of times in Enid when I was traveling that way, and earlier this year in Santa Fe when I was there for an archaeological conference. We all communicate by email occasionally.

"These recent reunions and recontacts are great. I valued the bonding with certain people while at OU. Not everybody bonds, but you learn how to get along with different people."

"You learned how to take care of certain house responsibilities. It is a financial operation like any business. I remember the annual assessments when they'd run short of cash.

"I am an archaeologist, and my career was spent at Cahokia Mounds State Historic Site (which started out as a state park) in Illinois. I am retiring in December after 48 ½ years there.

"I am married to Gloria and have a step-daughter and my oldest grandson is going to be going to Purdue, majoring in computer science. He was valedictorian at his high school. The other grandson is the jock in the family, into hockey and track and is a junior this year.

"When I was a freshman I almost flunked out. The partying and drinking about got me. When I joined DKE, Larry Wade, the Scholastic Chairman, was a big influence, and he kept telling me 'You've got to get your grades up.' He helped me a lot with study skills and I eventually improved.

"It's important to have an organized group (like the Deke house) to belong to. Social skills, learning how to communicate and work with others, social graces, manners, how to hold your fork. Dorms didn't have that.

"The commonality, the shared experiences were helpful to me. I wish I'd maintained the contacts. It gave me a different, valuable perspective on how different people get together and work together."

"The Dekes were a lot more than parties. It was about studying and also having fun with the other guys and getting dates. From my background, my mom was very formal and my dad was an officer in the Corps of Engineers so I knew all the etiquette rules that Mom Harris taught the pledges.

"George Patterson's girlfriend (and later wife), Nancy, would always fix me up with dates. The Deke experience helped me open up socially. Maybe you don't consciously use your social skills but you have them. Skills learned from the house may be unconscious after awhile but they're still there.

"I finally left the house and spent several semesters off-campus but maintained contact with the house and activities. People moved on."

Terry Miller
Cypress, TX

"In the Deke house, we shared something together, even with people who'd come to OU from other schools. One of the things I remember is the bonding with other members and how we adapted to different living arrangements. The Dekes were a kind of support group.

"One of the things I remember is the bonding with guys you normally wouldn't and how interesting they are when you get to know them. I'm still in contact with Legatski. I've been his best man. Twice.

"When I was the kitchen manager I had to fire the cook because she was getting kickbacks from the meat supplier. Brother John Barrett weighed the meat and compared it to the invoices and proved that.

"I was studying in the dining room one day and she came out and asked me if I would help her taste some whipped cream. I did and I said, 'Maybe you should use some sugar instead of salt.' I couldn't find a replacement for her, so we decided to wait until the end of the semester and then I let her go.

"John's parents thought he was backward in school. Once, when he was playing baseball in the outfield, a ball hit his head and they determined he wasn't dense, he just needed glasses. He eventually earned an electrical engineering PhD from Texas A&M."

Ron's memory of John is that he attended classes only for midterms and finals and was a practical genius. Terry and Ron laughed about the trials they'd both experienced as House and Kitchen Managers. The experiences had definitely become valuable life skills.

"I was in the Navy, on a destroyer off Vietnam. We went to Taiwan a couple of times, to Subic Bay, Philippines a few times, Hong Kong for R&R four times but our home port was Yokosuka, Japan. A brotherhood definitely forms on a boat.

"I was founder and first president of the Ship Association for 31 years, a group of Navy veterans. For 16 years, I edited stories for them. Rather than pay me, I asked them to give the money to my favorite charity. I also presided over the organizing of the USS George K MacKenzie DD-836 Association in 2004.

"In 2002 I was named Executive Director of The National Association of Destroyer Veterans, Tin Can Sailors, Inc. I still hold that position. Tin Can Sailors is a charitable corporation founded in 1976 and has 12,000 members who are former U.S. Navy destroyer veterans.

"Randy Morrison was someone who, no matter what he faced, he took it on fully. His death as a Marine combat medic (a Navy Hospital Corpsman) is a sad addition to the Wall."

Ron's note: The stone-cold bravery of combat medics isn't well understood, or appreciated by those outside the military.

378

"I worked for 14 years for Western Union and had four of my friends commit suicide. I feel bad that I was unable to help them.

"Volunteering for things one believes in is a learning experience. I learned a lot as a Deke pledge. Mother Harris taught me that you only oiled the piano with one drop of lemon oil or it would detune the piano.

"When a pledge played bridge with Mother Harris, she'd give each person individually-wrapped candy. I ate mine, put the wrapper in my pocket and then she said, 'You did that perfectly instead of putting it in that ashtray right there.' Those esoteric manners. They all come in handy.

"It was surprising to have Mom Harris attend the "Gross Gift Party" at Christmas. I remember someone giving someone else a bag of '.3875 cubic feet of flatulance.' The brother who'd received it, stepped on it and smashed the bag. Mom Harris was sitting next to him and she left the room.

"Brother Dave Cooper used to tell us that he 'emoted cool.'"

Terry and Ron reminisced about Cooper, who they'd both seen in television commercials.

During Dave's initiation, the members had required that, since he was so cool, he'd be able to carry ice cubes wherever he went and show them to any member who needed to see proof of his coolness. To his credit, he always did.

Bob Pickup
Gulfport, FL

"I don't recollect much other than bad grades, drinking scotch, my presidency and asking for the pot smoking to stop (leading to an exodus of members).

"My dad was an OU grad (class of '36). He talked many Wellsvillians into going there. Streb and I were high school classmates. DKE seemed to be the only house that wanted out-of-staters. I never regretted joining.

"Roundup goes back to George (Otey) and me. Somehow George got my cell number. We visited for a while and conjured up a reunion. Then Burnsie, Clowers and Fred jumped on board, and we were off. Burnsie was huge in the communications department.

"Except for Fred, I had talked to zero brothers in many years. I'm so glad we took the plunge."

Doug Mistler
Cary, NC

"After graduating, I served at Fort Carson. I was in an Army family, my father was in the Artillery and I grew up at Fort Sill (the home of the Artillery) and elsewhere.

"I joined the Artillery and then converted to Military Intelligence. The younger officers in the Military Intelligence branch who had no field experience nor context were at a disadvantage. I'd served a tour in Vietnam as an artillery forward observer prior to that and had that skill set to bring to the intelligence service.

"At one time in Vietnam I was with a battalion of Vietnamese Marines chasing the NVA back into Cambodia. We were once ambushed six times in one day.

"Delta Kappa Epsilon was like puberty: huge changes socially but we were learning how to become not buddies but brothers with wildly different people. Life lessons. My little brother was Joel Ketonen.

"At OU I worked in a Biology office maintaining the vault records for grain alcohol (Everclear - the basis of Purple Passion). "I would periodically be required to get rid of some of it because the professors would grab half a bottle and sign out for one entire one so I was told periodically to "get rid of the overage" and somehow it found its way to the Deke house."

381

"I regret I've lost touch with many from the house but it might have had something to do with the 'closed' sign on the Deke house in 1973. That might have convinced some brothers that they'd be trying to keep in contact with a lost tribe of the 70s, almost as if our fraternity had been officially closed.

"The Deke house was a formative experience that occurred during the time of life when you're changing, so the bonds were deep. You learned how to live with people from different backgrounds, different religions. I fell away from most of my brothers but I still have my Deke pin.

"One learns permanent values far beyond the contents of school. Life lessons, like 'Duty, Honor, Country, which apply to everyone in the military. The military builds character; that's a fact.

"After I retired from the military, I worked as an intelligence analyst. I started my own company and sold it 20 years later. I still have my clearances.

"I was rock climbing and fell 40 feet breaking my back and pelvis. I'm partially paralyzed and I walk with a cane.

"I'm writing a book now, too, with a neurology physician's assistant ,on managing the medical problems caused by my fall. The first draft is 360 pages. My book is for older persons, caregivers, doctors, nurses; it's a topic 'not discussed' because it's too intimate."

"My book started out as notes to myself, but I just kept at it as a mental health project. More on this when I publish.

"These days, I live in senior housing with professors and doctors, so it's a very stimulating environment. It's a different kind of brotherhood here."

Bill Nation
Germantown, TN

An Easy Friendship

"One of the longest running relationships I have in the house
is with George Otey, of course. I'm also a Tulsa native and I
have family there, so George is about the only guy that I saw
over the years from the house.

"Tierno and Streb and Pickup, I call them some of my
longest running relationships, too, because ten years ago or
so when we first started talking about reunions, it was like we
just picked right up where we'd left in college. We know each
other so well. And obviously we haven't changed that much.
Those are good relationships. They're just an easy friendship.

"You come out of high school, you're basically a community of
one, after trying to get through all the battles of the hormones
and the age-related issues. And you think you're the only one
who feels this way. Then you go through rush.

"After going through rush, and not really understanding it
then, but looking back on it the reason I was drawn to the
house was just that people were different. They weren't all the
same. It wasn't Todd, Todd, Todd and Todd. We had the good
classic southerners from South Oklahoma, we had upscale
guys from California, it was all so different and I wanted that,
that kind of culture to broaden my perception of the world. It
really provided that."

"My memories of the house were, of course, parties, they were the big time events. But the initiation sticks out to me because of the effort it takes and at the end of it, there's the acceptance. The band of Brothers. Just becoming one with all. It was quite a life-changing experience for me."

The Student Store

"The other thing that really stands out for me was the work that Tierno and I did with the student services. After putting it all together and getting the actual nonprofit going for us and getting the store going, that was kick starting it. When Bobby left, I took over.

"I inherited all of it and began building the rental programs, and got into just about everything that we could do from fans, rugs, bicycles, and refrigerators. The big one that came along, the really neat, new, tremendous technology called calculators. It was cool buying those $600 HP's and then after that came the engineering model. We made a bundle off those.

"I majored in two academic fields, finance and economics. I filled out majors on both of them. I was going to become a stockbroker, but my advisor, who was the Dean of Finance in the early 70s when the stock market was tanking, said, 'Listen, there's no future in it. The market will never come back. You ought to think about something else.'

"But the grounding I got from doing this stuff with student services whetted my appetite for retail."

"It was a great thing because I carried that all the way to the Board of Directors with Kroger's. I had a great run.

"I think it was because we had fun with it. I think that's what propelled a lot of success."

Risk Takers

"What pearls would I tell young freshmen? I'd tell them, 'One of the most important things in life is friends are forever.' You can bond with the guys and they will always be there for you. That's one of the major factors I got. All of those friends will make you richer in your soul because they will all be so different and you will learn from that difference.

"We had gathered a neat collection of them at the Deke house. My thought was, we were a bunch of risk takers. I learned from the risk takers. I mean we're all different, seriously. We have different attitudes, different aspects, different outlooks, we tried different things. That, I think, was an empowerment I took away from living with the men in the house.

"If I was speaking to would-be pledges I'd say the house was and should be a place where it's OK to have different opinions. And living together will teach you that it's OK. You can disagree. It's OK to be different. Have different ideas. It's not damaging. And it's not against the laws of nature .

"The experience of living with those who think differently will broaden yours. I think that's a very, very important lesson."

Don Burand
Anchorage, AK

"Brothers Bob and Ron, I have thought very often about how I would like to relate my experiences as a Brother in D.K.E. This book that you are compiling is just the catalyst that I needed to try to collect some of these thoughts. I hope my contribution is worthy. I hope to be in attendance at the Roundup this year. I may be sidelined due to doctor's orders.

"So here goes…My desire to be a pilot and my love of aviation had brought me to this point. Though it would be a few moments until I would learn what 'this point' was.

"My first officer, (co-pilot), is Christopher Dahl. A man who is impossibly young for what he has already seen in his lifetime. Chris grew up in a tiny place called Cold Bay, Alaska. He had started his life as a productive member of society by being a deck hand on a commercial fishing vessel. It was a demanding and difficult life, hauling salmon from one of the most productive wild salmon fisheries on the planet, Bristol Bay.

"Chris learned two things from this early experience, 1) fishing paid very well, and 2) the work was much too difficult and there must be a better way to make a living.

"Chris decided to take his earnings and invest in a dream. He bought a piper Cherokee, (the very same type aircraft that I soloed in when I was twenty years old)."

387

"Next, he hired a flight instructor. Our paths to becoming flight officers for Alaska Airlines had been quite different, yet here we were, some thirty thousand feet above the Alaska tundra headed to a place called Bethel, occasionally referred to as the "Paris of the Kuskoquim."

"Chris and I always enjoyed flying together, and we had done so dozens of times over the last few years. As we approached our destination, I called ahead to the station operations folks and reminded them that I would be leaving the airport property for a few minutes to get a pizza for the crew.

"Moments later, Chris spke out of the clear blue and said, 'Don, you are a gentleman and a scholar,' to which I replied, without missing a beat, *'and* a jolly good fellow, but not necessarily in that order!'

"A few seconds lapsed until Chris, his eyes a bit wider than moments before, said, 'Don, are you a Deke?'

"'I am,' I replied, 'how did you know?' And that was how I met my first DKE brother from another chapter, some forty years after my initiation into the brotherhood at Rho Lambda.

"My experiences as a Deke have many punctuation points, and it is a very difficult choice finding the ones to memorialize into print. But as I look back, I can remember that some parts of the journey were very significant to me. The first was the realization that I had 'made' it."

388

"The headiness of this realization was still spinning in my brain as I stepped out of the back door of 700 Elm St, into the parking lot and the crisp, cool air of a spring morning in 1969, … and saw my father.

"It was the last thing I expected at that moment.

"My dad had not encouraged me to become a fraternity member. In fact, he had done his best to dissuade me from even going to college. It was his choice that I go to a Vo-Tech (Vocational – Technical) school of some kind, since he viewed college as a waste of time.
"Imagine my shock that only moments after being presented the Diamond Pin of Brotherhood by no less than the National President of Delta Kappa Epsilon, I am looking into the eyes of my father, and he is inviting me to breakfast! It was an amazing moment for me, and one that, for a while, brought me closer to my dad than I had ever thought possible.

"I think we went to Denko's, since it was the only place I knew would be open on a Sunday morning.

"Not long after initiation I was made Rush Chairman for the upcoming summer and following school year. (I would go on to serve as rush chairman for two full years.) I was able to parlay this position into permission to stay in the chapter house during times when it was normally closed to occupation, specifically the long winter break between semesters, and the summer.

"I was the sole occupant of the house, when I met two brothers whom I will always remember, but for very different reasons. The first was Stan Tubbs.

"Stan showed up one cold night during the semester break. He was on his way home to Sapulpa, OK, a town south of Tulsa. Since it was late, he was hoping to find a place to bed down for the night. He had seen cars in the parking lot and a light inside, and knocked on the door hoping to be welcomed in.

"My good friend Jerry Keating and I were in the basement watching TV when we heard the knock. Stan introduced himself and then made the offer to 'liven up the party' by supplying a few bottles of single malt scotch. I had no knowledge of what 'single malt' meant, but I knew well the concept of 'free,' so Stan was welcome. To this day, the smell of single malt scotch makes me nauseous.

"It was a similar circumstance that brought me to meet another Brother.

"I was staying in the chapter house over the summer break when a stranger showed up asking if he could spend the night. He introduced himself as Randy Morrison. Randy said he was about to 'ship out' to Viet Nam. I was glad for the company, and happy to meet another Brother, even if it was just to be for a short time. We visited late into the night, talking about 'stuff,' though I can't recall just what 'stuff' included. I did learn that he had a girl, and he was looking forward to getting the 'Nam thing behind him and getting on with life."

"The next morning was the last time I would see Brother Randy.

"We sent another Deke to 'Nam shortly after my initiation, Brother Ron Sorter. I think it may be the fact that Ron did return to us still alive, though badly broken, that added to the elation of his return.

"I will always remember the night that several of us went to Will Rogers World Airport in Oklahoma City to welcome Ron home. He landed in a Braniff 727, significant only in that the aircraft had an aft stairway, which allowed us to enter the airplane and help Ron from the jet.

"I remember that we partied that night in Norman at one of our favorite watering holes, rejoicing the evening away, glad that he had returned alive.

"We had several Brothers, who like myself, had chosen to join R.O.T.C. The motivations for this action were probably as varied as the number of Brothers who had done so. Mine was quite specific. I wanted to be a pilot, and I knew that my one most likely path to that end would be through the military.

"Some used R.O.T.C. as a way to avoid the draft. That evening the first Draft Lottery was conducted, many of us assembled in the basement to watch the drawing of the numbers on TV. Brother Fred Streb showed up that evening with a couple of six-packs and proclaimed that he had decided to "take (his) chances" with the lottery and had resigned from R.O.T.C."

"It was his intention to watch the lottery, with the aid of his domesticated beverages, until his number was called. His was the first number chosen!

"We would learn that the next day Brother Fred asked for and received reinstatement into Army R.O.T.C. Brother Fred finished a career with the Army, just as many of us would do with our military experiences.

"I have many fond memories from the days in 'the house.' I remember that there were the non-stop card games, (your choice of Pinochle or Bridge), mixers, parties, and 'The Undertakers.'

"Among my favorite memories was our participation in 'The University Sing.' Brother David (Butler?) announced one night in Chapter that he believed we could win the competition and that he had a plan.

"Where most competing groups followed the 'boiler plate' format of choir-style grouping, with semi-formal attire and carefully rehearsed show tunes, Brother David proposed that we go against the grain, (now considered thinking outside-the-box), and put forth a remarkably different show.

"On the day of the performance we Deke's showed up in blue jeans and cotton shirts, to the obvious disdain of the other competitors. However, less than halfway through our presentation of Petula Clark's 'Downtown,' when we broke into a bugaloo dance step, the audience was wowed!"

392

"The finale was our rendition of 'Ain't Nothin' Like a Dame' from the musical *South Pacific*. We won the competition hands down.

"My mother was in the audience and she told me later that she was so embarrassed for us when we came out on stage looking so ragged and out of place, but that she was as proud as she could be when we stole the show with our animated performance!

"What wisdom would I share from the fraternity experience with brothers of a newer generation? That could be another book!

"For me, being a part of the shared experience that was fraternity put me a giant step ahead when the time came for me to face the various challenges of life. In fact, that very word challenge is important to how I have developed my attitude about life.

"Many people, when confronted with a difficult situation, are likely to identify it as 'a problem.' For me, calling something a problem, implies that there may not be a solution. I prefer to use the word challenge, because that means a solution just has not yet been found."

Kerothen,

Don Burand
Rho Lambda '72

Richard Burns
Denver, CO

"I didn't go through rush week. I'd met Bob Bradford in the Young Republicans and he invited me over to the Deke house for dinner. Bob had a couple of brothers who were Dekes, too.

"I was kind of introverted so the house of brothers really made an impression on me. It became important to me.

"I think the Deke house was unusual since it was a collection of guys from a lot of different places and were all different kinds of people.

"Serving our times in the military probably helped us drift apart, too. Life gets in the way. Clowers and I were best friends in the house and he and I've kept in contact.

"Streb and I would reconnect every 8-10 years but Dennis and I kept in communication over the years."

I mentioned that each of the brothers I've interviewed for this book had commented on the value of the spreadsheet of contact information Burnsie had put together for use with the recent reunions.

"I asked him about who and what had driven the reunions which have been so welcomed by the brotherhood, especially the reconnections between brothers made possible after such a long diaspora."

"George Otey spoke to Bob Pickup and they first talked about a reunion. Then Pickup called Clowers and Clowers called me. I really jumped in the middle of it to repay what had had such a big effect on my life. I'm a petroleum engineer and I know spreadsheets. So I made a simple one for contact information.

"That was easy. Tracking down the brotherhood was the effort. To locate everyone, to find the communication threads. There were several brothers who didn't respond to email so I called them and got a surprising amount of information by asking them to come to the reunions. Those personal connections are more powerful than an email.

"I do like to hear about the connections that have happened because of the spreadsheet that has come out of the reunion idea."

I told him how his comments fit perectly with the book Bob and I are writing about brotherhoods, about our original connections at the Deke house, and how the recent connections between brothers who are sharing such meaningful times together again. He was humble about that, saying the work wasn't such a big thing.

The thing that troubled him the most was collecting personal contact data which might be shared without a brother's approval, so for several years he shared it only when necessary but eventually, after explaining the context and asking for input from the brotherhood about the situation, it was finally decided to share it.

It's been a good thing, a powerful thing. Not only to enable brothers to reconnect with those they haven't heard from in fifty years but to create a digital chapter room, in a way, where topics of every kind can be discussed, as if it were yesterday.

Thank you, Burnsie, for your part in that.

Dave Johnson
Tulsa, OK

"My law career has taken me, via the Air Force as a AFJAG, to Thailand, then back to Tulsa where I joined an energy company, Cities Service Company, as a corporate attorney. An assignment with the company was with a subsidiary in Brazil for three years. I returned to Tulsa, where I've lived to this day.

"After ten years with Cities, the company was acquired by Occidental Petroleum and I left to start my own law practice. Some years ago, I joined BoescheMcDermott law firm and have continued my career with the firm.

"I have stayed in contact with a number of Rho Lambda Dekes including George Patterson and Jim Mullen. Interestingly, Harry Seck and I have ended up being next door neighbors!

"Randy Morrison was my pledge brother. We were good friends." Ron told Dave that he has a rubbing of Randy's name from The Wall and that, after returning from Vietnam, the house gave him the Randy S. Morrison Award, which he treasures. Randy and Ron were friends, too.

"I think one of the reasons the Deke house closed is that almost everyone had a military duty after graduating which distanced them physically from Norman and the house. At the time we did not have the easy and quick modes of communication like email and FaceBook."

"There were insufficient local alums to keep up any momentum that had been built to keep the house going, and if my memory serves me correctly, the house faced another cycle of the Greek Community becoming somewhat unpopular during the Vietnam period.

"In any event, it's my thought that the house did not exist long enough for an alumni group to reach family and economic stability where the resources of time and money were available to make it work when a downturn, for any reason occurred. Also, unfortunately, life events have a way of unplugging relationships.

"When I was President, the house was divided into two groups: one was serious about their scholarship, about graduating and partying wasn't the main goal. The other group felt the opposite: that a good party and bending rules was the priority and good grades needed to be sufficient to remain in school.

"Both groups had folks that cared deeply about the house, the philosophies were just different. The tension between both groups played out every day. Looking back, I would wish that more effort could have gone into finding a better blend of approaches."

"There are others that deserve to be in the history if someone has not already brought them to your attention. Bob Rose was the house president when I pledged. I had the privilege of spending a lot of time with him and learned so much."

"He was a great mentor for many and always had a positive word of encouragement. He was the stability of the house for the time that he was in Norman. Similarly, Jim Ellis cared greatly about the house and was always available to younger members with advice and a kind word.

"Mom Harris was the person who held the house together year after year and president after president. She had the 'institutional memory', a wealth of contacts in the Greek System and was respected by the University Administration and could pick up the phone and call any alum.

"She taught several generations the advantages of good etiquette and manners, and turned more than one pledge into a gentleman. With a laugh, I have to say that it took more than the pledge year for some of us!"

Author note: Dave was President when Ron's theft of the concrete lions blew up into such an embarrassing episode. During this interview Ron told Dave how much he regretted all the facetime Dave had suffered with the Dean because of his actions. Dave had gravitas with the Dean so Ron is convinced his intervention, with a promise of a written confession from Ron for the Dean's files, helped him be able to remain at OU.

Of course, Ron is also convinced that Dave was not only one of the best presidents our house has ever had, he's never heard anyone say different.

Definition Of A College Prank (Ron Sorter)

In early 1965, Ron Sorter's two dorm roommates and fellow
Deke pledges Jim and Alex were cruising the "most desired
area of OKC," Quail Creek, where they discovered a pair of
concrete rampant lions, lions with alternate paws up in the air.
They being the symbol of the Dekes, they were duly
appropriated, their weighty mass bottoming out the springs of
Bud's Chevy all the way back to Norman.

They were quickly installed on the front porch of the Deke
house, but not before the right paw of one was broken off. It
was used by another brother for a paperweight. Soon, those
lions were stolen off the front porch.

Shortly thereafter, Ron and a few other Deke pledges were
driving to a restaurant in west Norman and saw identical lions
on the porch of an expensive home. With the same paw broken
off. "These people stole our lions!"

Ron returned to the Deke house, got the paperweight paw,
sneaked up to the porch holding the lions and...it didn't fit.
Not even close. How could that be?

Separately, the Norman police raided a party at an apartment
complex in east Norman and, in the process, discovered two
lions, one missing a right paw. Aha. Remember the house in
west Norman?

The owner had finally filed a complaint: Grand Larceny.

400

The lions had cost him over $500. He had the receipt. The busted party guys said, 'No way, we're innocent, we didn't steal the lions from that guy, we stole them from the Deke House.'

Detectives visited the Deke house president. The President visited with Ron on the second floor, by the bulletin board:

I remember it like it was yesterday. The Prez is pre-law. "Here's the deal," he says, "if you don't confess, the entire house gets drawn into this. You need to save the house by proving you stole those lions from wherever you stole them from. Do you agree?" I swallowed. He was right.

Here I am, by myself, at the door of the fancy house in north OKC where we, I, stole the concrete lions. I've had to tell my family what I did.

I had to write a confession for the Dean of OU for him to keep in my file until I graduate. Or not, if the owner of this house wants to send me to jail. My commission, my entire future is on the line. I knock on the door and face my doom.

A woman answers. I tell her my story, she listens then walks away and a man returns with her, an important, rich-looking man. "Tell him," she instructs me. I do.

He doesn't say anything for a while. Then he says, "It must have been tough for you to come here and tell us. You get points for that."

"If my insurance hadn't recompensed us for those lions, I probably wouldn't be saying this, but let's say this is a lesson learned for you. I won't press charges. Now you better leave."

I did.

The Norman detectives confirmed the above and I was free.

The college boy becomes a college man ,and Dave Johnson had a hand in that transformation. Brotherhood.

Appendix

A Brief History of Rho Lambda of Delta Kappa Epsilon
By George Otey, PΛ '73

We'll Sing to Phi and Rho Lambda
And Dear Old Delta Kappa Epsilon

Founding

In the spring of 1951, a group of men living at Oklahoma University's Whitehand Hall won both University Sing and Sooner Scandals, student talent shows where Greek lettered societies traditionally garnered the trophies.

The experience solidified a deeper bond among them, sparking enthusiasm to affiliate with an organization not already on campus. Banding together as the Charter Club, they pursued Delta Kappa Epsilon.

The club adopted Rho Lambda as their Greek name and were subsequently recognized by the University's Interfraternity Council.

By 1953, Rho Lambda's membership included Howard W. Byars, Morris L. Dunlap, Riley G. Goldsmith, Roger A. Hansen, Jerry L. Johnston, Howard L. McMillan, Mike Sandlin, George L. Scott, J. F. Van Ryder, and Jerry Wood; the officers being: Howard Byars, President; Howard McMillan, Vice President; Roger Hansen, Secretary; Morris Dunlap, Treasurer; and George Scott, Social Chairman.

They secured an accommodating structure at 701 DeBarr Ave (see above), and employed the services of Mrs. Isla "Mom" Harris as Housemother.

Chartering

By 1953, the men of Rho Lambda believed a foundation existed for recognition as a chapter of Delta Kappa Epsilon.

Morris Dunlap, Riley Goldsmith, Howard McMillan, and Mike Sandlin traveled to Deke's 109th convention being held December 28-30, 1953 at the Royal York Hotel in Toronto, Canada. There the Rho Lambda delegation presented its formal petition bearing a dedication to Dan C. Kenan (ΓΦ, '15) [former Mayor of the City of Okmulgee, OK] with support from Howard Taber (Φ '49), a Deke alum living in the state, and Oppie Watson (ΩΧ '28), known as Mr. Deke of the Southwest. The faculty sponsor for the group was OU history professor Donnell M. Owings, (ΨΦ '34).

Rho Lambda received approval of its application to become the 63rd Chapter of Delta Kappa Epsilon at the convention which had just installed the Honorable George A. Drew (ΑΦ '17) as the fraternity's 28th Honorary President.

Following acceptance, Rho Lambda was officially chartered on February 21, 1954 with the 16 Petitioners being: George Dooley, Morris Dunlap, Riley Goldsmith, Roger Hansen, Ronald Holcomb, Cleo Maddox, Howard McMillan, Byron Parker, Charles Sanders, Malcolm Sandlin, Bob Scott, George Scott, Brady Stewart, O. A. Thomas, Preston Trimble, and John Woody. The Chapter's first pledge following acceptance was James Howard.

700 Elm

In the fall of 1956, Rho Lambda seized the opportunity to move to a more suitable location by purchasing the former Tri-Delt house at 700 Elm.

Located at the corner of Brooks and Elm, on the West side of the OU campus, the house allowed the brotherhood to be centered within the north Greek community and provided higher visibility for the Chapter.

The three-story red brick Dutch Colonial Revival style, included a full basement and space for expansion.

Facing Elm Street, the structure was visually pleasing from the street with the west half of the front façade being covered with English ivy which provided year-round green foliage.

Upon entering the house, to the right was the dining room with hardwood floors and chandeliers.

On the walls was a partial set of the striking panoramic wallpaper called "Views of North America."

To safeguard the wallpaper at the Deke house, someone painted the walls with a clear lacquer. Unfortunately, this had the reverse effect of permanently discoloring it.

The Placid '50s and '60s

As the 25th fraternity at OU, Deke was one of the youngest Greek houses on campus.

The Chapter wasted little time living up to Founder Jacobs' characterization of a Deke being a "gentleman, scholar, and jolly good-fellow."

By 1958, the house had grown to 55 members and pledges. Deke's campus leaders included: Sherrill Whitten, OΔK; Jerry Duncan, TBΠ Honorary Engineering Society; Derrill Whitten, OΔK, TBΠ, and BMOC; Rick Kingelin, OU varsity baseball; Bill Whitaker, OU Rifle Team; Randy Robbins, OU varsity tennis team; Walter Milligan, Convair Air Cadet Award; and Tim Miller, a Westminster fellowship recipient. During this period Max Weitzenhoffer and Larry Wade joined Deke. Larry and Max eventually represented Rho Lambda on the Deke Council before Deke changed its governing structure.

Both Max (a Tony Award-winning producer in New York and London) and Larry (editor of the Elk City newspaper) became members of the OU Board of Regents with each serving in the capacity of chairman. Max was named one of six Oklahoma Living Treasures in 2006. Founder Preston Trimble was elected as District Attorney for Cleveland County and later District Court Judge through the 1980s.

Under the leadership of Brothers Jim Burdett and Walt Millington, the house created an award winning comedy troupe called "The Undertakers" which became a sought after act especially for Sooner Scandals. The cast of five dressed in black suits, white shirts, black bow-ties, and black derbies with one member holding an open umbrella. Taking inspiration from a televised Ernie Kovak skit, they developed a series of mime-like skits lasting approximately two to three minutes. With dead-pan looks, the Undertakers went about the macabre business of finding a person (inevitability their victim) in need of their mortuary services. The Undertakers were active on campus until 1972.

The Chapter continued to round itself with a variety of social events including an annual Founder's Day banquet, spring and fall formals (eventually merged into an annual Deke Diamond Formal), the traditional Prohibition party (later renamed the St. Valentine's Day Massacre Party), a Western Days BBQ, and the Morbid Meal and Reincarnation Ball (the last two eventually combined into the Graveyard Party).

The Tumultuous '70s

The college scene at OU remained sedate and seemingly unchanged from the 1950s and well into the 1960s but by the end of the 1960s, changes occurring on college campuses around the nation finally caught up to OU. The Greek system, long recognized as a bastion of traditional college life, found itself a not so subtle target of those demanding social change and seeking to uproot "the Establishment." Fraternities found themselves caught in the middle of this culture war and Rho Lambda was no different.

The years 1966-70 were a watershed for the Chapter. In 1966 Mom Harris retired and Mrs. Ouwita "Mom" Moran assumed the task as housemother. Also that year Dr. Owings retired and Professor Charles C. Suggs replaced him as the Chapter's faculty adviser, remaining in that position until the Chapter's demise. Professor Suggs' tie to Rho Lambda was strengthened as his son Charles Suggs, II and later his nephew Tom Norman both joined Deke. In a gesture of support, Dr. Suggs, a Sigma Chi, spent hours hand crafting a Deke and a Rho Lambda crest both of which were works of art.

The 1966 Distinguished Air Force Cadet went to Brother Dave Johnson, a recognized BMOC.

While other fraternities on campus fit a "cookie-cutter" mold of Greek houses, Rho Lambda accentuated its difference by reflecting Deke's tradition of strong individualism. This leadership characteristic was exemplified by Rob Stites, OΔK and BMOC, and Hank Helton, a campus police officer, who held the presidency of the RUF/NEKS, the nation's oldest male pep organization which is responsible for driving the iconic Sooner Schooner at football games. Additionally, Deke was diversified for its day, being the only fraternity on campus open to Jews, except the Jewish fraternities.

Until 1968 Rho Lambda leaned heavily on out-of-state recruitment because of Deke's international prominence. In 1968, largely due to the efforts of Rush Chairman David Cooper, Rho Lambda's numbers grew when over 20 pledged, most coming from Oklahoma.

In the spring of 1969, the symbolism of initiating 15 new brothers (the largest class since the Founders) during the 15th anniversary of Rho Lambda's founding, was not lost on the brotherhood and served as an encouragement that serious growth of the Chapter was eminent. With the new initiates scheduled to move into 700 Elm, over the summer of 1969 the entire backyard was converted to a paved parking lot for the burgeoning house. The 1968 success was amplified when the 1969-70 pledge classes grew to nearly 40 men, mostly from Oklahoma.

In the fall of 1969, things appeared to be going extremely well. All rooms in the house were filled with 40 members, the new parking lot was nearly filled to capacity, the Chapter had a 30-man pledge class, there were another 15-20 active upper-class members living in apartments, Dekes had a number of recognized campus leaders, and Deke International had recognized the creation of the first chapter of "Deke Little Sisters."

Deke was about to get caught in the culture war of the 1960-70, centered on the anti-war movement, demands for social and political changes, and an overall anti-Greek feeling on campus. Although other fraternities were experiencing the same pangs, Deke's youthfulness proved a disability with a small alumni base and a large number of out-or-state members.

Many fraternity members attended OU on military ROTC scholarships. Rho Lambda was no different. But larger political and social issues became internalized and controversy over house social and political policies arose late in the spring semester of 1970 and remained unresolved through summer rush.

That fall Deke attracted only 10 pledges. Nevertheless Dekes continued to bring leadership laurels to the house when Bill Millar served as president of the RUF/NEKS, Bob Pickup was OΔK, and Bob Tierno was OΔK and BMOC. Dissension continued, ultimately leading many brothers to leave the house mid-year at the end of fall semester 1970 and no longer participated in fraternal activities.

411

This had a negative impact on summer rush. At the beginning of the fall semester 1971 the Chapter attracted fewer than 10 pledges. Yet Deke continued to provide leadership for the campus when Brother T. Ramsey Cantrell became president of ΑΦΩ service fraternity, and Brothers Bob Tierno and Bill Nation started the Student Store.

While news media focused on war protests, radicalized racial relations with the emergent Black Panthers, a burgeoning feminist movement, and the birth of environmentalism, little attention was paid to the student's rights movement with its demands for curriculum changes for "relevant" courses and more student participation and decision-making power in both policy and everyday campus life.

Believing students empowered at a grassroots level provided more valuable life skills than protesting, a number of Dekes decided to venture into the area of direct student involvement. The idea was simple: be radical but not revolutionary; as such, developing a student owned and run business providing student jobs and offering merchandise priced to assist limited budgets. The Student Store was born.

Beginning in the Fall of 1970, Brothers Bob Tierno and Bill Nation began working with the OU Student Association to obtain the necessary $10,000 investment and use empty space in the University's Muldrow Tower at Adams Hall. Many Dekes, led by Fred Streb, volunteered hundreds of man hours to build out the facility. After months of promotion and publicity, the Store opened on March 29, 1971 with Brother Tierno as store manager assisted by Brother Nation.

Brother Nation brought on Brother Rick Hagar as the accountant. Despite lack of support from the School of Business, the Store became an overnight success, selling sodas, snacks, and study aids as well as renting refrigerators, calculators, and bicycles.

By September 1971, the Store had grossed over $50,000. When the Store obtained a license to sell beer University officials intervened even though private vendors sold beer at the Student Union. Brother Tierno used the situation to negotiate better terms for the OUSA with the University.

A snack bar and grill was eventually added (with Brothers Dennis Caufield and Mike Shipman being the cooks) and in the spring of 1972 Brother Bill Nation expanded to a satellite location at Ellison Hall, catty-corner to the Deke House, which served a breakfast of an egg, a piece of toast and two pieces of bacon for a dollar. Although Deke's committed participation in the Store's success was recognized across the campus, it was not enough to overcome anti-Greek sentiments and did not translate into attracting rushees.

From 1970, the declining pledge numbers resulted in an inability to keep the house sufficiently occupied and ultimately made it impossible to keep the doors open. Mom Moran retired in the spring of 1972, her replacement being Mrs. Margaret "Mom" Lester. At the start of the spring semester 1973, Mom Lester resigned; there were approximately 20 active members remaining on campus with only 6 brothers continuing to live in the house.

Another Deke emerged in a campus leadership role when Al Sherer was elected as President of the RUF/NEKS. Unable to attract more than a handful of pledges, that semester alumni informed the brotherhood of the impending sale of the house at the end of the school year. In an ironic twist, Deke's overall academic rating at the end of spring 1973 was No. 1 on campus toppling Beta Theta Pi from its long held monopoly.

The 1973-74 school year marked the demise of Rho Lambda. Not wanting to disband and hoping for some revival, four remaining brothers rented a house on the corner of Flood Ave. and Lindsey Street. The rolls continued to reflect about 15 "active" members, all upperclassmen. The location, five blocks from campus, held no attraction for potential pledges. The Chapter continued at that site until a fire over Christmas break destroyed the structure. The members then moved into separate apartments and the fraternity ceased to exist. Its memorabilia was ultimately sent to Deke Headquarters.

Rejuvenation

704 West Lindsey

A short-lived three year rejuvenation occurred from 1990 to 1993. A group of men, disenchanted with efforts to recolonize the Acacia fraternity, turned to Deke in the spring of 1990. The brothers resided at 704 W. Lindsey (corner of West Lindsey St. and Chautauqua Ave.) and decorated it with composites and crests returned from Deke Headquarters.

Although located on the fringes of Greek housing the brothers asserted their presence by volunteering to assist with the Special Olympics' regional competition held at Norman High.

The brothers hosted monthly parties from September through April, opening the festivities to the campus while complying with the IFC policy against uninvited guests. This reinforced Rho Lambda's commitment to promote a diversified membership. Although one of the smallest houses on campus, the fraternity expanded to include men from Malaysia, Canada, Nigeria, Germany, France, Taiwan as well as having Latino, Cherokee, Cheyenne-Arapaho, Shawnee, and Native-Alaskan backgrounds.

Deke welcomed Christians, Jews, Atheists, and Taoists seeing the open exchange of ideas and cultures as nothing more than a real life application of the fraternity's fundamentals expressed in the Objects.

Isolated by geography from other Deke chapters the brothers made unsuccessful attempts to connect with Dekes at Kappa Delta at Louisiana Tech and Omega Chi at Texas.

Yet one of the most satisfying events occurred in September 1991 when a group of Sigma Alpha Dekes traveled from Blacksburg, VA to Norman to see Virginia Tech take on the Sooners at Owen Field (OU won 27-17).

For the visiting brothers, Rho Lambda rolled out the red carpet, quickly covering it with plastic to shield it from spillage when it became obvious that fraternal bonds were turning the weekend into a long revelry, the stories of which are mercifully perishing with the fog of memory.

In 1992, the chapter allowed its lease at 704 W. Lindsey to expire and Rho Lambda again faded from campus due to an inability to sustain membership.

Roundup Reunions

In the spring of 2013 upon learning of the chartering of Omega Mu Chapter at Oklahoma State University, a call went out to Rho Lambda alums to meet in Norman for the inaugural Rho Lambda Roundup reunion at the upcoming fall homecoming football game. The Friday night before the game, 14 brothers with their spouses met for dinner.

Brother Fred Streb, acting as emcee, presented awards of recognition with Brother Dennis Clowers receiving the Ron Sorter Rho Lambda "Goal Post" Award. The "Goal Post" is a segment of a Cotton Bowl goal post from the 1956 OU-Texas game bearing the score: OU-45 Texas-0. It hung in Ron Sorter's room at 700 Elm, until he left for Vietnam.

It graced a basement wall at the house until its mysterious disappearance in 1973, only to resurface at the 2013 Rho Lambda Roundup along with a letter from Brother Sorter.

As alums from around the country journeyed to Norman, old friendships were revived and new ones made when 12 men from Omega Mu traveled from Stillwater to Norman for introductions and participated in the tailgate before the game. The successful 2013 gathering has resulted in annual Roundups since then.

The 2014 Roundup marked the 60th anniversary of the chartering of Rho Lambda. The Friday gathering drew nearly 30 alums, many with their spouses, along with Deke's Executive Director Doug Lanpher, Deke alumni from other chapters, and representatives of Omega Mu.

Founder Howard McMillan attended, and received a standing ovation. Brother McMillan and Executive Director Lanpher both made remarks with the evening festivities closing as Brother Richard Burns received the Ron Sorter Goal Post Award.

One of the highlights of the reunion came the next day when 30 Omega Mu brothers traveled from Stillwater to Norman and hosted a tailgate for the alums at 700 Elm.

The reunion of Dekes from each era of Rho Lambda's existence combined with meeting the brothers from Omega Mu underscored the fraternity's open motto *Kerothen Philoi Aei*.

Letter from a Battalion Commander

(Editor Note: A Light Infantry Battalion typically consists of 920 soldiers when fully staffed and has four rifle companies. 1st Lt. Sorter was the commanding officer of Charlie Company, a unit of the 1st Battalion, 20th Infantry, aka Sykes' Regulars. The battalion was then commanded by Lt. Col. Gordon Lynch)

28 November, 1970

Dear Ron:

It was wonderful to hear from you and to know that your spirits are high, they are treating you the way you should be treated and that your wounds are doing well.

Charlie Company is indeed driving on. They CA'd north of Big Red the day before Thanksgiving with an RF company and two PF platoons. The results have been unbelievable.

Everyone is focused on cleaning up eastern Mo Duc with an enthusiasm and spirit of cooperation I've never seen before. We've killed 44, captured 122 VC/VCI and had 10 Chieu Hoi's, really since the 15th of November. Also we've taken 20 tons of rice, AK's, M-16s, pistols and documents by the pounds. The men have really caught on to "hole hunting."

Today, a new E-7 came into Charlie Co. His name is SFC Boyd. He served with you at Ft. Carson and was anxious to do so again. He sends his regards, as do all those you served so well.

Believe it or not, all the rifle companies are up to TOE strength and we've gotten in a number of senior NCOs as platoon sergeants and now have some E6's as squad leaders.

My orders came down last week, I'll be turning over the battalion on or about 14 December to person unknown at this time. On 18 January, I'll be back at the books for a year to get my degree at the University of Nebraska at Omaha. A real change of pace.

I know there were times when I seemed unmerciful in my fanny biting but I want you to know that I was proud to count you among my commanders, you did a superb job and we are all forever grateful and humble to the Lord who spared you.

If there is ever anything I can do for you, just write or call.

Sincerely,

Gordon Lynch

1973: Bob writes a letter to President Nixon
Here is the official reply

UNITED STATES DEPARTMENT OF JUSTICE
BUREAU OF PRISONS
WASHINGTON 20537

March 1, 1973

Mr. Robert Tierno
% W. R. Sorter
3205 South Parker Road
Denver, Colorado 80232

Dear Mr. Tierno:

Your letter of January 29, 1973, to President Richard M. Nixon has been referred to me for response.

Correctional Officer positions in the Bureau of Prisons are filled by competitive appointment from a list of eligibles maintained by the United States Civil Service Commission. When we recruit, we must consider applicants who are referred to us by the Civil Service Commission in the order of their assigned comparative ratings. A recent check with the Washington Area Office of the United States Civil Service Commission indicated that your application has been received and rated. You were rated eligible for the position of Correctional Officer with a rating of 101TP, and you are on the list of eligibles for the Englewood Institution. Your chances for early employment are favorable.

I have advised the Englewood Institution of your interest in employment. I want to assure you that if your name is referred to the institution, you will receive every possible consideration for employment.

Thank you for your interest in the Bureau of Prisons.

Sincerely,

NORMAN A. CARLSON
Director

420

Michelle Anne Sorter
September 3, 1944 - March 5, 2019

Michelle Anne Sorter, age 74, passed away peacefully at her home in Sequim, WA on March 5, 2019 after a valiant fight with dementia. Enfolded in the love of her husband and her children, she drew her last breath in their arms. She is survived by her husband Ron, her children Chelle Struve and Mike Struve (wife Ilsa and sons Billy and Paco), and her brother Mike Herrick (wife Barb and daughter Emily). She was preceded in death by her beloved parents.

Michelle was born September 3, 1944, in Burlington, IA to Anna and Dave Herrick. Her mother enjoyed telling anyone who would listen that Michelle was born with a smile that never left her. She attended a dozen schools as she, her mother and brother followed their father in a succession of jobs.

He rose eventually to be the Director of the U.S. Forest Service's Rocky Mountain Research Station. She loved meeting new people wherever she went and had countless adventures flying with her father in his small plane. She once surprised an aunt in Iowa by landing in a field behind her house.

When her family lived in Alexandria, VA she attended Southern Illinois University, pledging the Sigma Sigma Sigma sorority. She always insisted she had no earthly idea how she won a beauty contest there. She later worked at the Pentagon, where she was the youngest employee with a Top Secret, Eyes Only clearance.

In 1967, she married Bill Struve with whom she had two children, Chelle and Mike. She was a mother foremost and forever yet found time to work in several executive positions for EF Hutton, TAO, Inc., and other corporations in San Diego, CA.

In 1994, she married Ron Sorter. They lived in Redstone, a historic mining town of 92 souls on the Western Slope of Colorado where she reveled in the high country. She'd snowshoe in winter with a friend with whom she had an "8 at 8" rule: if it was warmer than eight degrees at 8 a.m. they'd trek three miles into the back country then return home for coffee outside in the sun.

With her husband she was awarded the Redstone Outstanding Community Service award for their work obtaining grants to preserve local historic sites. A fond memory of her husband is seeing her unflinching insistence to a large bear that he depart from her kitchen. Her lifelong love of books was on display in the library Ron built for her collection.

After surviving a cerebral hemorrhage in 2013 with minimal aftereffects she was cared for by her loving husband and in 2015 they moved to Sequim and bought a home next door to her son and his family. Everyone involved with her care—caregivers, doctors, nurses and therapists—always remarked on the smile that never left her face. One of her closest friends once told her husband, "Michelle is the nicest woman I've ever known."

Her absence is heartbreaking but her memory warms them as a beloved wife, mother, daughter, sister, grandmother and friend. A woman's life, wonderfully and truly lived.

Services with the family have taken place.

After her husband's death, their ashes will be commingled and final services will be held as they're interred in Arlington. Should friends desire, memorial contributions may be sent to Volunteer Hospice of Clallam County, 540 E. 8th St., Port Angeles, WA 98362.

Author Bios

William "Ron" Sorter

Colorado native Ron Sorter relishes the challenges of leadership. In 1970, he was a Captain in the Infantry and as a 1st Lieutenant, commanded a rifle company in Vietnam. After eight months in combat, he was severely wounded, losing his right leg. After recovering from those wounds, he's spent his life making lemonade from lemons. His life is a story of leadership, in the public, private and community sectors.

Ron led the Denver and San Diego Prosthetics services for the Veteran Administration, later serving as a consultant for them. After obtaining a graduate degree in Artificial Intelligence from San Diego State University, he worked in the private sector as the Director of Prosthetics for the San Diego firm which had purchased his graduate thesis, as they began developing their own computerized prostheses.

After meeting the love of his life, Michelle, they retired to Redstone, CO and immersed themselves in volunteer work. Ron was project director of the award-winning acquisition and restoration of the town's major historical landmark, the Redstone Coke Ovens, while co-leading the development of the local Caucus' master plan for the entire Crystal River valley. In his free time, he rebuilt and doubled the size of their home.

After his beloved wife suffered a debilitating illness in 2013, they moved to Sequim, WA, where he cared for her in their home until her death in 2019.

424

Ron has been awarded the Combat Infantryman's Badge, the Bronze Star, and Purple Heart which hang proudly on his living room wall next to the Olympic Torch he carried during the 2002 Salt Lake Olympics. He holds an MSBA from San Diego State University and a BBA from the University of Oklahoma.

He received the 1974 award for Courage and Inspiration from the Denver Naval Reserve Association, the annual Hands And Heart Award from the Veterans Administration in San Diego, the Redstone Outstanding Community Award with his wife Michelle for their volunteer work and has been honored many times on TV for his service to other members of his Purple Heart brotherhood.

Ron lives next door to his grandsons. When he's not playing golf, painting or working on his memoir, he's building race cars and skateboard half pipes for them and teaching them about brotherhood.

Robert "Bob" Tierno

Bob has been around the block, and the cell-block.

In his storied career (and there are many stories), he has been a correctional officer, federal prison systems regional manager, Intel automotive marketing manager field sales engineer, district sales manager, a Bed & Breakfast owner in the Gold Country foothills of the California Sierras, a franchise business coach and a semi retired consultant.

What ties it all together for Bob is the knack for leading business growth strategies and then executing on them, relentlessly. He enjoys the gift of quickly learning the intricacies of diverse industries. Never one to rest in the comfort zone of a silo, he is experienced in sales, marketing, business development, and operations.

Bob holds an MBA from Pepperdine University and a BS in History from the University of Oklahoma. He served as a Captain in the U.S. Army Reserves from 1972-1986. He has always been passionate about communication, integrity and leadership. He is the author of the 2019 medical memoir: *The Prostate Chronicles: Detours and Decisions following my Prostate Cancer Diagnosis.*

Bob lives near Denton, TX, with sweetheart Karen and his one-eyed cat Toby. You can find him on the Robson Ranch pickleball courts most every morning, or swinging the old tire iron on golf course

426

CPSIA information can be obtained
at www.ICGtesting.com
Printed in the USA
LVHW040947151019
634129LV00022B/3605/P